IMAGES
of America

PRISONS OF
CAÑON CITY

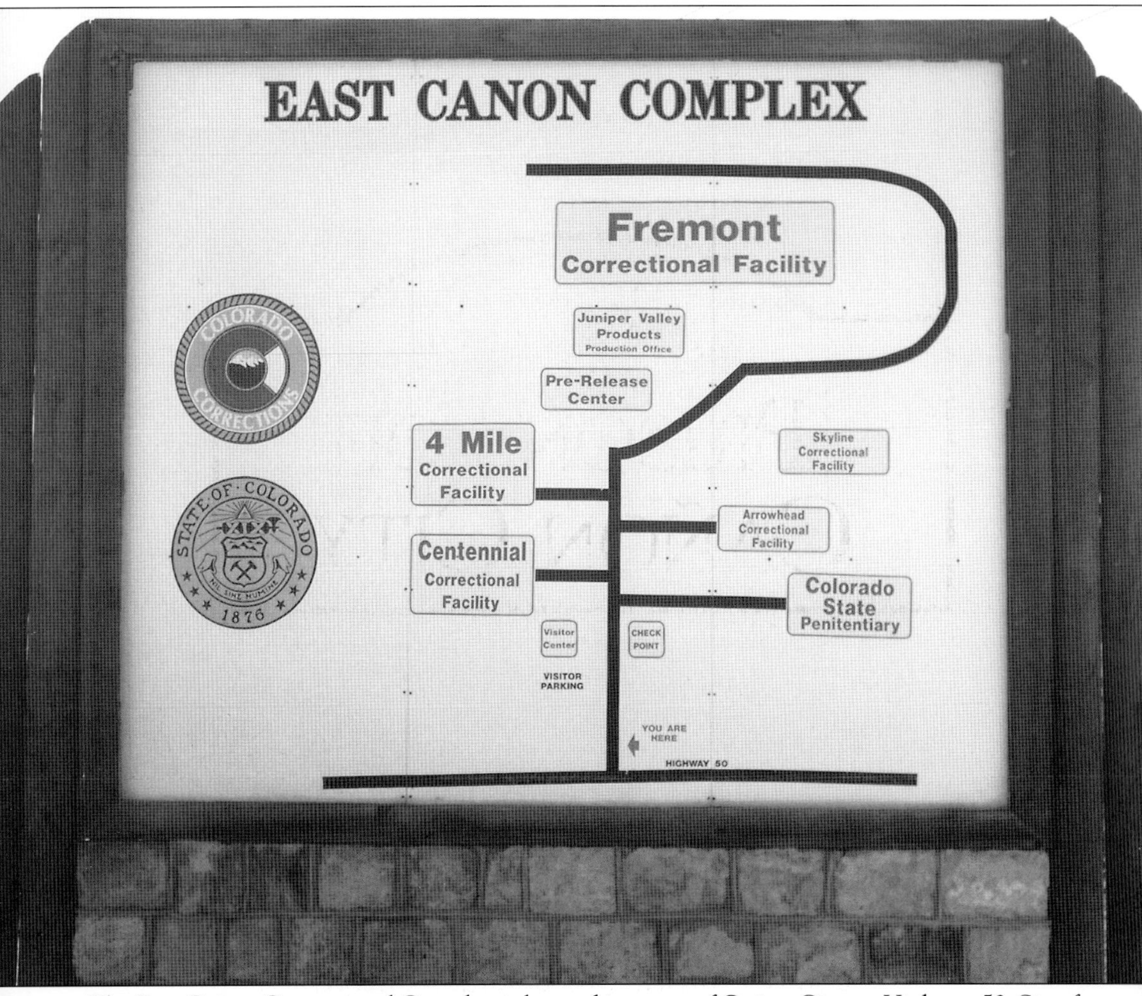

The East Cañon Correctional Complex is located just east of Cañon City on Highway 50. Six of Cañon's eight facilities are situated in this area. In the early years of the prisons, the region was called Ranch Five, as it had been home to the piggery and turkey and chicken ranches. Although the prerelease center is no longer used, six facilities, fleet services, Colorado Correctional Industries dairy, canteen services, the wild horse program, and the furniture shop remain in operation. When Colorado State Penitentiary II is built, it will be connected to Centennial Correctional Facility and will house over 1,000 offenders. The women's facility stands just west of the East Cañon Complex, and the Territorial Correctional Facility stands on the west side of Cañon City, on the site of the original facility. Now it is much larger than the single building of 1871.

ON THE COVER: In the late 1930s, Colorado State Penitentiary entered a float in the Cañon City Blossom Parade. The float, sitting in front of the prison administration building, shows what products the prisoners made at that time. Actual convicts were used to pull the wagon and ride on the back. The prisoner on the float is John Cox, No. 4307, the oldest convict to be housed by the state. Cox entered prison in 1898, following a bar fight from which he received first-degree murder charges. During his incarceration, he became well known for the bits and spurs he created for guards. Some are worth thousands of dollars on today's market. Cox was eligible for release in 1937 but asked to stay because he had no family or friends. In 1940, he died of natural causes while still in prison.

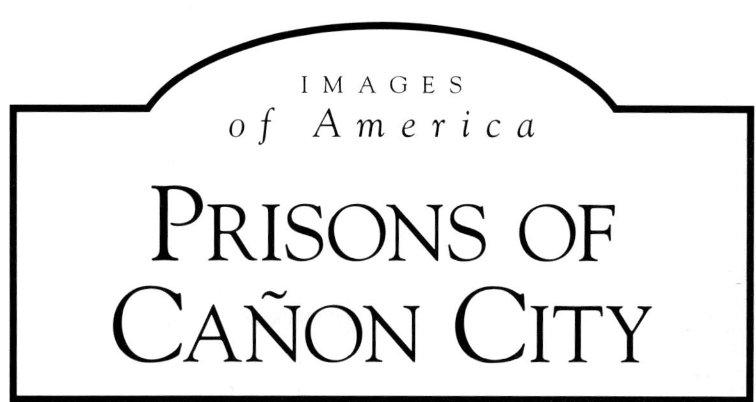

Victoria R. Newman
and the Museum of Colorado Prisons

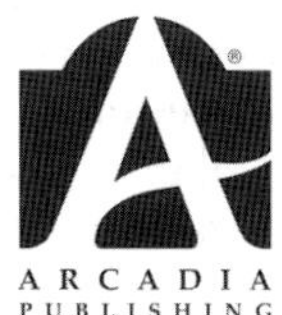

ARCADIA
PUBLISHING

Copyright © 2008 by Victoria R. Newman and the Museum of Colorado Prisons
ISBN 978-0-7385-4845-6

Published by Arcadia Publishing
Charleston SC, Chicago IL, Portsmouth NH, San Francisco CA

Printed in the United States of America

Library of Congress Catalog Card Number: 2007936586

For all general information contact Arcadia Publishing at:
Telephone 843-853-2070
Fax 843-853-0044
E-mail sales@arcadiapublishing.com
For customer service and orders:
Toll-Free 1-888-313-2665

Visit us on the Internet at www.arcadiapublishing.com

This book is dedicated to English teacher Warren Babilot.
Carl Sanburg said, "Nothing happens unless first a dream."
Thank you for helping realize one of my dreams.

CONTENTS

ACKNOWLEDGMENTS

Heartfelt thanks go to the Museum of Colorado Prisons and the Department of Corrections for their meticulous record keeping and preservation of the artifacts and photographs that made this book come to life. Without the support, friendship, and guidance from the curator of the museum, Pat Kant, this book would not have been written.

I am grateful to the employees of the Colorado Department of Corrections—both past and present—who have dedicated their lives to their work, put their lives on the line daily, and made the ultimate sacrifice.

Thanks go to all who have made the pictorial history of the prison possible, especially Heather Ward, former Department of Corrections officer and current director of the Museum of Colorado Prisons, and Tim Bennett, retired Department of Corrections fire marshal.

I am grateful for those who have taken the time to visit with me and put stories with the photographs that disappeared before my time. Dean Marshall, retired Department of Corrections employee, provided great stories. Melvin Cole at Minimum Centers gave a great tour and offered guidance in the shots we needed of the current-day facilities.

Thanks to Hannah Carney, my editor at Arcadia Publishing, for the support, concern, and guidance that got me through this process.

Mom and Dad, thank you for encouraging me every step of the way and believing in me. Geoff, Heather, and Kelly, for telling me that I have the best stories locked inside of me and if I do not write them down, they will disown me. And to my crazy family, who has given me tales to tell and love and support when I have needed them the most. You are my life, and I love you all. And these people have shown me that life is not to be taken too seriously and that a sense of humor gets one through the good as well as the hard times.

Within these pages, you will find mistakes. Unfortunately dates and people's memories are often confused. What you read in these pages is as accurate as the books, manuscripts, and the thousands of written documents provided by the Department of Corrections allow. Unless otherwise noted, all of the images in this collection come from the archives at the Museum of Colorado Prisons.

INTRODUCTION

Cañon City, Colorado, has been described as "a prison town," "Prison Capital of the World," and "the place where all the inmates live." Home to eight state prisons, it is indeed all of these things, but the beauty and mystery of the area surrounding Cañon City make one forget.

The land is rich in apple, plum, and cherry orchards, among other fruits. Each year, the town sponsors the Cañon City Music and Blossom Festival with bands from all over the United States and Mexico performing in the competition. The festival is held the first weekend of May, when the trees are usually in full bloom for the parade—that is, unless snow or a cold snap kills the blooms. Late winters can surprise residents with large snowfalls and very cold weather until the end of May. For the most part, though, winters in the area are on the mild side.

At an elevation of 5,332 feet above sea level, the area originally belonged to France and was part of the 1803 Louisiana Purchase. Zebulon Pike and his scouting party camped at the Grand Canyon of the Arkansas (now known as the Royal Gorge) in December 1806. Because of the mild weather in Cañon, the party spent the winter here.

In 1859, the Old West town of Cañon City was established using the Spanish spelling of the name. In 1883, archeologists recovered a 53-foot brontosaurus fossil north of the area. Skyline Drive, overlooking Cañon City and built by inmate labor in the 1930s, has dinosaur tracks that have been pushed up by the movements of the mountain ranges and hills.

Many Native American tribes lived in the area, including the Sioux, Cheyenne, Kiowa, Blackfoot, and Comanche, who followed the buffalo here in the spring. The region is rich in arrowheads and artifacts. At Soda Point, a hot mineral spring in Cañon City, the Native American tribes used the springs for medicinal purposes.

Cañon City boasts a population of 29,931 as of the 2007 census, but inmates are included and take up approximately 5,000 of that figure. The Department of Corrections employs around 1,600 staff members in the Cañon City area. It is the number one employer in the county.

One

IN THE BEGINNING

The first prison in the Colorado Territory was built in 1868 and opened its doors in 1871 as Colorado Territorial Prison. When Colorado became a state in 1876, the federal government turned the facility over to the state to run, thus creating Colorado State Penitentiary. The first prisoner to arrive was No. 1, John Shepler, followed by No. 2, William H. Henderson, on June 13, 1871. Imprisoned for larceny, Shepler received one year and was released on November 28, 1871. Henderson was given a sentence of five years for manslaughter, serving until September 18, 1874.

In the first year, the prison admitted 24 male prisoners. The facility employed four full-time guards at $25 per quarter to cover 24 hours a day, seven days a week. The warden at that time earned $208 per month. In the early days after Colorado's statehood, the warden was appointed by the governor, but now the position is hired by the state.

By the 1920s, Colorado State Penitentiary had grown in population, staff, and structure. Two new cell houses and a dining area had been added, along with a separate building for women. Up until then, women had been housed in the same unit as the men, separated only by bars. Towers were added to insure that the prison was seen from above all hours of the day and night. Industries provided the facility with self-sufficiency. The gardens, tag plant, soap plant, tailor shop, and dairy were all added to keep the inmates busy and contribute to the prison's revenue. Though no longer self-sufficient as everyone would like, the prison is well run, and revenue from the industries helps the system operate smoothly.

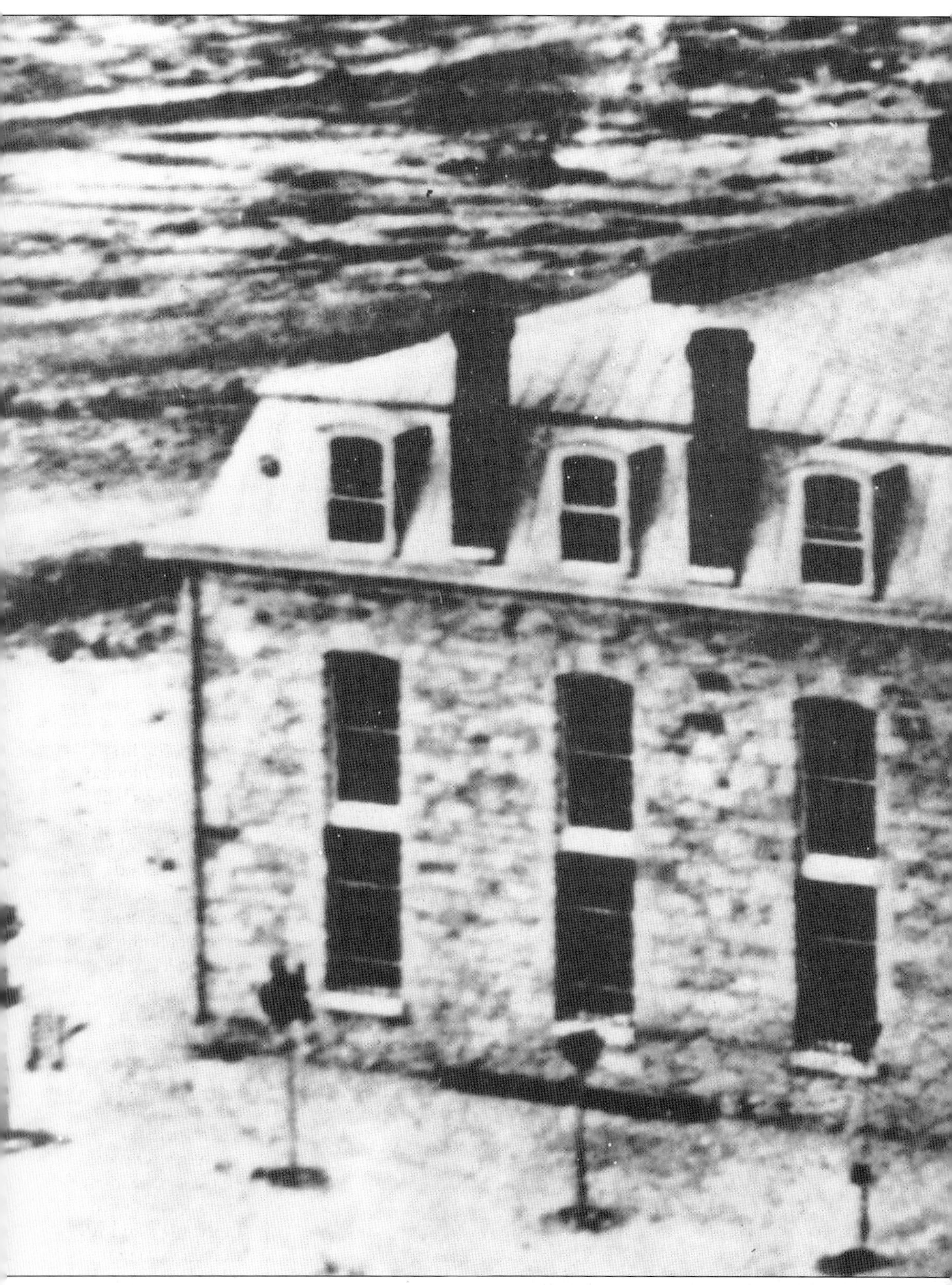

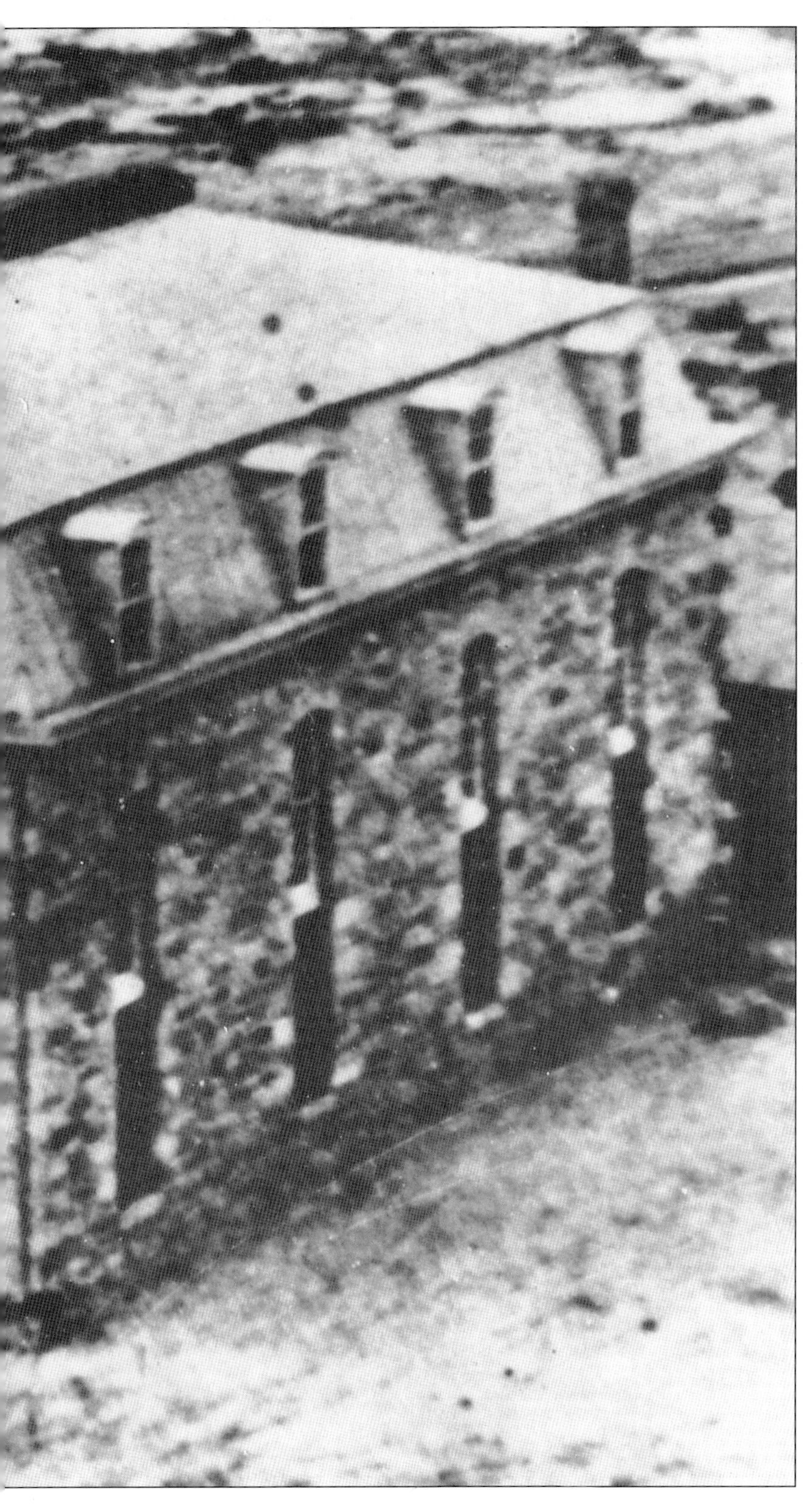

In 1868, the first prison in Colorado Territory was built, becoming Colorado State Penitentiary upon statehood in 1876. The facility consisted of one building with no fence or wall surrounding it. There was no formal town at that time, and Cañon City grew up around the prison. There were no age restrictions on employees, so many of the guards were in their 60s and 70s; women were not allowed to work.

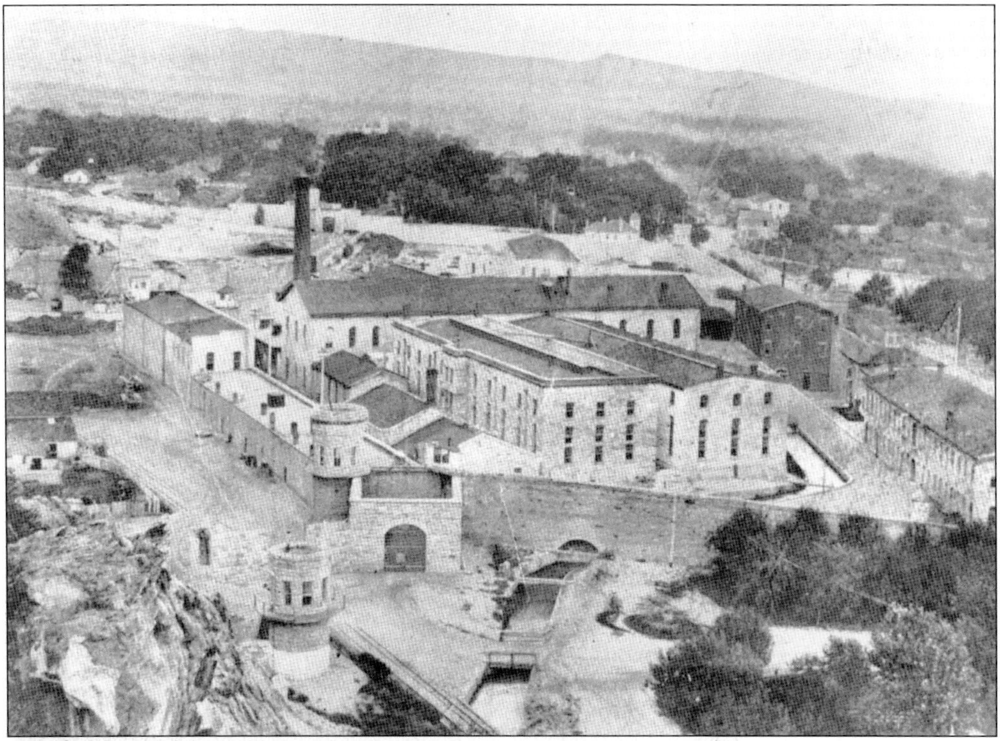

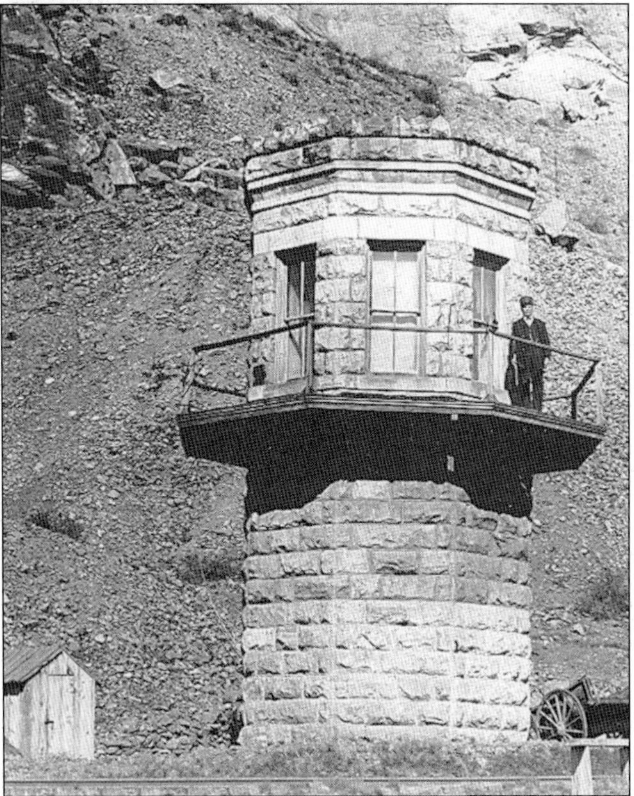

By 1920, the prison had grown not only in size but in inmate population. The continuing influx led to many years of nonstop construction. A women's prison was in the plans, but until 1935 the women were housed in a separate building within the facility.

Towers have always been a mainstay at prisons, as they give the guards (now officers) an overview of the happenings down below. Many times, tower guards have spotted trouble before anyone on the ground is aware of a problem. Towers are normally armed, while the ground staff is not, and personnel above can fire warning shots and break up problems before they escalate. In the 1880s, a guard stands watch in a tower that was later raised in height for better protection of the employees.

The north gate at Midway was the hub of the prison's internal works. The day shift captain had an office in Midway, where inmate clerks would also run errands and complete paperwork. Guards would be called to Midway during their shift for assignments. The site still functions in the same capacity today.

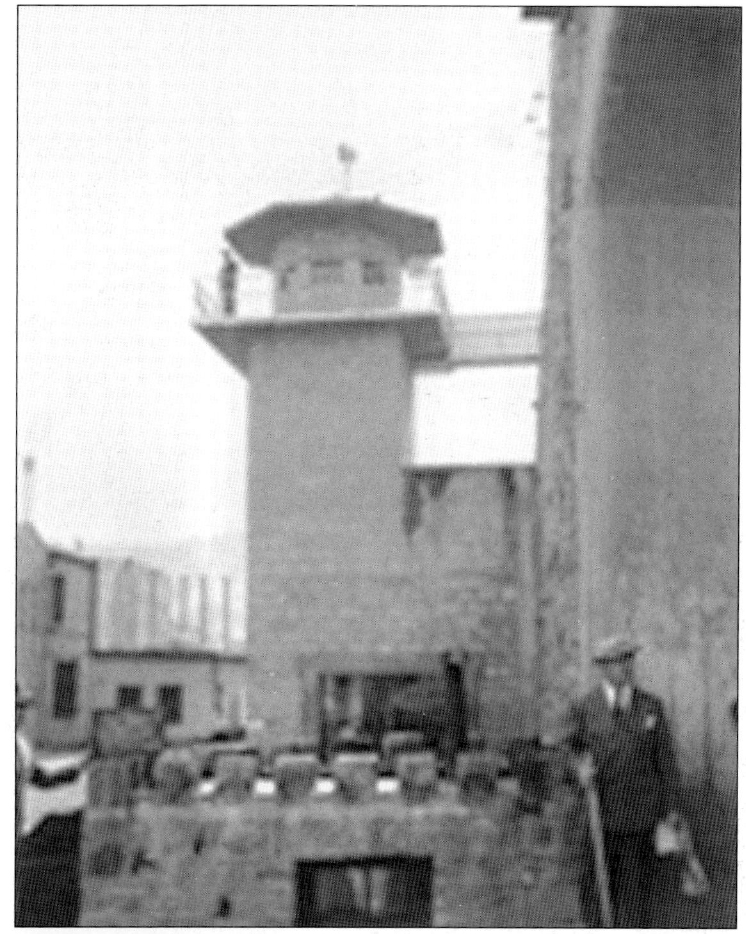

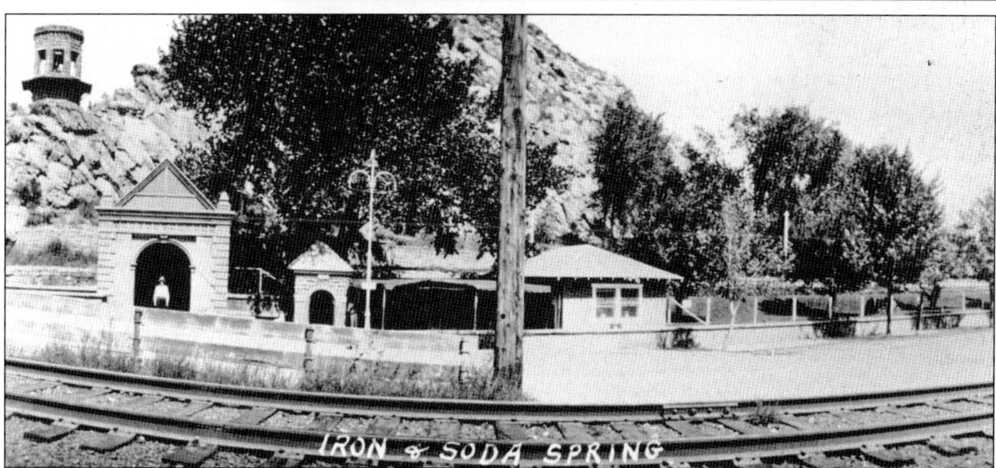

Soda Point, which sat just west of the grounds, was guarded by a tower called Soda Point Tower. The hot springs attracted many tourists to the area. Prisoner Joe Nunez lived in the greenhouse directly behind Soda Point and painted from that location. Many of his paintings now hang in the prison museum. Soda Point was torn down in the 1920s, thus leaving only memories of the beautiful springs.

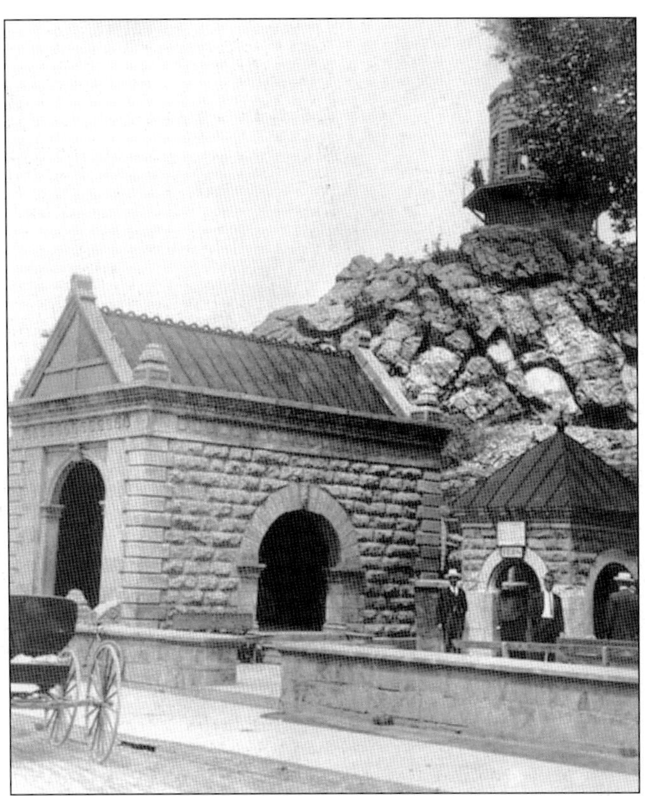

The area surrounding Soda Point was—and still is—beautiful, bounded by mountains and ripe with wildlife. Pres. Franklin D. and Eleanor Roosevelt visited the springs to ease the president's polio. Native Americans would frequent the warm mineral springs for medical purposes as well.

Prisoners stand next to their racks of bread at the bakery in the early 1900s. Bakers were on the job by 3:00 a.m. to make enough bread to feed the inmates and guards for the three meals. They worked seven days a week and received less than 50¢ per day for their long hours.

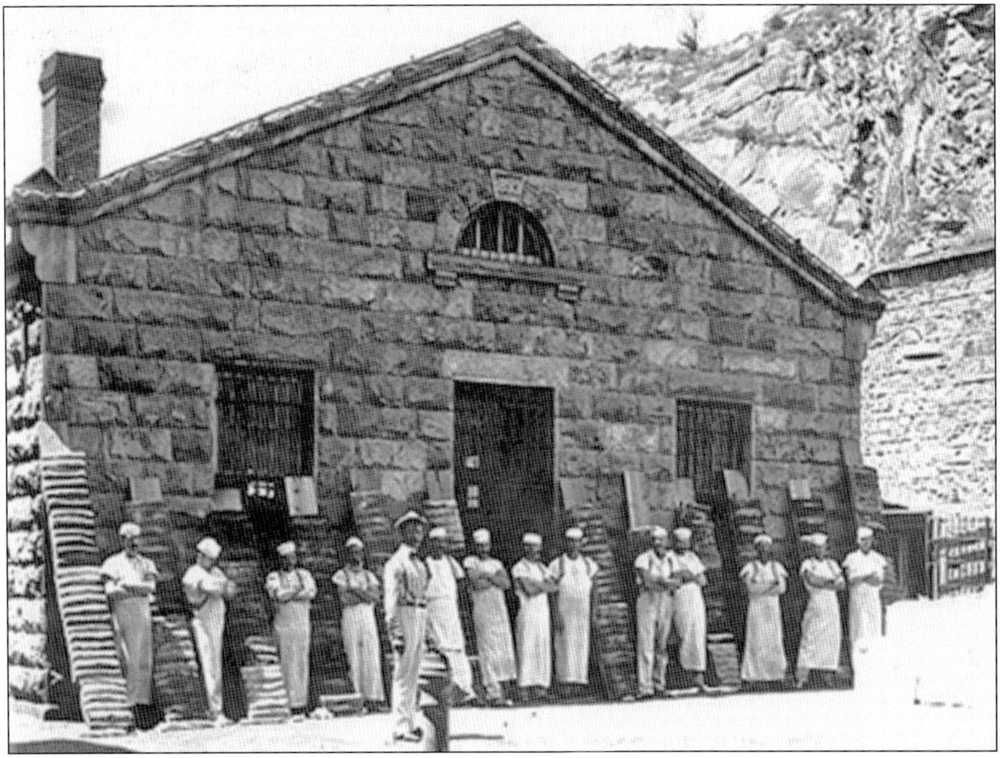

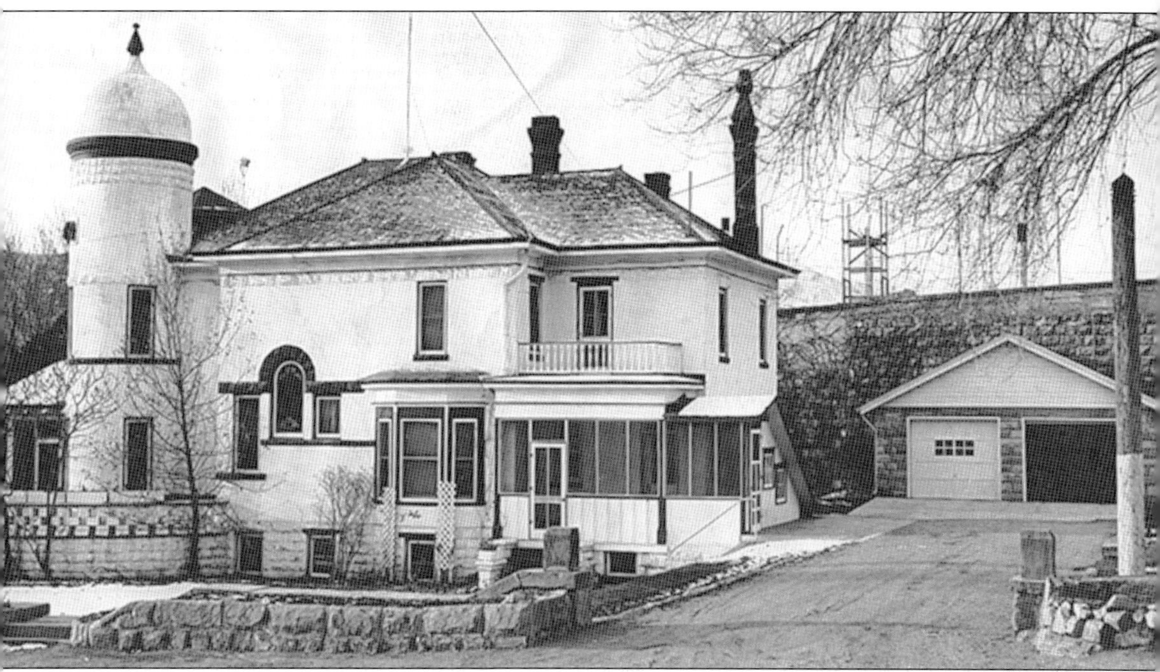

In 1902, the deputy warden's house, later referred to as C-House, was built outside the east wall of the prison. The structure was used in that capacity until the 1930s, when it became finance offices. The beautiful Victorian home boasted four staircases, servants' quarters, and its own garden tended by prisoners. The deputy warden's house stood beyond the wall, while the warden's residence remained inside, so that at all times one officer or the other would be off prison grounds in case of trouble. Now standing empty, the home is still stately—a beautiful building waiting to be renovated and brought back to life. The Department of Corrections hopes that it will find grant funding to renovate the old residence to its original condition and use it for much needed office space.

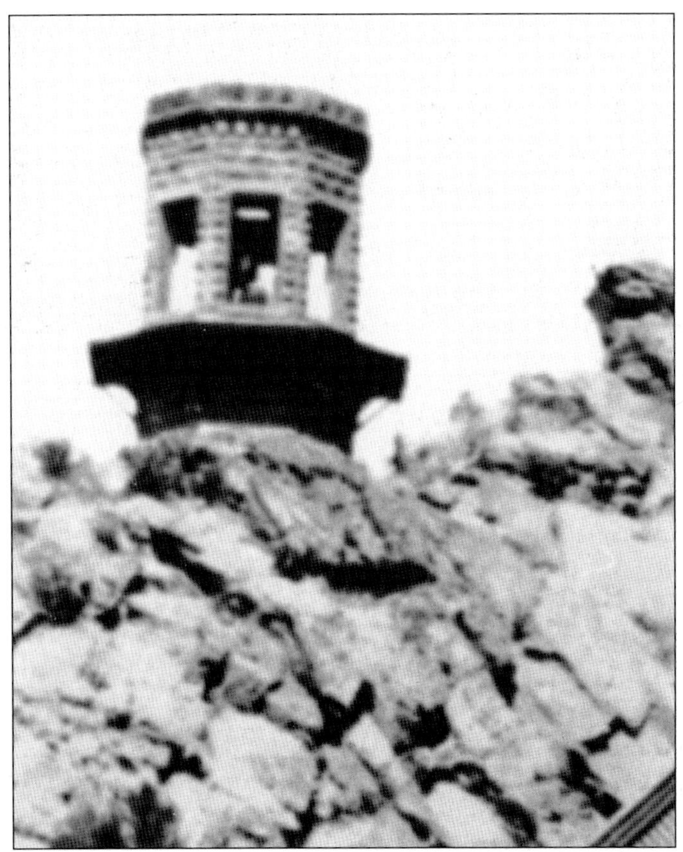

Soda Point Tower was constructed for the protection of the prison but also that of tourists who visited Soda Point because of the close proximity to the grounds. Warden Roy Best's first wife, Mabel, often climbed to the tower with her art supplies to paint the wonderful scenery.

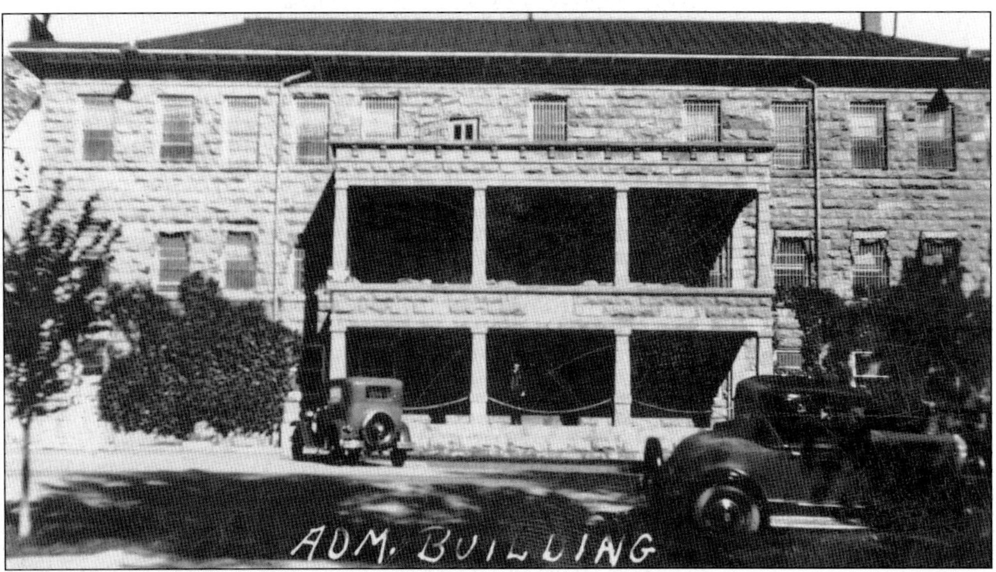

In the early days, the administration building stood directly on the main road going through Cañon City, and the public had access to the prison. A guard was stationed at the front doors to insure that people could not walk in with idle curiosity rather than business as their motive.

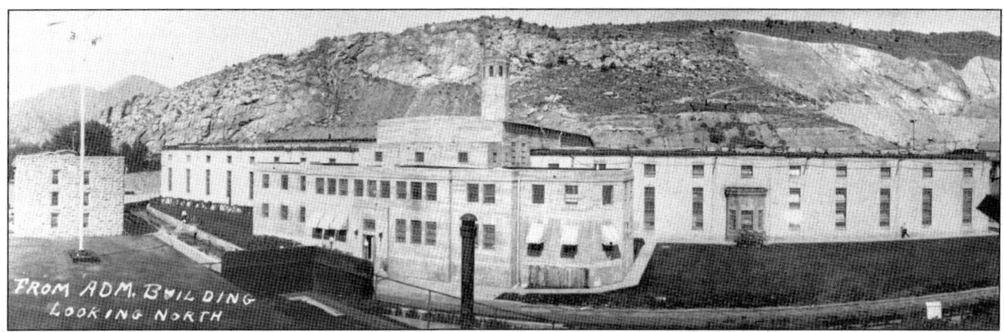

Directly behind the administration building was this area. When a guard entered the front door, he encountered the on-duty desk sergeant, who would provide the work assignment for the shift. Next to the sergeant's desk was the ready room, or roll call, and behind that was the deputy warden's office. Upstairs was the guards' tailor shop, where the uniforms were cleaned and shoes shined.

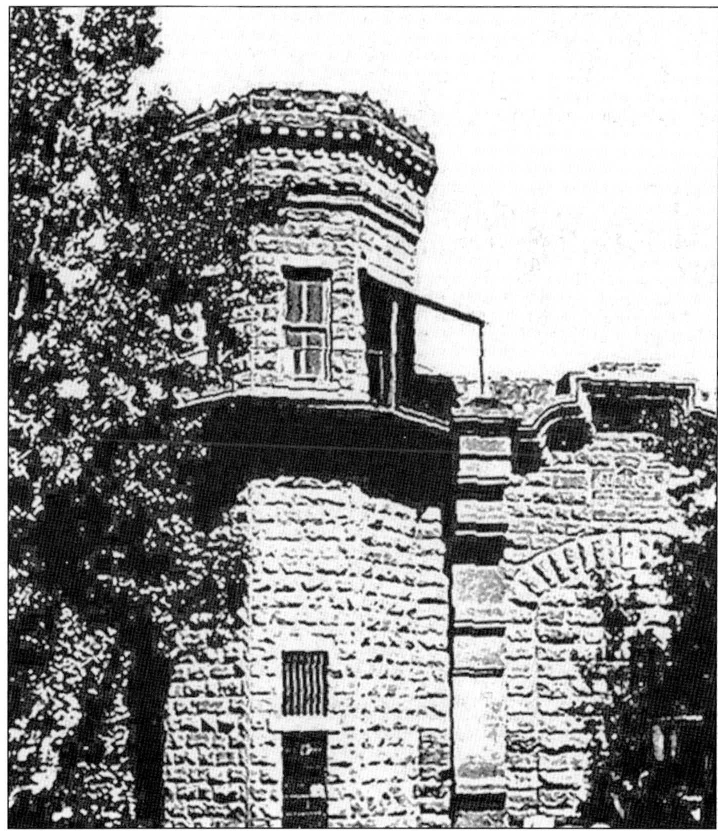

State vehicles entered the prison at this gate, where a guard stationed on the ground searched all cars passing through. Vehicles leaving the prison were also searched. The same method is used today to control contraband and catch possible escapees.

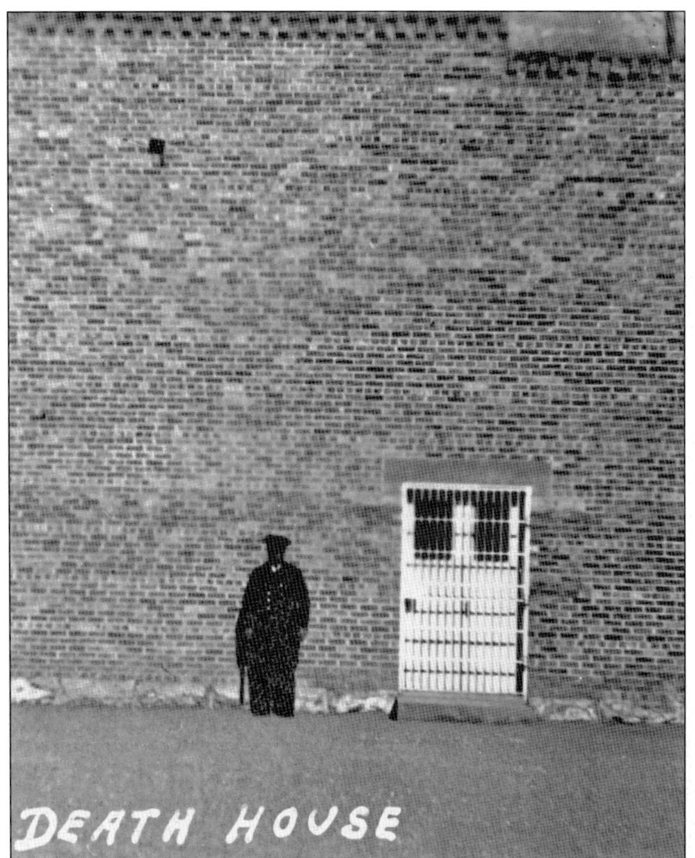

From 1871 to 1933, the method for executions in Colorado was hanging. The building at left housed the prisoners during the week of the scheduled execution. In 1933, when the method of execution changed to gas or cyanide, the building below held the gas chamber. The original chamber was a two-seater, and in 1933, brothers John and Louis Pacheco, Nos. 18012 and 18013, were put to death together for the murder of a rancher and a 16-year-old living with them. The rancher's wife was left in a burning house but lived to testify against the Pachecos. In Colorado, 45 prisoners have died by hanging, 32 by gas, and 1 by lethal injection. The gas chamber is on display at the Museum of Colorado Prisons.

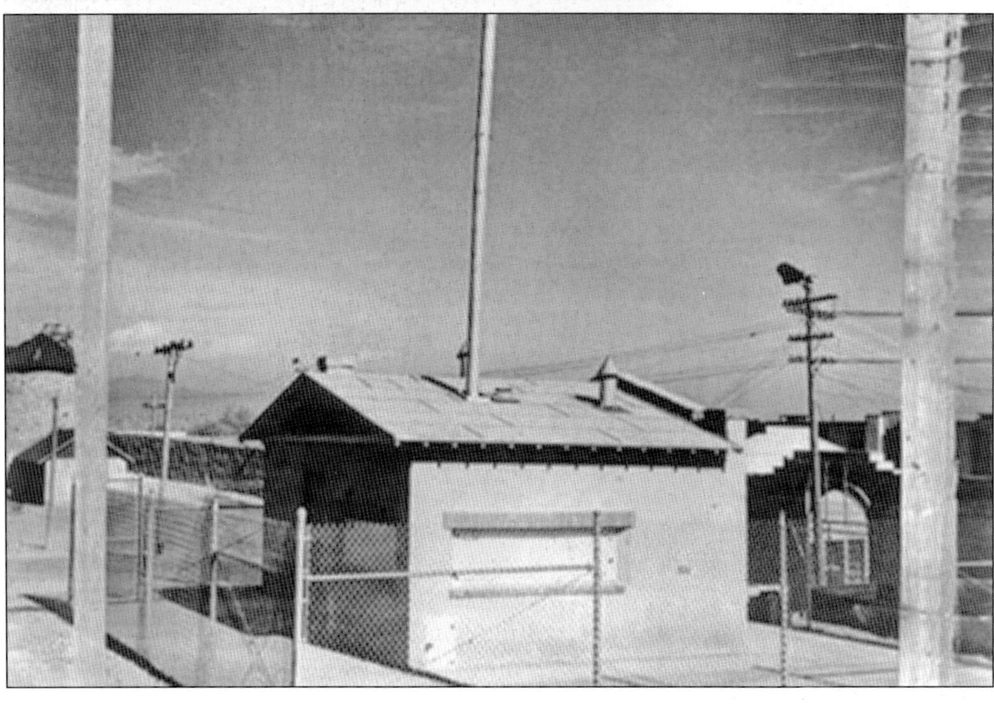

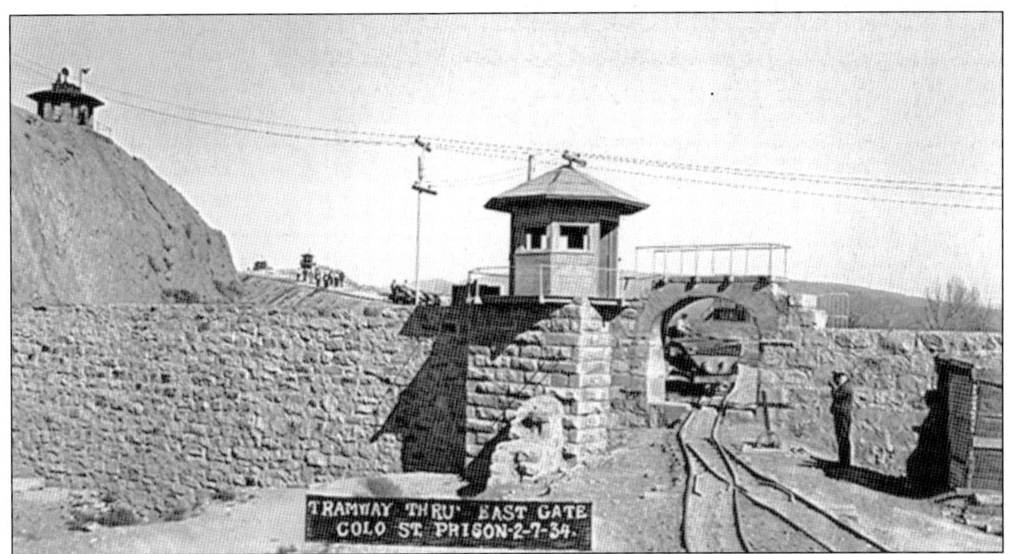

The only manned tower on the east wall, Tower 6 watches over the tram used to travel through the east gate. The tracks are gone, and the east gate was sealed up after the 1971 Alsip and Bell escape. The sealed gate is still evident in the parking lot for the Museum of Colorado Prisons.

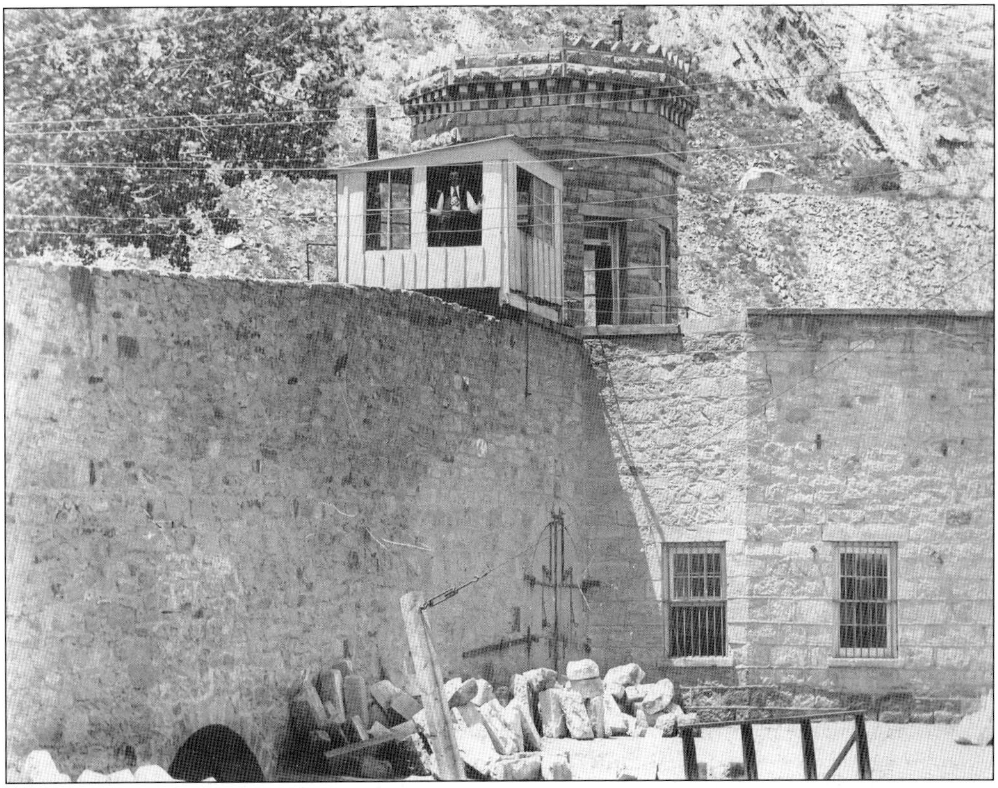

Inmates left through the west gate for outside work gangs, the quarries, and the gardens. The Shake Down Room, where prisoners were stripped to insure the absence of contraband, was located below the West Gate Tower. The manned tower was temporary while the one in the background was being raised.

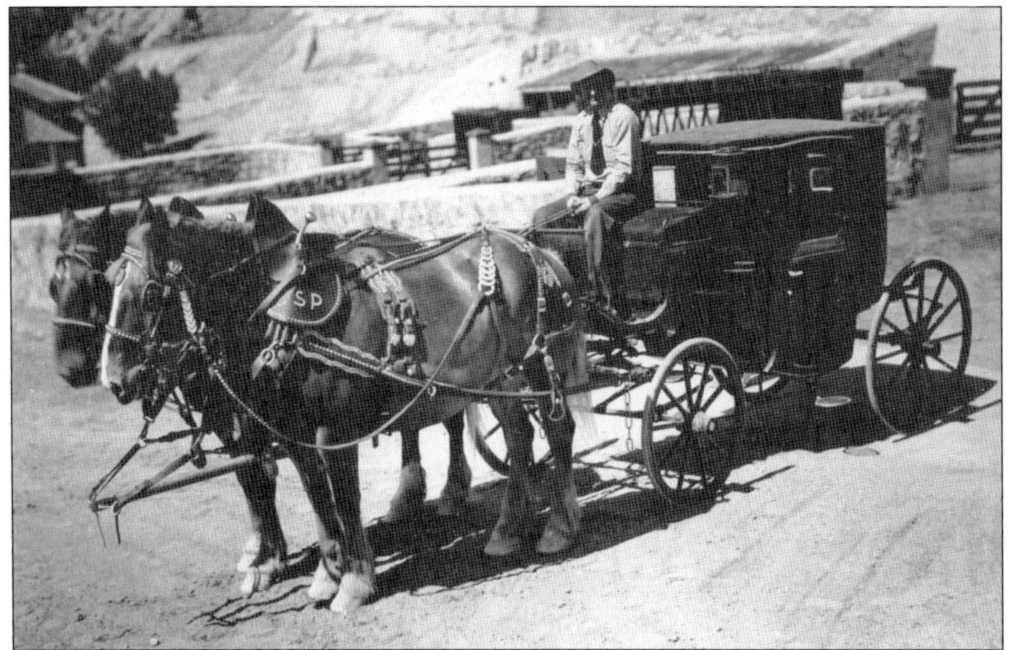

Employee Don O'Neil is seen here with the coach and horse team on the north side of the prison. Note the intricate leatherwork on the horse gear, made by prisoners and marked "CSP" for Colorado State Penitentiary. Many guards owned fine leatherwork created by inmates. Saddles were also made at the prison.

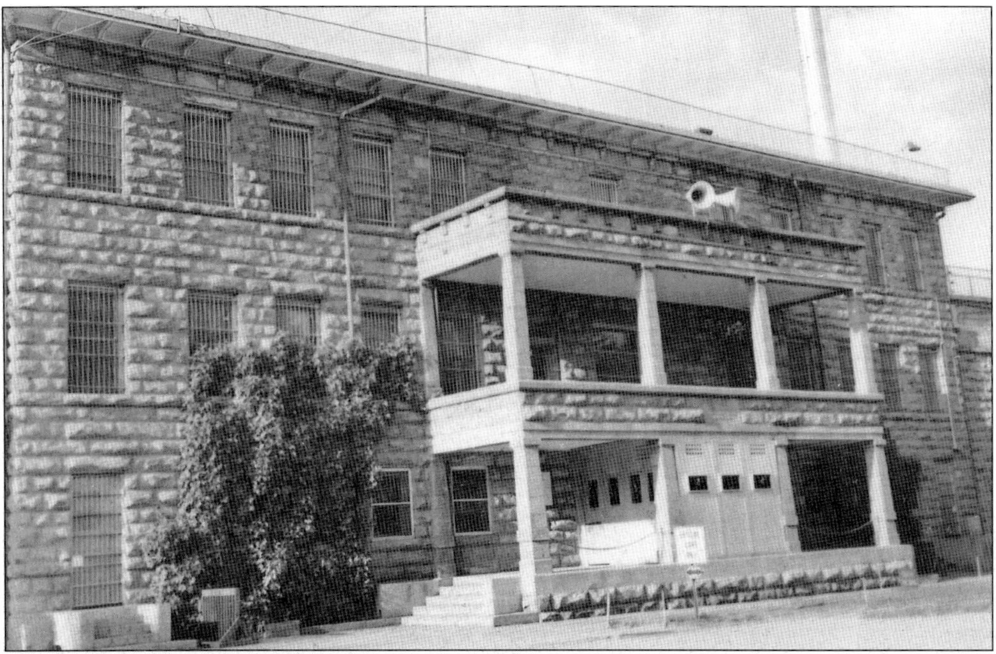

During Roy Best's days, an electric eye was installed. Much like airport security today, all staff, civilians, visitors, and prisoners had to pass through the eye to enter the prison. It detected any metal object, like a gun or ammunition. Most prisons now have some form of the electric eye at their entrances.

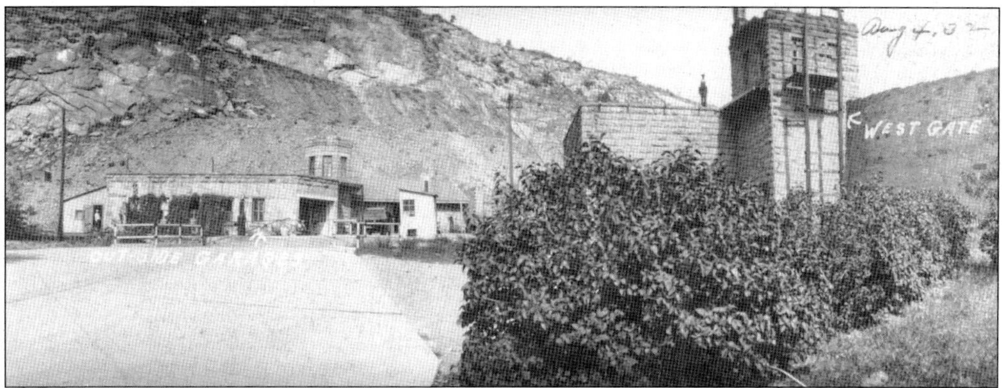

Les White ran the garage at the west gate for many years. State vehicles were serviced here, and what the prison called prowl cars were readied. Inmates drove the prowl cars and state vehicles, chauffeuring the staff to doctors' appointments, the warden's and deputy warden's children to school, and others to meetings and state-related business.

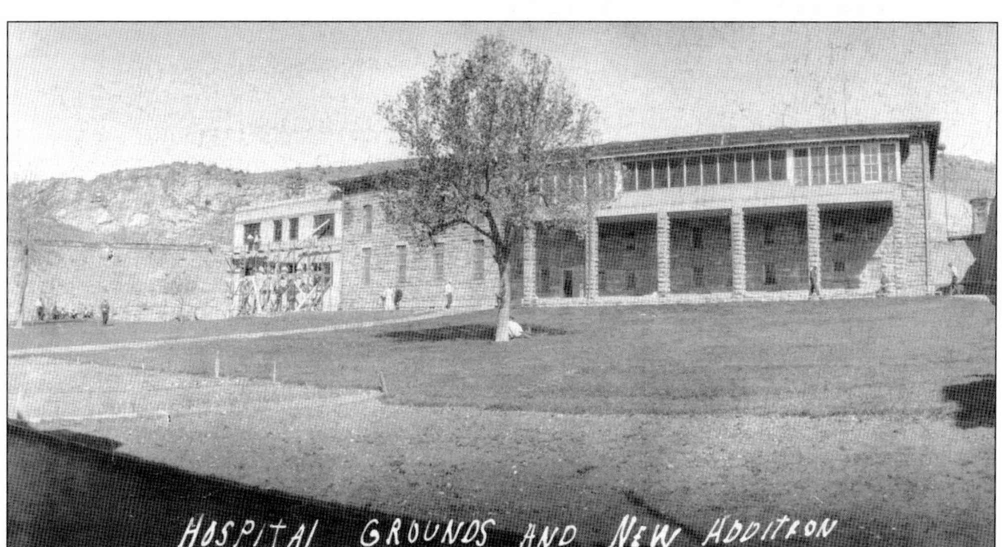

In the 1940s, a new addition to the hospital was constructed. Prisoner Joseph Corbett, No. 33322, the Coors kidnapper and murderer, served as the X-ray technician for years. One elderly prisoner was allowed to live upstairs in the hospital until he died because if discharged he had no place to go. He was allowed to come and go from the prison as he pleased.

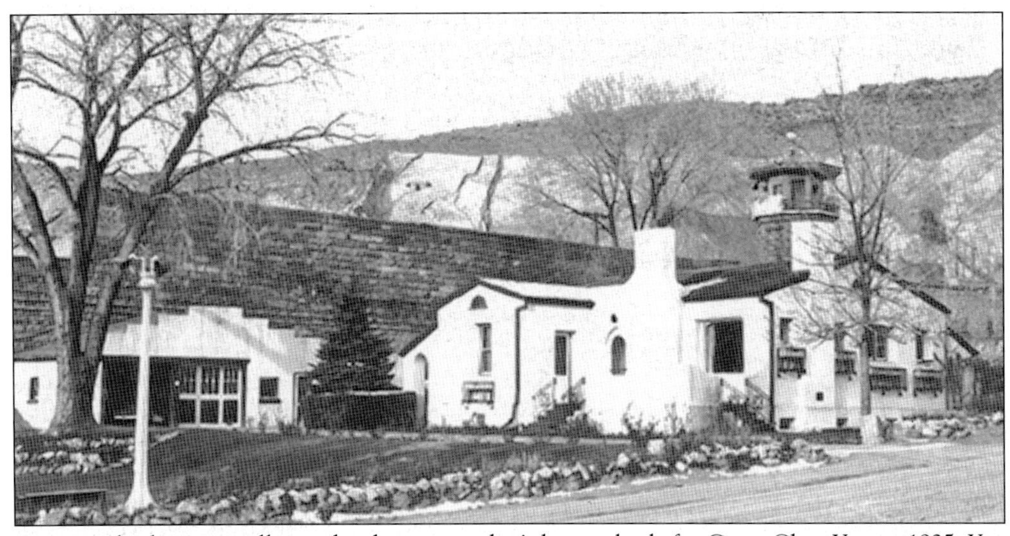

Just outside the east wall was the deputy warden's house, built for Capt. Chet Yeo in 1935. Yeo lived here for a few years prior to it becoming finance offices. During an escape in 1971, two death-row prisoners jumped on the roof of a shed in the back of the house before being killed by alert tower guards.

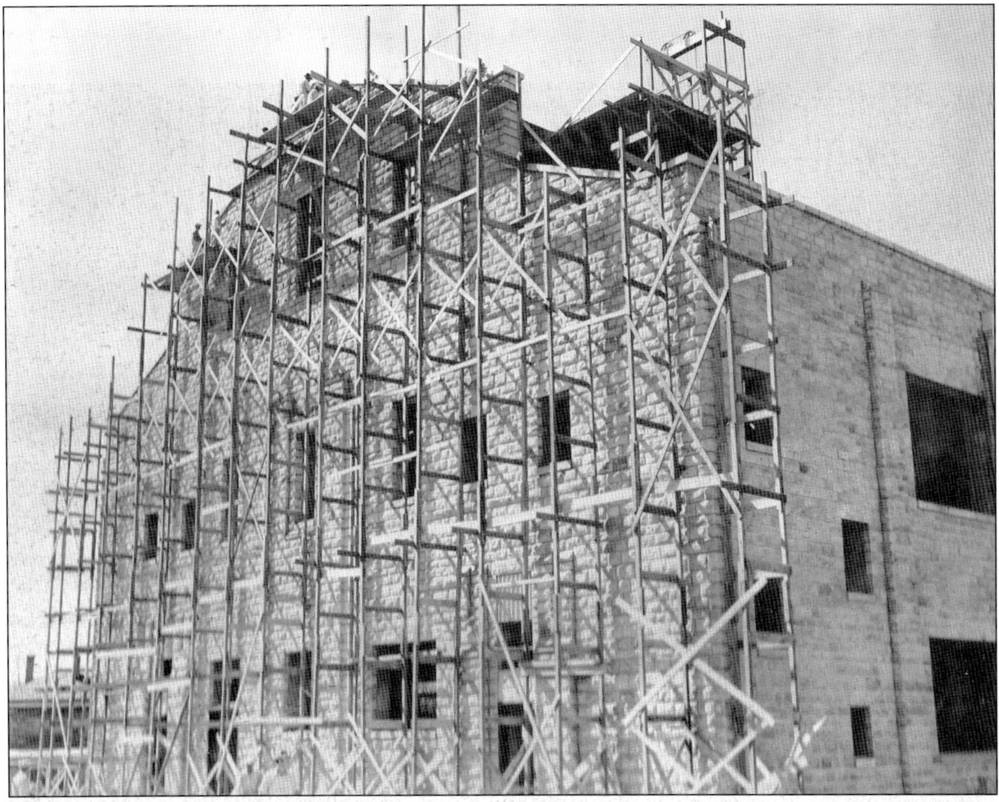

This two-story building was constructed in the 1930s, with the upper story housing the auditorium where prisoners watched movies on Sundays and the lower story holding the new mess hall and chow hall. The old auditorium had been destroyed by fire in a 1929 escape attempt and riot.

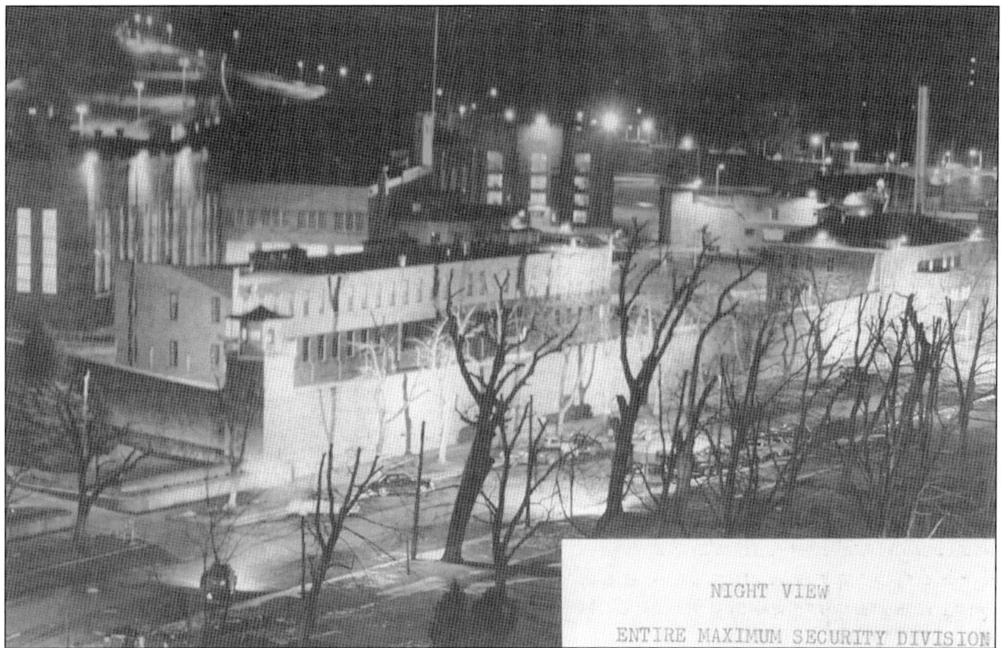

The penitentiary could be an awesome sight at night, as it was well lit for safety reasons. Here the Maximum Security Division, Cell House 3, is seen in an aerial view. In the 1930s, the main street of Cañon City ran directly in front of the main gate.

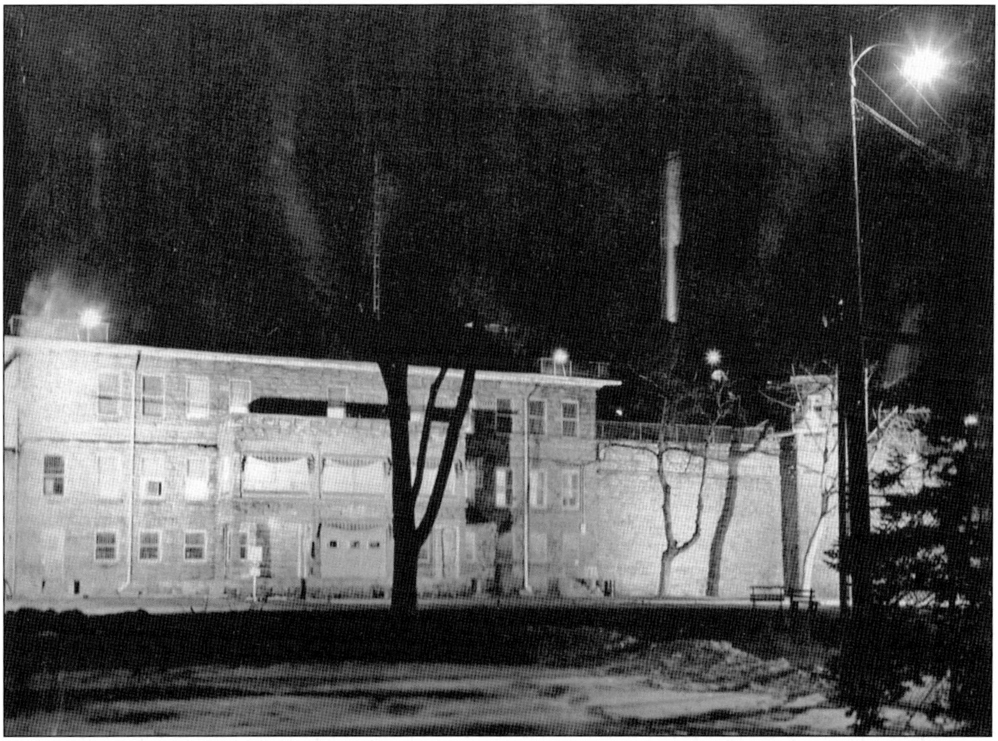

The administration building was also well lit to insure proper security. Once inside the electric eye at the front doors, one saw the main desk and the wardens' offices beyond.

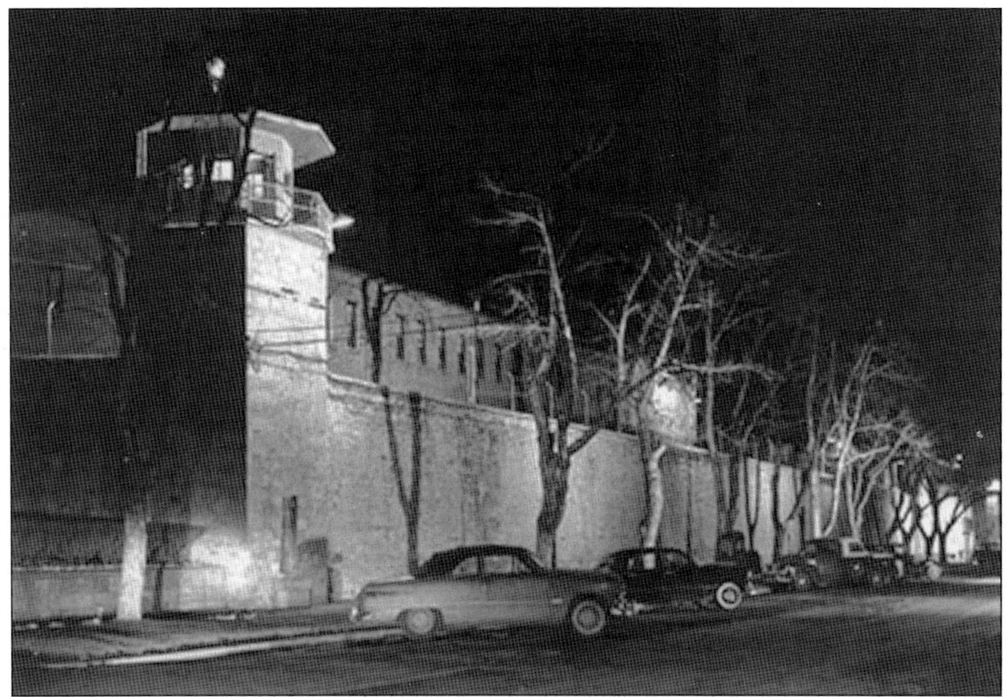

Tower 1 was positioned at the southwest corner of the prison's front wall. Manned at all hours, it overlooked Maximum Security and provided a vantage point for movement on the street in front of the prison. Lighting on the outside of the building illuminated everything in order to maintain tight security and keep people from tossing things over the wall for prisoners to retrieve.

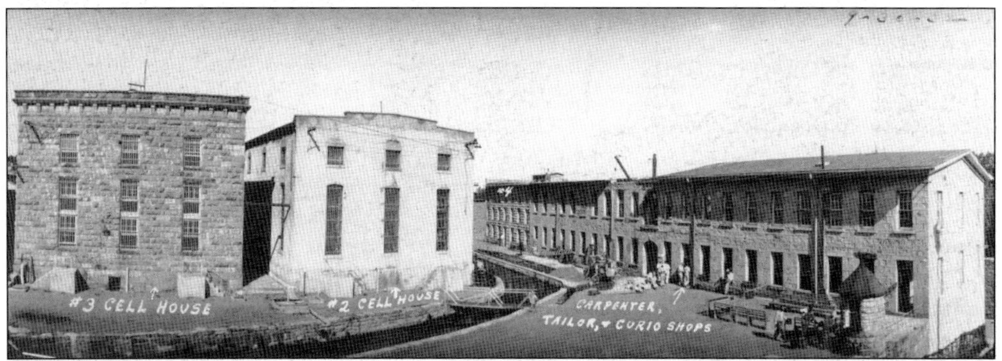

Cell House 3 housed maximum-security prisoners and death row and stood adjacent to Cell House 2. Across from the cell houses were the carpenter and the curio shop, where prisoners could display handcrafted items. The tailor shop made prisoner and guard uniforms, and the prisoners' footwear was also issued from the tailor shop.

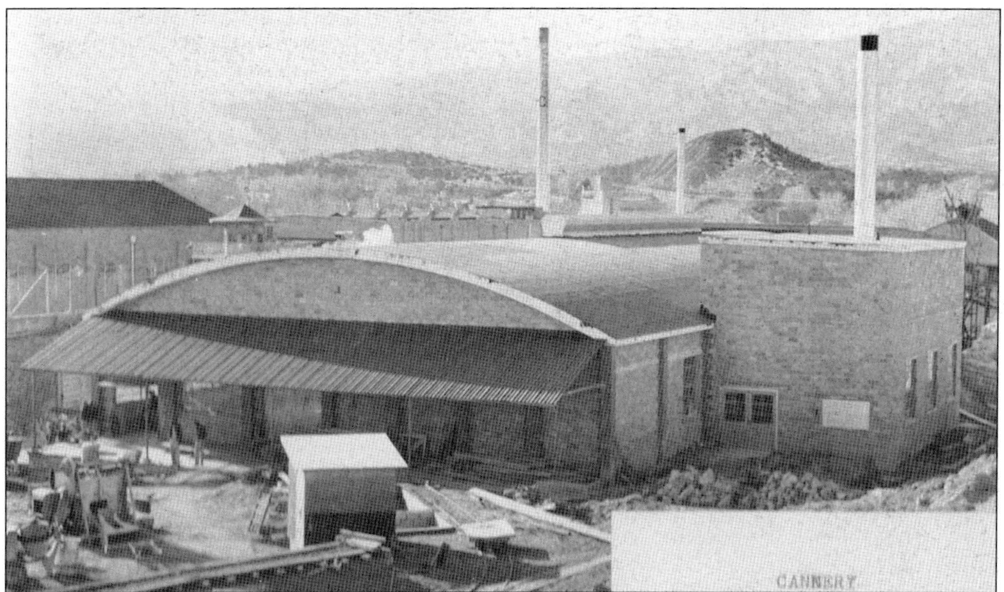

Built in the 1930s, the cannery was in production for many years. Prisoners tended the gardens that produced the vegetables to be packaged and then served at the mess hall. The canned goods were also sent to other state agencies such as the Colorado State Hospital in Pueblo. With livestock raised for meat and a prison dairy, the prisons were self-sufficient in the early days.

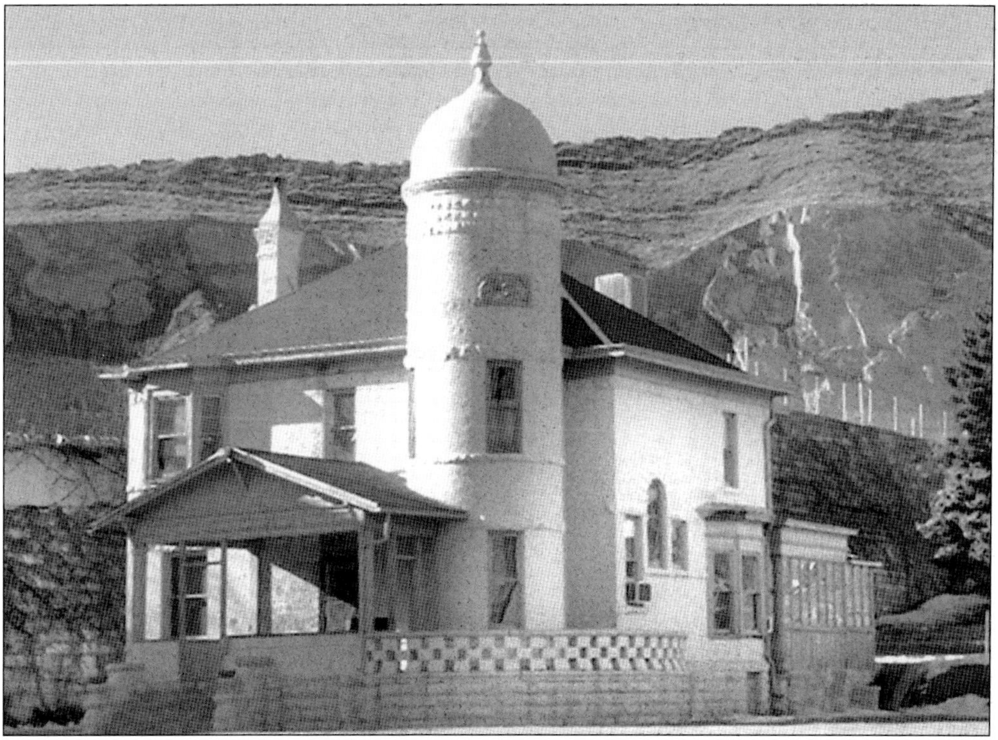

The deputy warden's house, viewed from the front, stands next to the east wall of the prison and in front of the museum. Although condemned at the present because of structural damage, the still-beautiful building will hopefully be brought back to life.

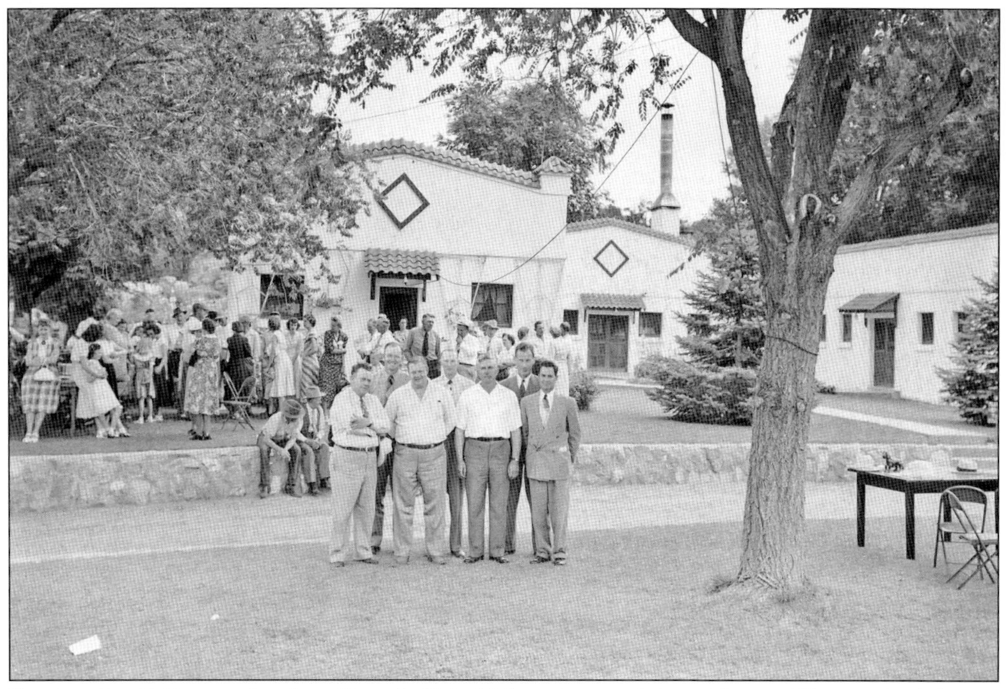

During the 1940s, warden Roy Best (left) held functions at his residence. The warden's house remains today, now holding communications for the prisons. During its glory years, the warden's section included a pond, tennis court, garden, and a beautiful, prisoner-maintained yard. A pet cemetery for Best's and other warden's deceased pets is still maintained on grounds.

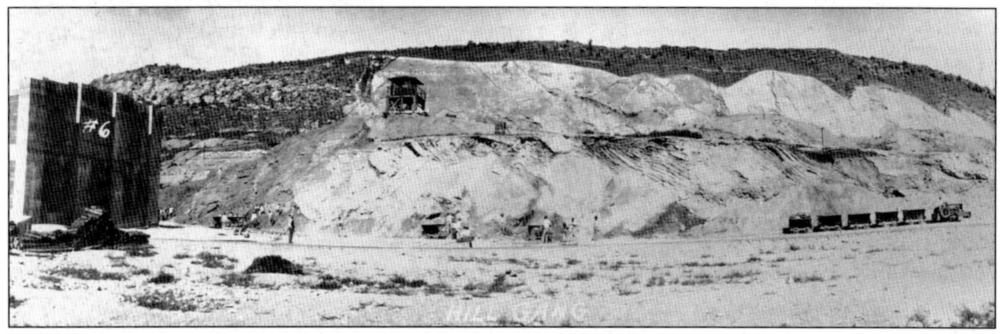

Before the north wall's completion, the hill gang worked at the quarry for the bricks to build the future wall. This train toted the stones from the quarry to the brick factory and brought prisoners to and from work. The train is now a permanent fixture on the front lawn of Colorado Territorial Correctional Facility, where it can be viewed by the public.

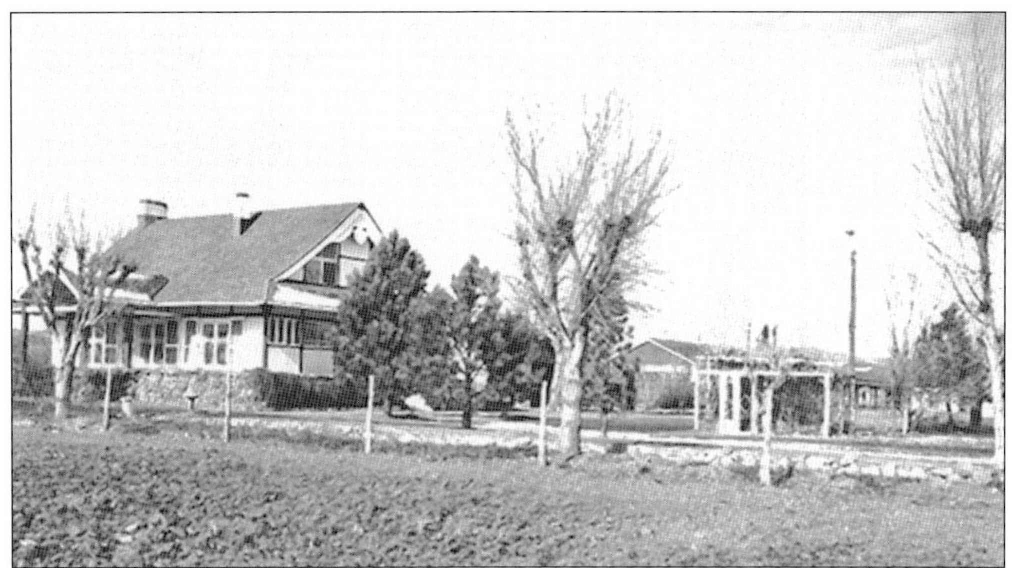

Ranch 1, constructed at the current location of the Holy Cross Abbey Winery, was a multiple-use operation with a garden, turkey ranch, and dairy. The property was later traded to the monks of the Holy Cross Abbey for the land that would become Fremont Correctional Facility. The abbey needed the water provided by Ranch 1, and the prison needed the large parcel of dry land.

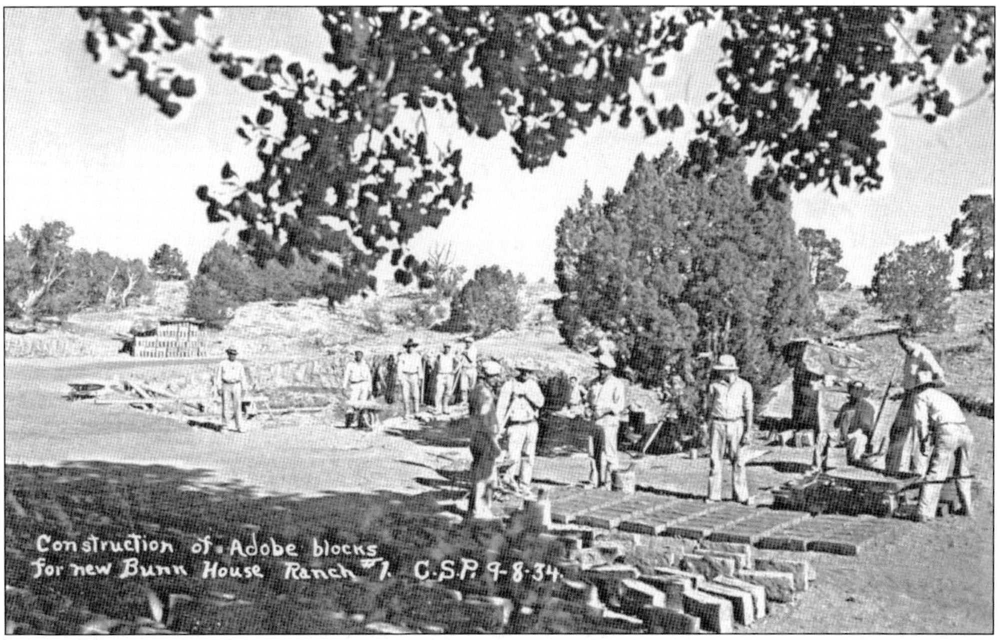

In 1934, prisoners were busy making adobe bricks for the new bunkhouse at Ranch 1. The adobe was poured into forms and left to dry in the hot sun and then stacked until used. The inmates worked long days to complete enough bricks to get the bunkhouse up in just over two month's time. Those who worked at Ranch 1 lived on site and were watched by guards assigned to the ranch.

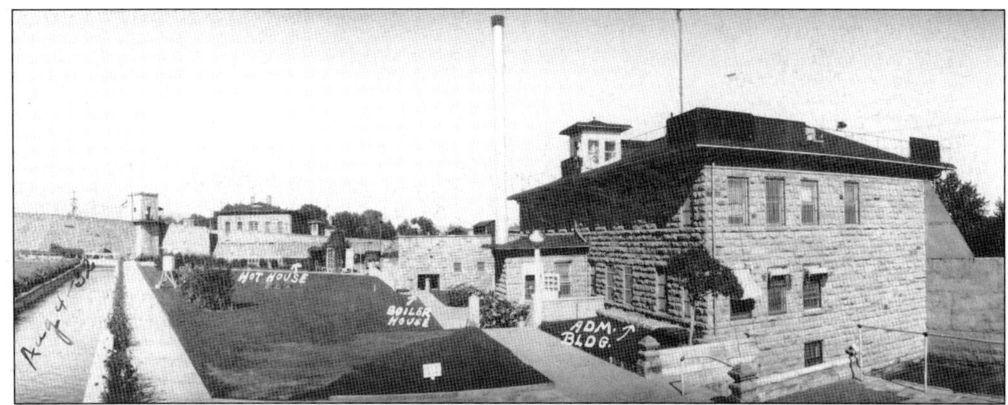

At the back of the administration building stood the boiler house, the hospital, Tower 8, and the ditch, shown here in 1932. Guards could live on the top floor of the administration building, provided they were single. At the right front of the building, where the fence runs, was the grudge pit. Prisoners with beefs could make an appointment on Saturday morning and fight it out here. Guards and prisoners watched the action from the sidelines.

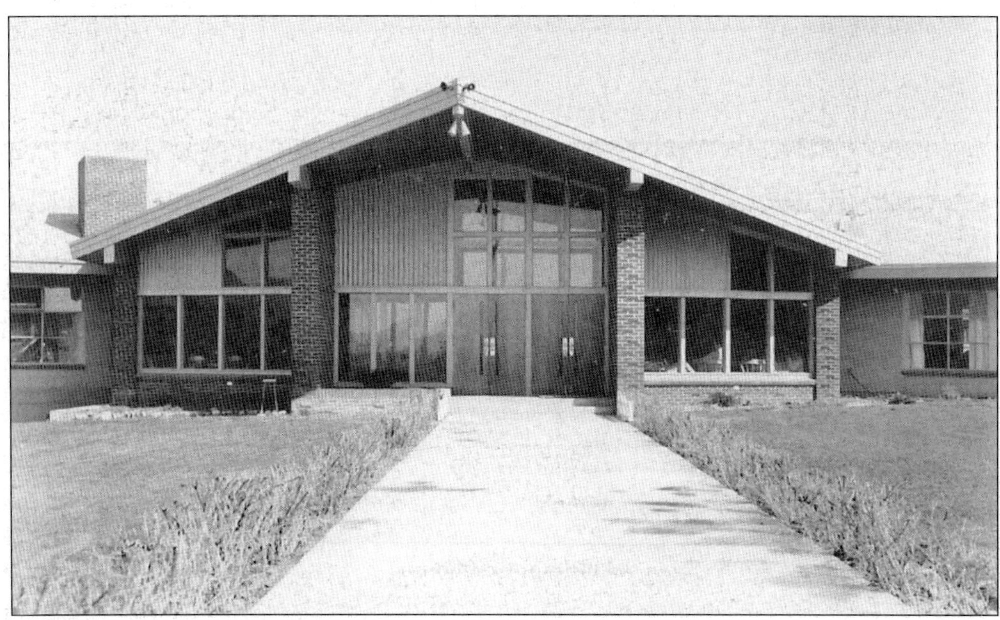

In 1956, the State of Colorado completed its second prison, Skyline, east of Cañon City. It was built as a pre-parole system and housed prisoners who would be hitting the streets soon. Now East Cañon Complex, classified as a minimum-security facility, it has a capacity for 249 inmates due to double-bunking. It remains without a retaining wall.

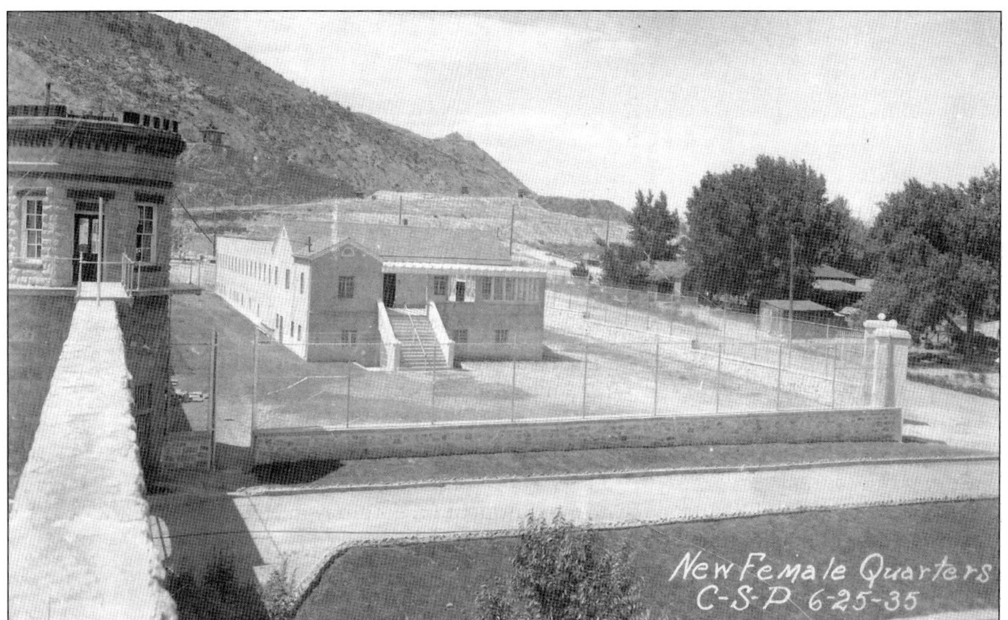

Colorado Women's Prison was constructed outside the east wall in 1935. With a capacity for 42 women, it had outgrown itself by 1968, when a new women's facility was built in Cañon City. The women's facility is now home to the Museum of Colorado Prisons and is the only prison in the country that sits next to a working prison. Tower 6, pictured, overlooks the museum.

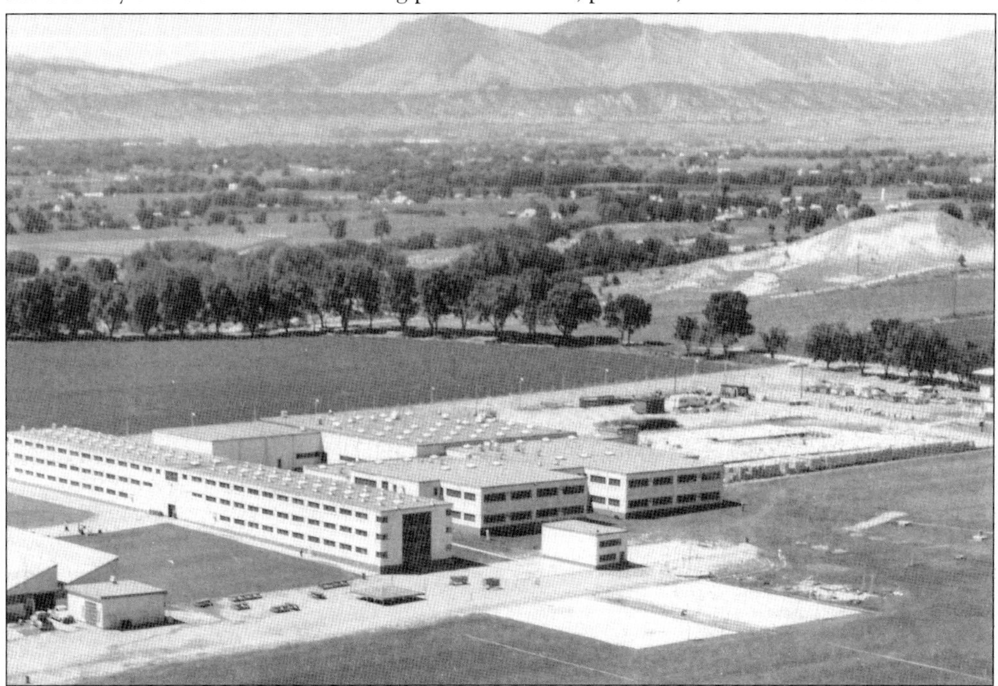

The year 1959 brought yet another prison to the area, Medium Security (more commonly MS). Not until the late 1970s did it actually get a name: Fremont Correctional Facility. Shadow Mountain was built directly west of Fremont Correctional in 1980, and in 1991, the two merged, making Fremont at that time the largest in the state. It now houses 1,471 inmates.

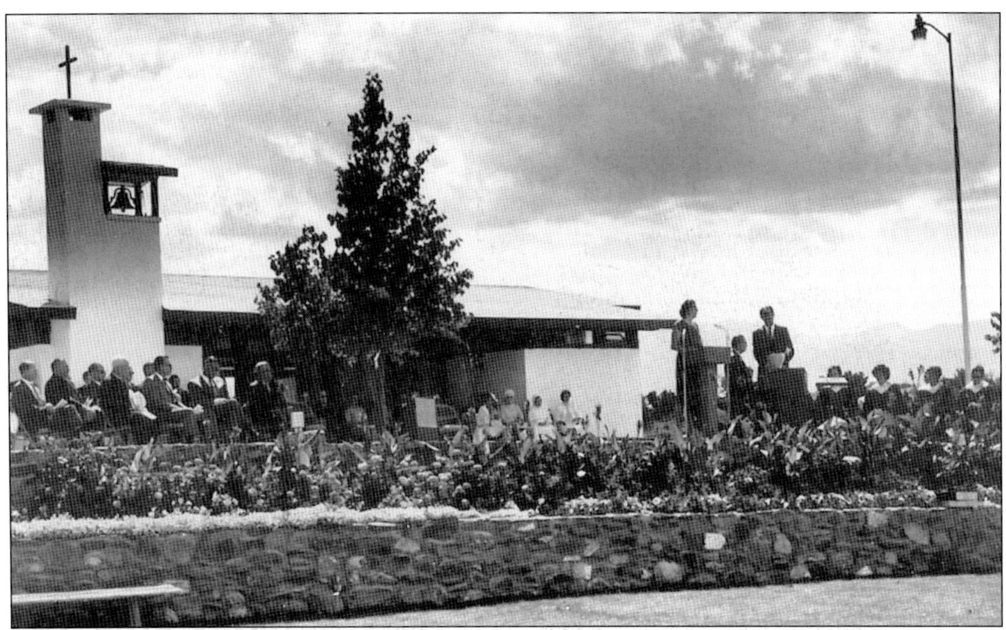

In the 1980s, Skyline prisoners built a chapel in front of the prison for all denominations. It is still used and well maintained by staff and inmates. On Skyline's grounds is a cemetery where eight prisoners have been interred. It is a beautiful little plot of land overlooking the mountains and Cañon City. Some of the names have deteriorated, but five still bear the names of the inmates buried there in the mid-1970s.

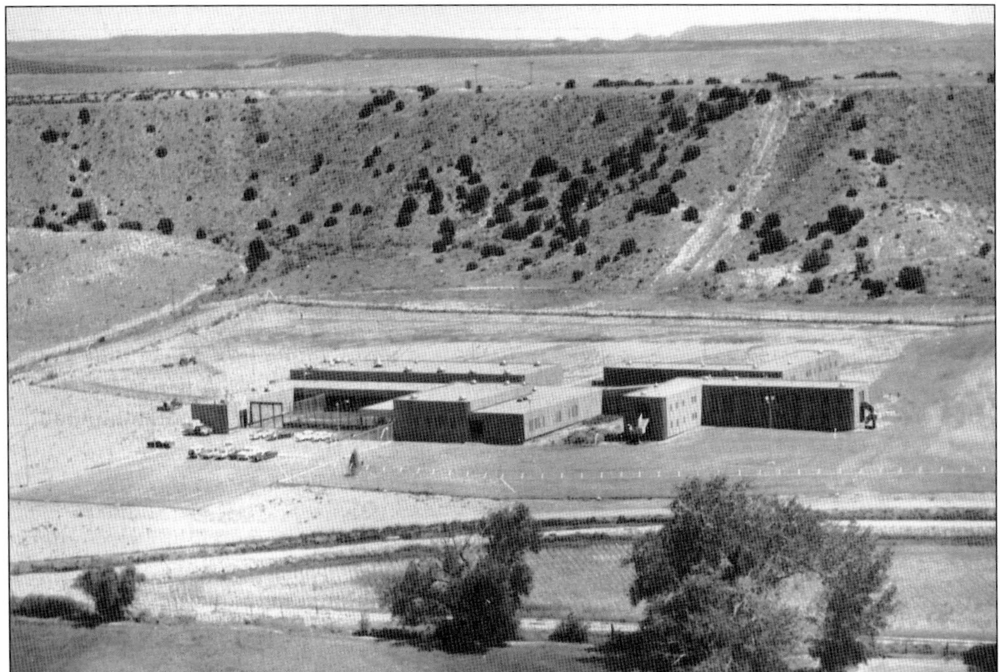

In 1968, the women prisoners outgrew the current building, and the state built a new facility east of Cañon, just west of the East Cañon Complex. With a capacity of 90, it consisted of 37 female officers and an average population of 50 to 60. It now has 210 beds and 14 segregation beds (inmates in lockup).

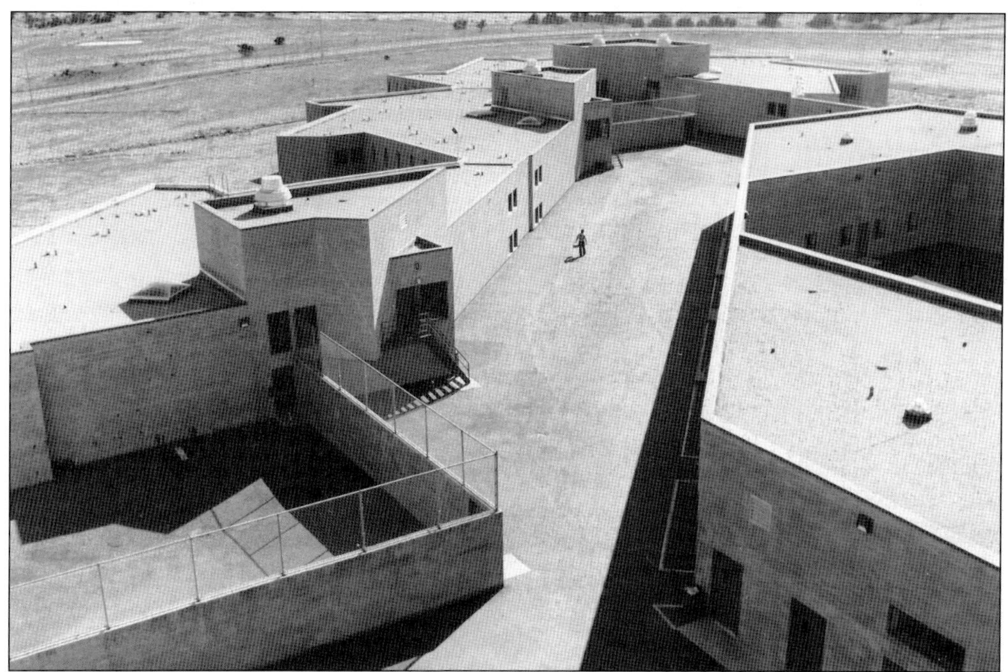

Centennial Correctional Facility opened in 1980 as the new state maximum prison, housing Colorado's most violent, dangerous, and disruptive offenders. It also included death row. Now it is a Level IV facility that has a combined 330 inmates on its Pro, Progressive Reintegration, and Diversion Units.

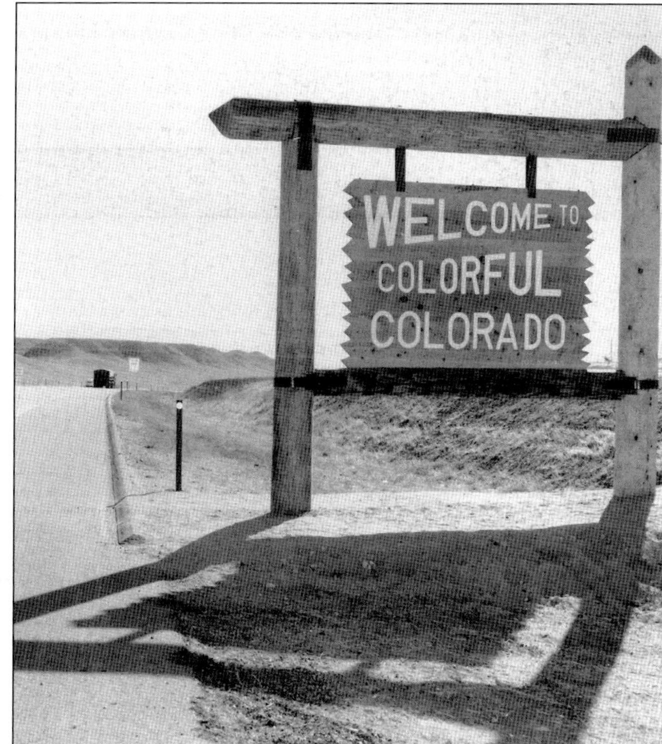

The signs seen while driving through Colorado—both wood and metal—were more than likely made by inmates. At the Territorial Correctional Facility, signs were made for the highways, parks, and national forests within the state. Some have been replaced by the Department of Transportation, but many of the originals remain.

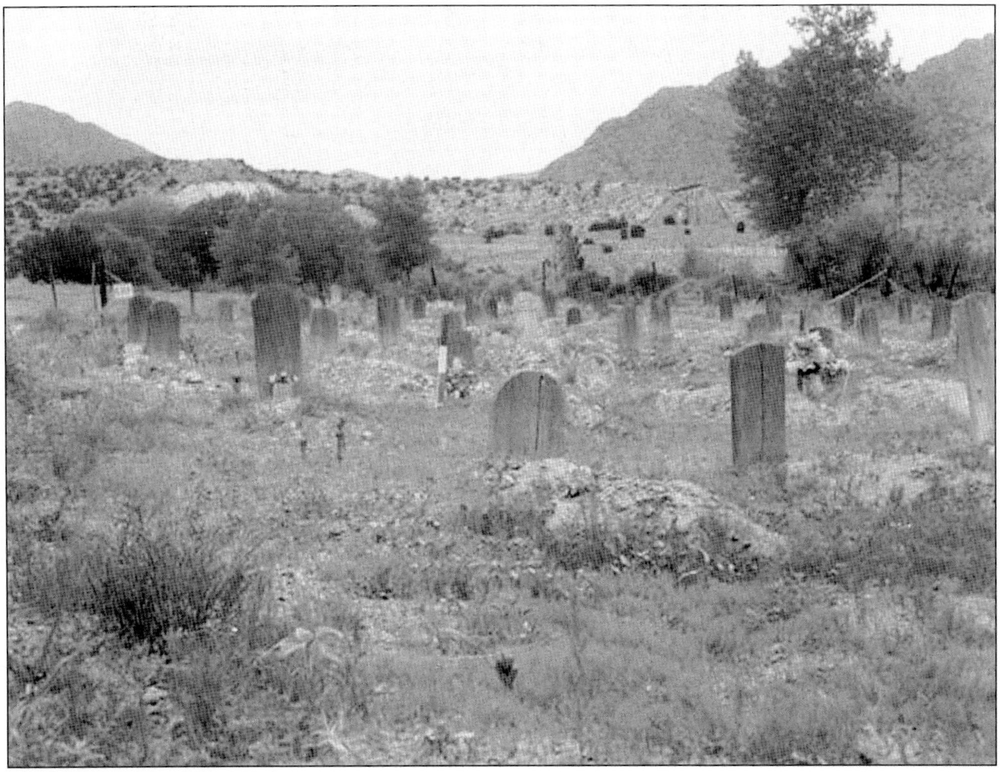

From 1872 to 1971, prisoners who died while incarcerated and whose families could not claim their remains were buried by the state at the Greenwood Cemetery. The section was named Woodpecker Hill by the inmates.

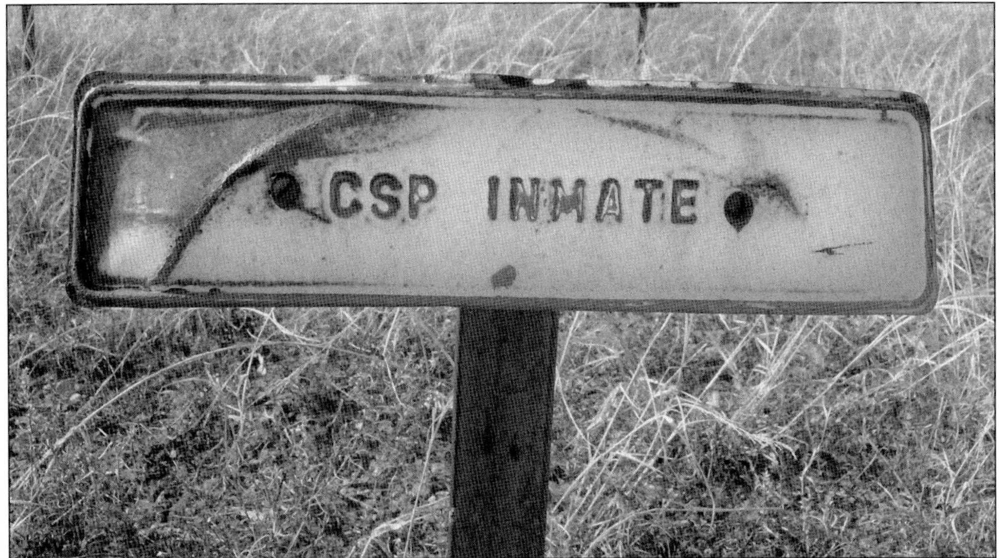

Approximately 600 prisoners are buried on Woodpecker Hill, but only 350 of the graves are marked with either a name plaque or a metal plaque simply reading "CSP Inmate." The old wooden slabs seen here were the original markers, and the woodpeckers would peck at the bugs in the slabs until they were fully destroyed. That is why the name *Woodpecker Hill* stuck.

Two

THE WORKINGS OF A PRISON

Although no images exist of the first prison's interior, it was described as a two-tiered structure with a kitchen, shower room, and guard office—very few bells and whistles compared to today's facilities. The six-by-eight-foot cells contained one bed, one mattress, a sheet to cover the down-filled mattress, one very thin blanket, and one pillow. Two uniforms were worn for a one-week period and then turned in to be laundered. Most prisoners would wash their own uniforms between laundering and hang them on the tiers to dry. Later, in the 1920s and 1930s, prisoners could possess more personal items and decorate their cells with personal touches. Families were allowed to send items such as clothing and sheets, blankets, and bedspreads that added a homey touch to the cells.

Now inmates are double-bunked in a cell about one foot wider and one foot longer, and all items must be purchased through a list approved by the Department of Corrections. Families can mail money with which the inmates may buy canteen items, but families cannot send items directly. A few things, such as hobby materials and books, are allowed from the outside, but they also must be purchased and sent from an approved vendor or store. To prohibit the introduction of contraband, restrictions on outside vendors are strongly upheld.

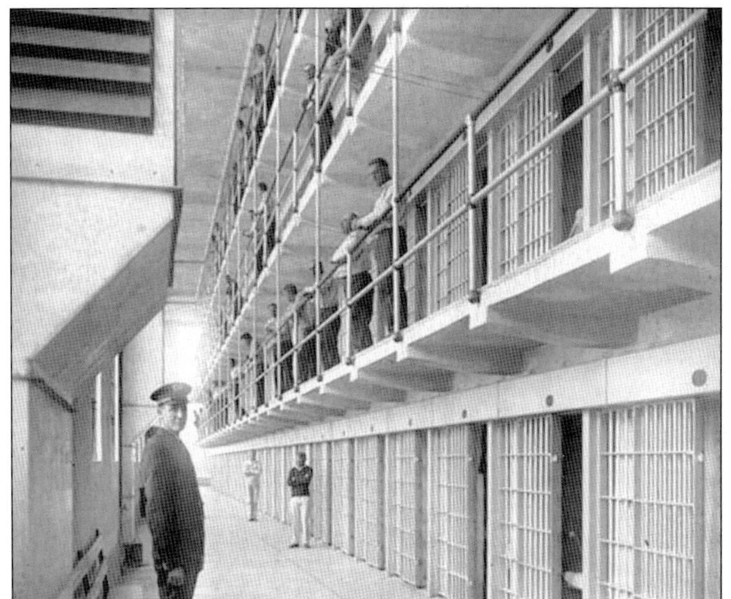

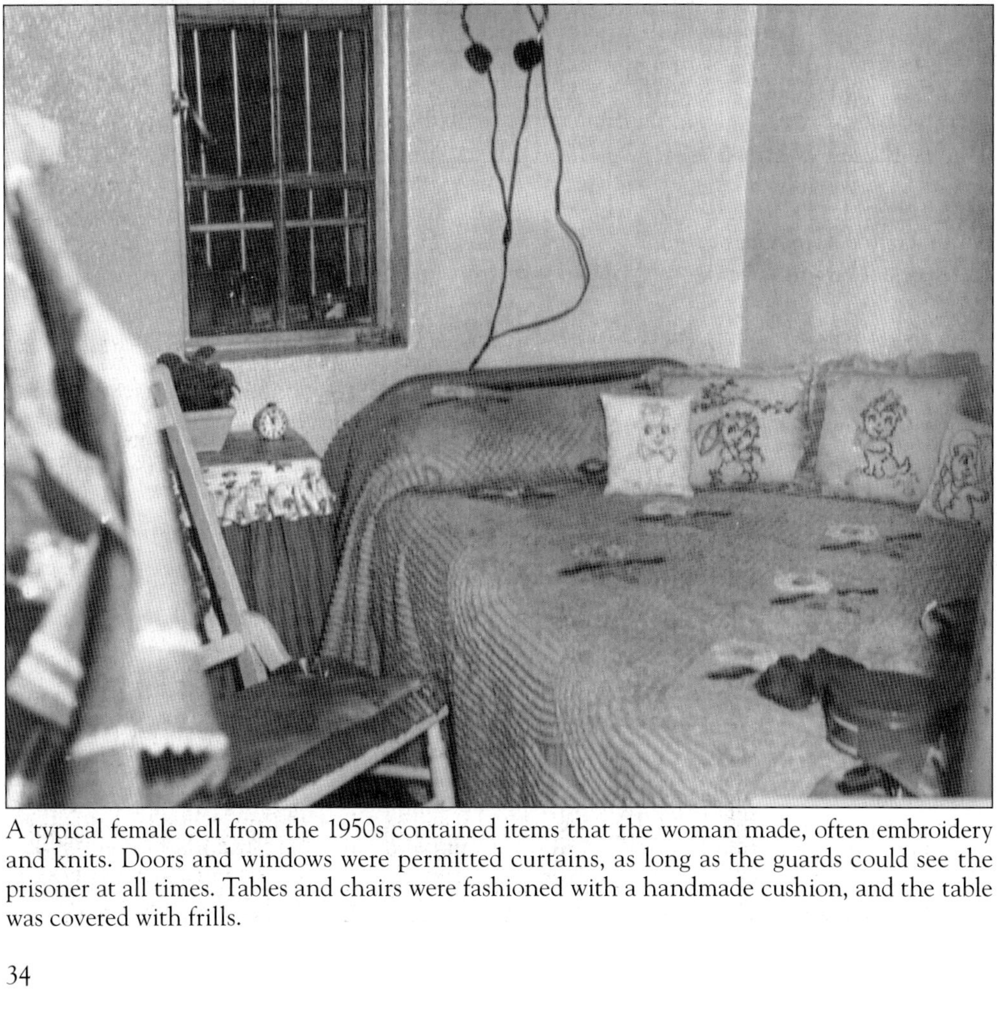

A typical female cell from the 1950s contained items that the woman made, often embroidery and knits. Doors and windows were permitted curtains, as long as the guards could see the prisoner at all times. Tables and chairs were fashioned with a handmade cushion, and the table was covered with frills.

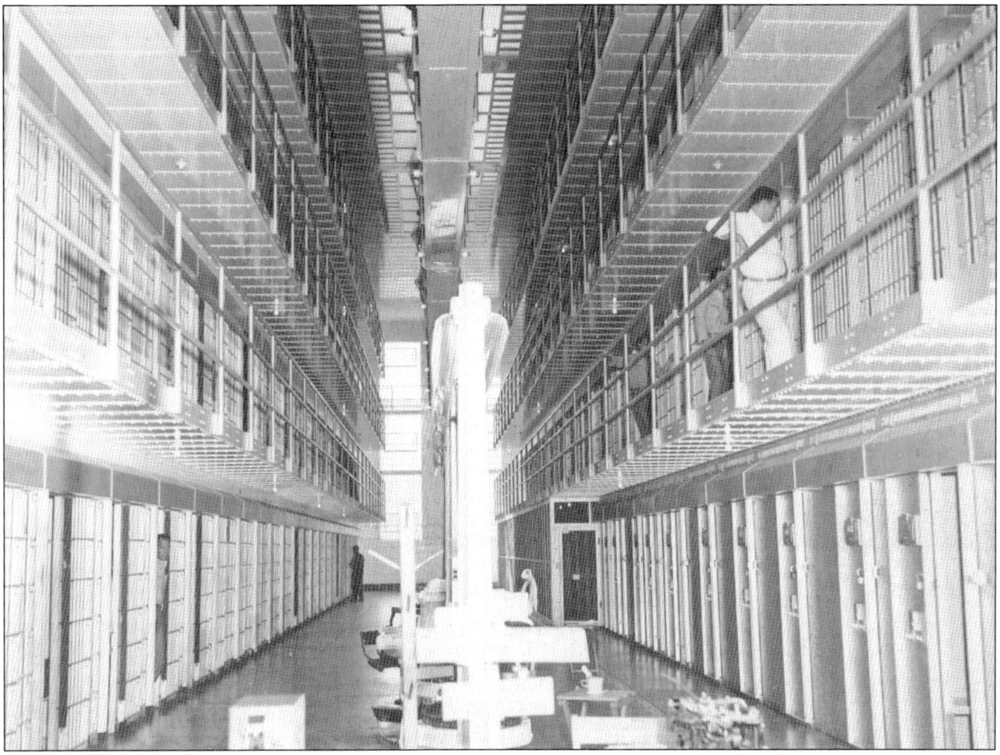

The cell houses were generally wet cells, meaning they contained a toilet and sink. A communal shower room was located at one end of the cell house and was used by all prisoners assigned there. Barber chairs lined the main corridor, and both prisoners and guards received haircuts from cell house barbers. One rule of thumb for the corridor: always walk under the overhanging tier so nothing can be dropped on one's head from above.

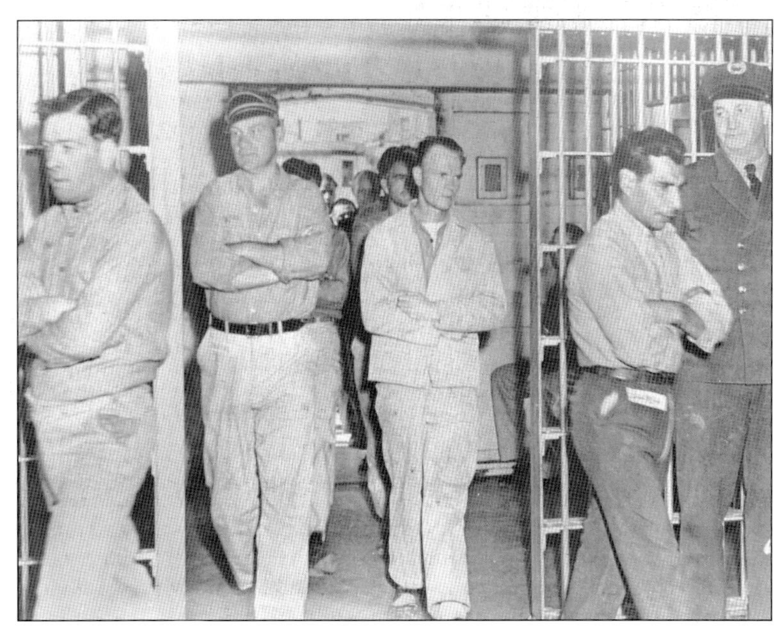

When prisoners moved from one area to another in a group, they were required to cross their arms in front of their chests. This pose is evident in many photographs throughout this book. Guards escorted prisoners to and from the job site, to chow, and to night lockdown.

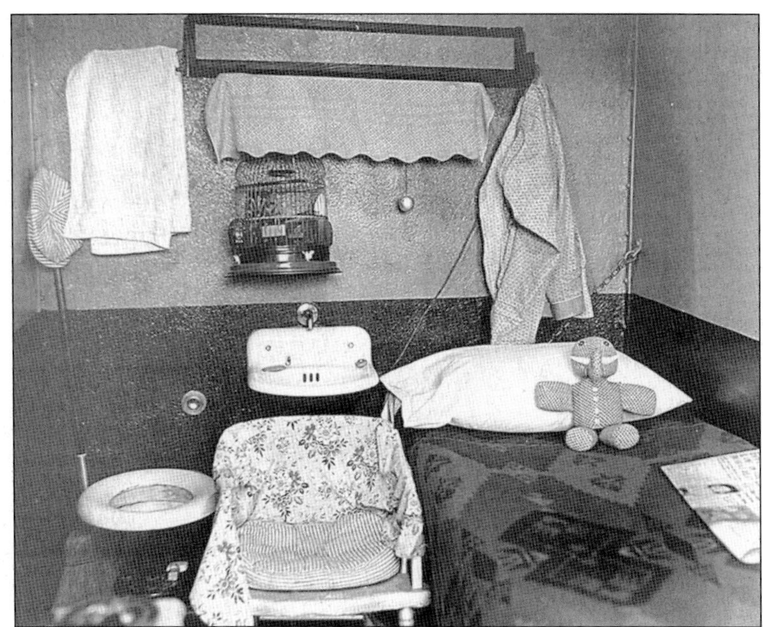

A male prison cell from the 1920s sometimes contained a bird in a cage, as inmates of that era were permitted pet birds. They could also decorate their rooms with personal touches. Now there are two inmates in most cells, and personal items are basically limited to purchases from the prison canteen.

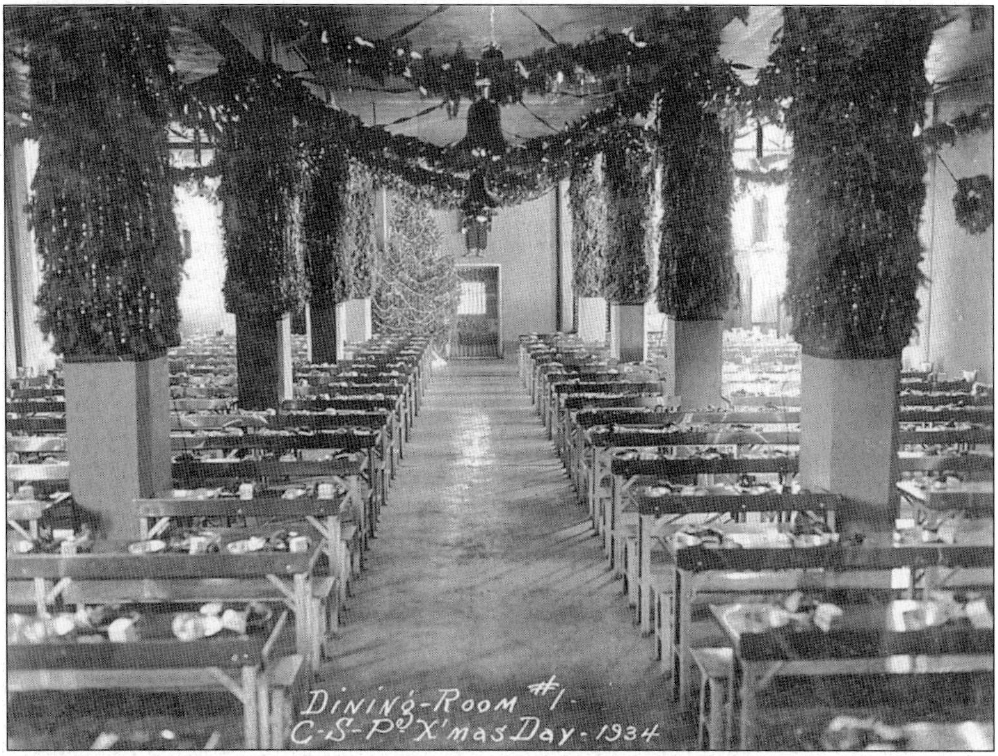

Christmas is celebrated in different ways by prisoners. Here the dining area is festooned with garland and a tree. The Department of Corrections recognizes many different religions, and prisoners are free to worship any faith. If it is not a department-recognized religion, inmates are prohibited from possessing items associated with its practice.

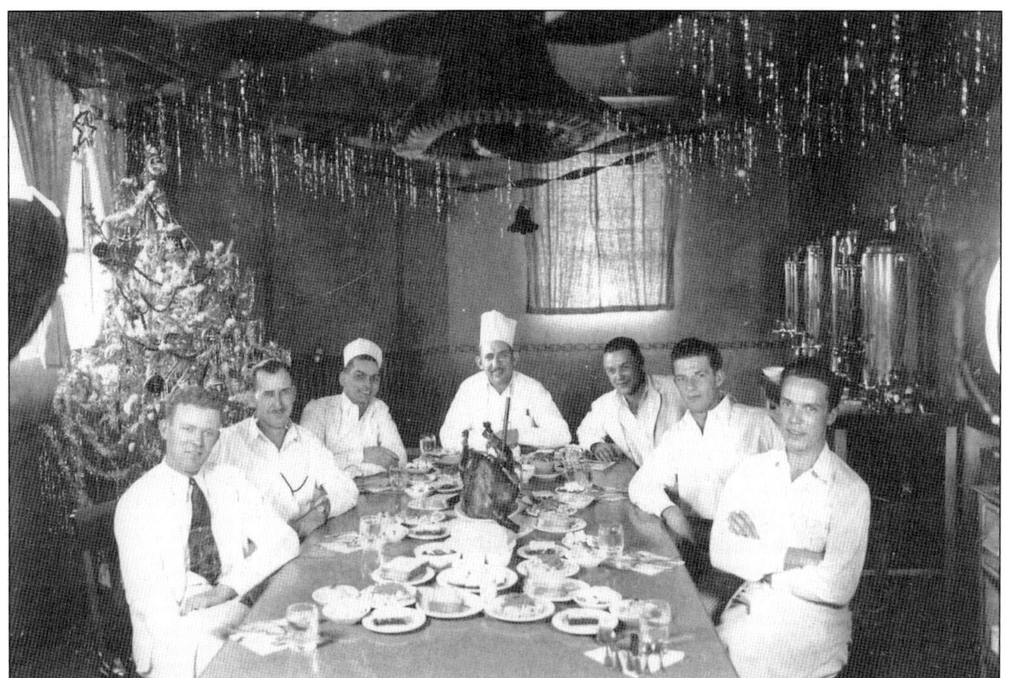

In the early 1900s, kitchen staff and the prisoners working in the kitchen share a Christmas dinner with all the trimmings. Usually guards who had the misfortune of working on Christmas would be joined by other guards to share the meal at a table such as this.

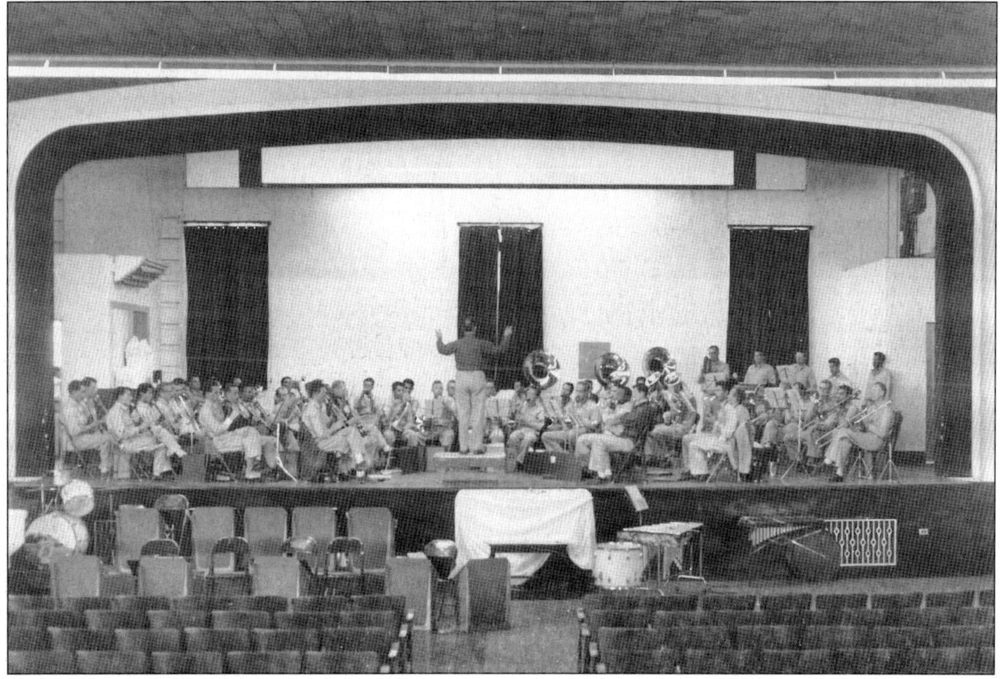

The prison band, seen here in 1938, performed for the public, often leaving the prison to give concerts. Band members also marched in the annual Blossom Parade in downtown Cañon City every May. And of course concerts were put on for the prisoners on holidays and special occasions.

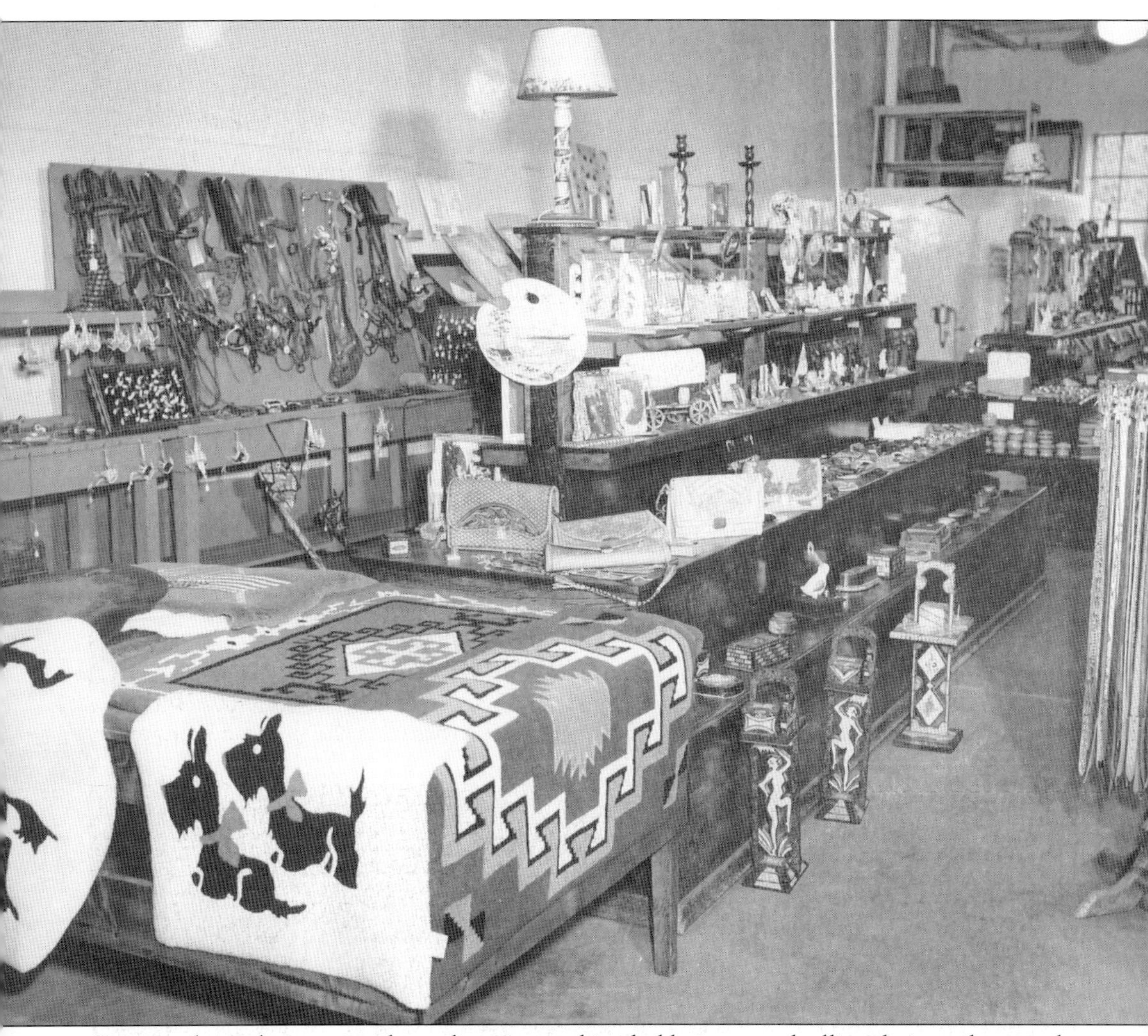

Prisoners have always enjoyed spending time making hobby items and selling their products to the public. From the early 1900s until the 1970s, Territorial had a curio shop just inside its front entrance where tourists and citizens could purchase prisoner-crafted goods such as rugs, lamps, handcrafted jewelry, leather wear, and bits and spurs. Some people simply bought for the novelty of owning something made by a prisoner, but many items where well crafted and made to last. Today the curio shop is no longer open, but items can be purchased in the Museum of Colorado Prisons.

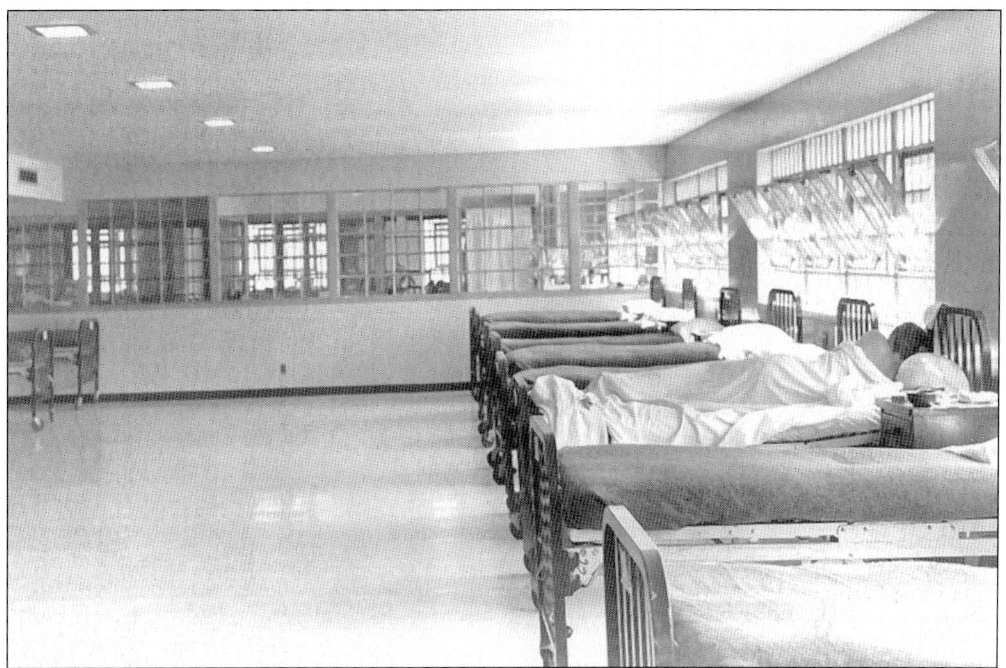

A new infirmary was constructed as an addition to the existing hospital in the 1960s. With four new prisons in the area, more beds were needed at the infirmary. To this day, the infirmary at Territorial is used as the medical unit for all eight facilities.

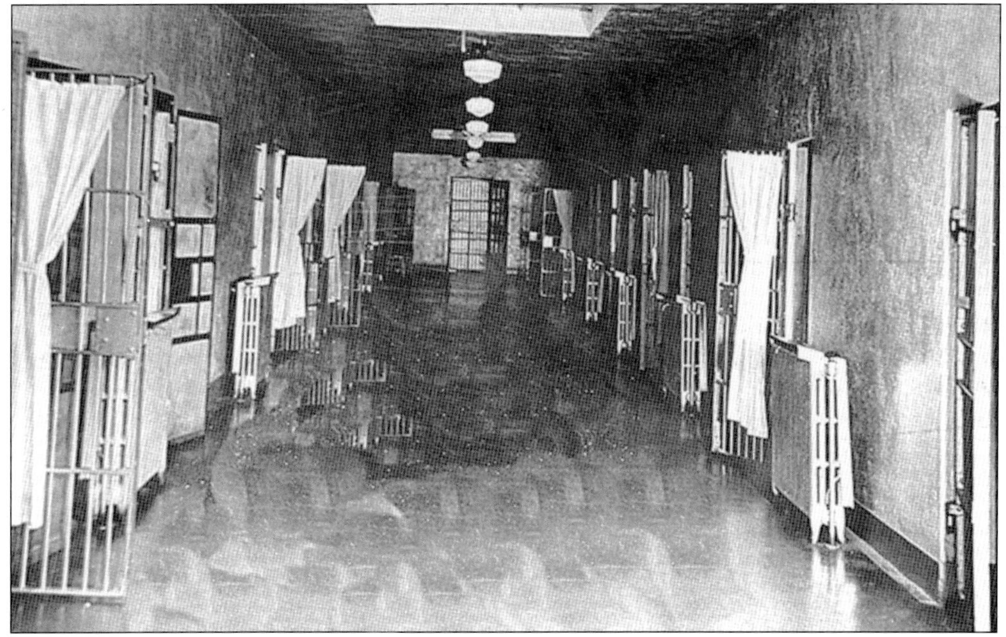

In 1935, Colorado Women's Correctional Institute was built outside the east wall, under the protection of Tower 6. It included 32 cells, along with 2 isolation cells in the basement; these were wet cells with their own toilet and sink and a community shower in the hall. The dining and laundry areas were downstairs. The old women's institute is now home to the Museum of Colorado Prisons.

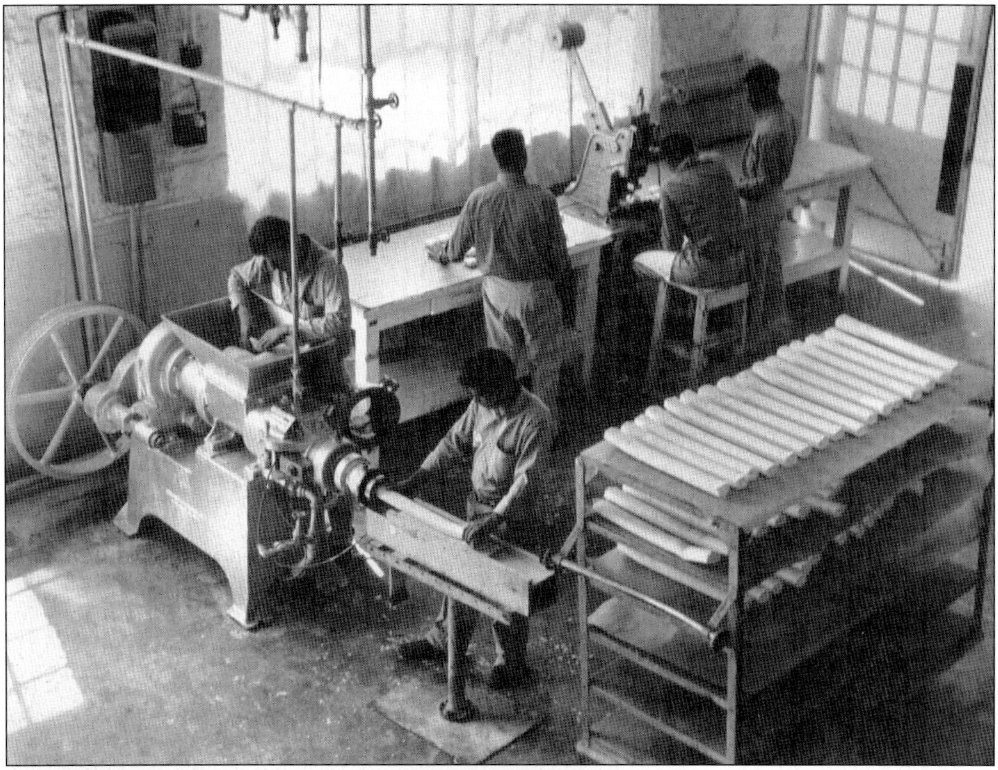

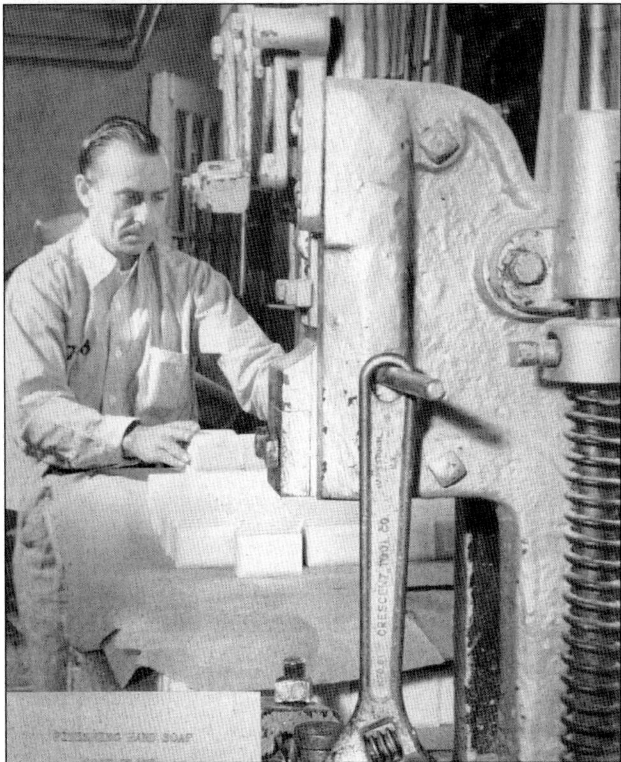

In the 1930s, soap was a big business in the prison. Here inmates make the soap in a long rope, sending it through the machine to form, shape, and cut. This lightly scented soap could take the bark off a tree. Prisoners were also warned that dropping the soap in the shower could be hazardous to their health.

The next step in the soap-making process was to mark it with the prison logo and package it. The original soap was marked simply "CSP" for Colorado State Penitentiary. Later, when Roy Best became warden, it was changed to "Roys Best Soap." The soap was made in two different colors: white and pink.

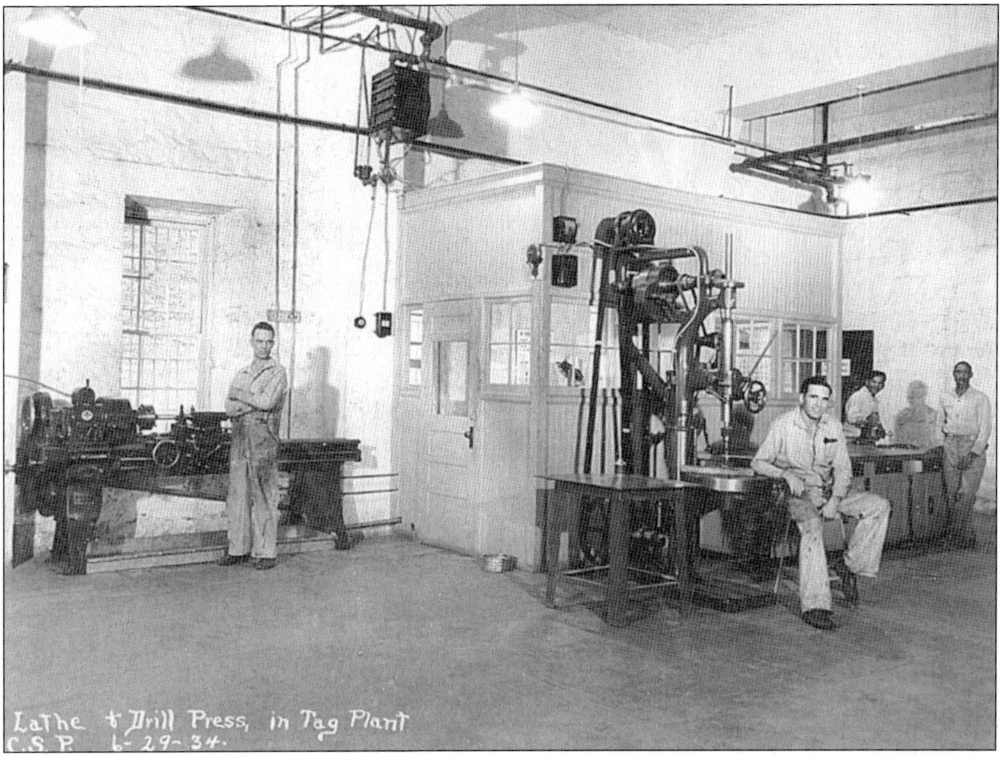

Colorado was the first state to use prison labor to manufacture license plates. Many prisoners were employed in the tag plant; today it is still a busy shop that produces tags for all vehicles licensed in Colorado. Here inmates use a lathe and mill to cut the plates to size in June 1934.

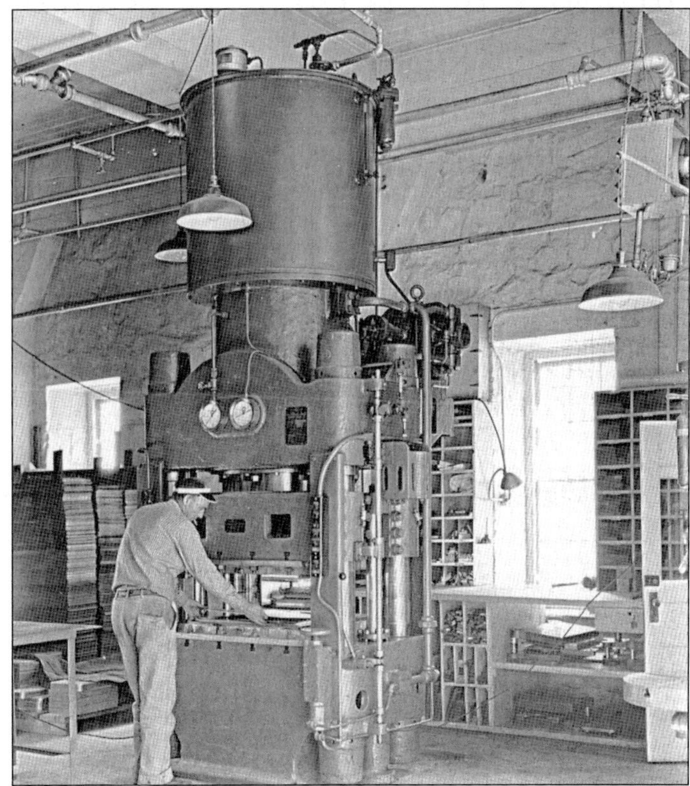

After the plate was cut, this machine imprinted it with the Colorado logo, tag number, and in days before sticky tags were used, the month and year. Now with tags specialized for different organizations and military groups and with the infinite possibilities of vanity plates, the plant keeps very busy.

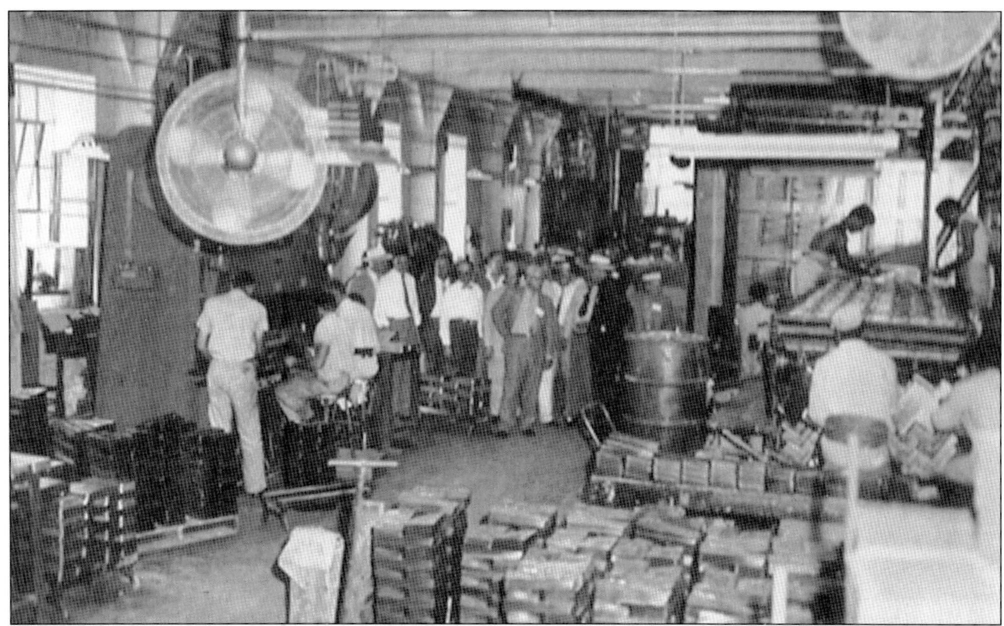

Since Colorado was the first to manufacture plates in the prison system, many states sent representatives to see how the operation worked. Here a group, including Colorado dignitaries such as the governor, visits the plant. Many states now use the prison system to manufacture license plates.

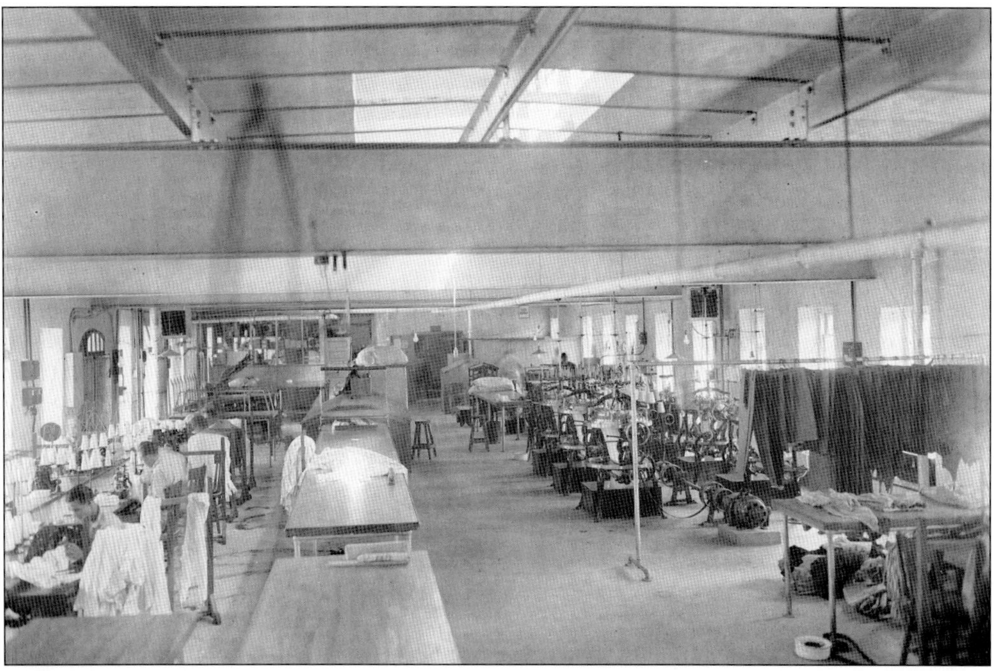

The sewing shop made prisoner as well as guard uniforms. The uniform was hemmed and marked with the prisoner's name and number. After pressing and folding, the clothing was sent to the laundry, where it was issued to the inmate.

Three

WE ARE ALL IN THIS TOGETHER

From the beginning in any law enforcement setting—be it police, sheriff, or corrections—there are unspoken rules among employees: stick together, protect, and always stand up for a fellow worker. In the Department of Corrections, it is always to protect those in blue. One has to be able to trust and count on those he works with because it could mean the difference between life and death.

In the early days on the hill gangs, outside work details, and inside the cell houses, the prisoners outnumbered the guards. Most guards were armed because there may not be another guard covering his back, and all he had between himself and a crowd of angry prisoners was a gun to ward them off. Now officers are unarmed, but help is just a radio call away; others can be there to assist in a matter of seconds in most cases. Situations can still arise in a few moments and escalate before help comes, however. An officer is often left alone in a very stressful situation, but today the Department of Corrections trains its employees in all scenarios so that they are prepared to handle whatever happens.

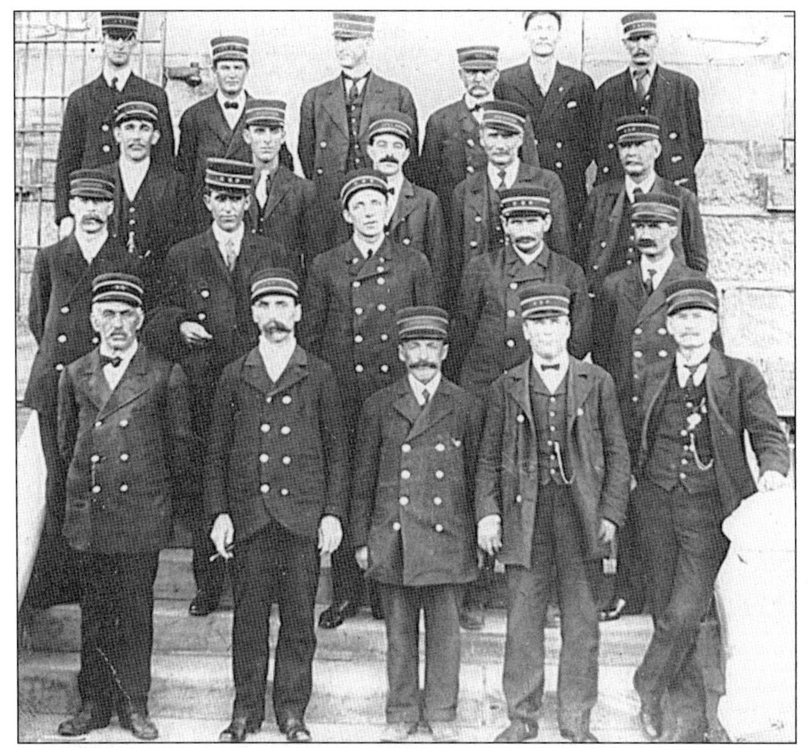

In the late 1800s, prison guards stand in front of the cell house for a group photograph. At the time, this was the extent of the staff. They were not called guards but rather overseers and turnkeys. Women were not allowed to work at the prison, and many of the men were over 70.

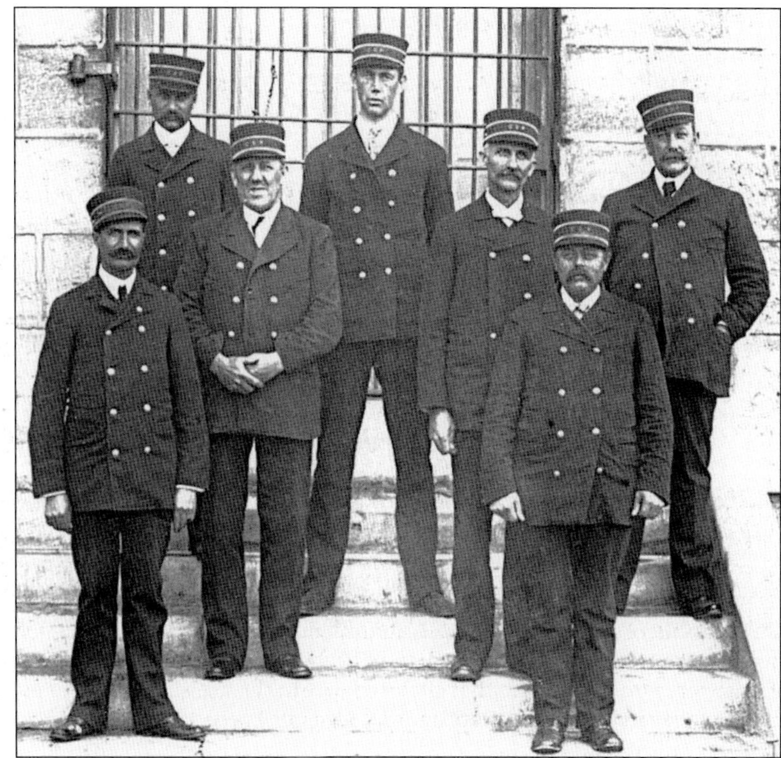

In 1871, overseers and turnkeys were paid $25 per month, while the warden received $208 per quarter. The warden was a governor-appointed position during that time.

Hiring at the prison in the early 1900s was an easy task, considering many men needed the work. No high school diploma or college degree was required, and there was no age limit. This hospital steward looks ready for retirement but probably worked for a few more years.

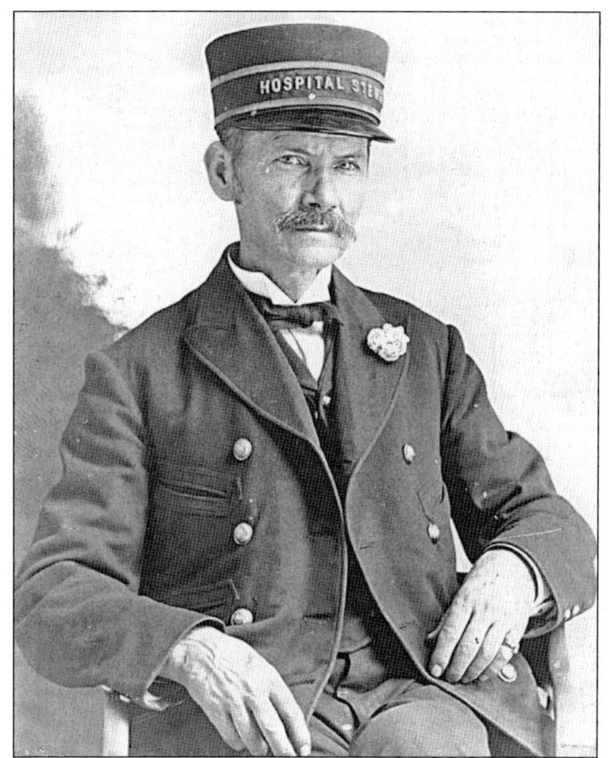

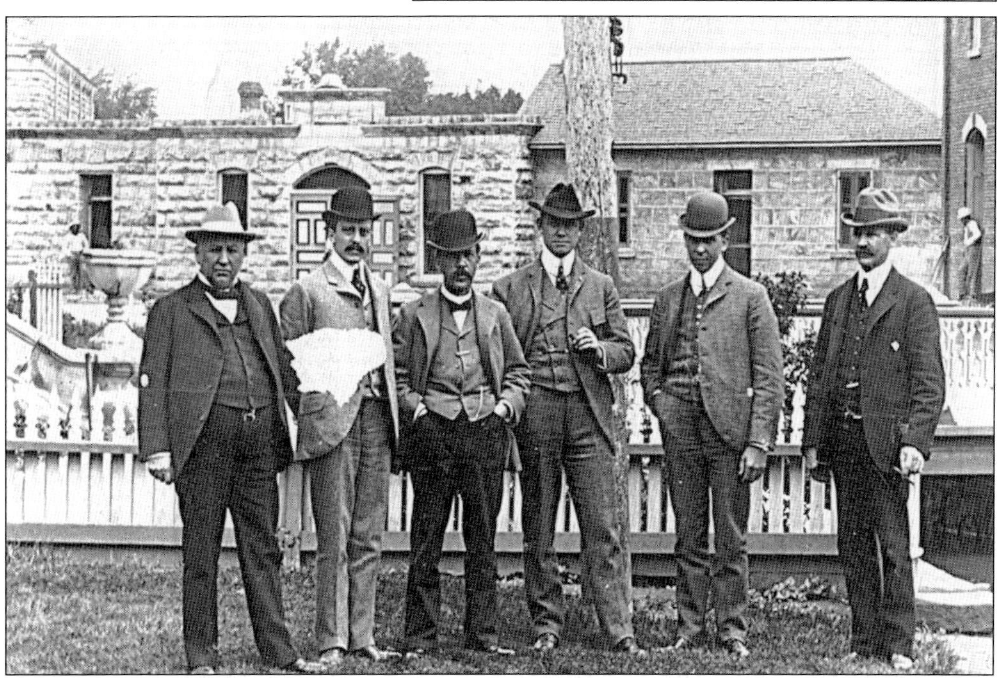

Here dignified-looking men stand in front of the firehouse. Territorial had a fire brigade consisting of prisoners who fought fires that occurred within the walls. In 1929, flames erupted during a riot and hostage situation in the prison, and inmates burned down a cell house, the dining room, and the auditorium.

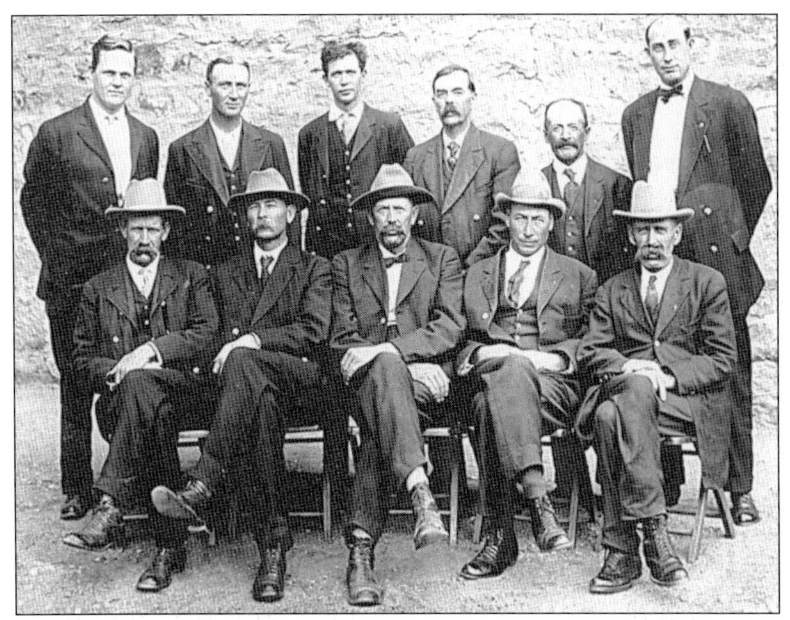

The caption for this photograph reads, "Famous Western Lawmen." Like those in so many images, these people were not identified. Lawmen came to the prison to drop off outlaws from different counties in Colorado and then stayed to tour the prison. They also came to see prisoners from their jurisdiction hang for their dirty deeds.

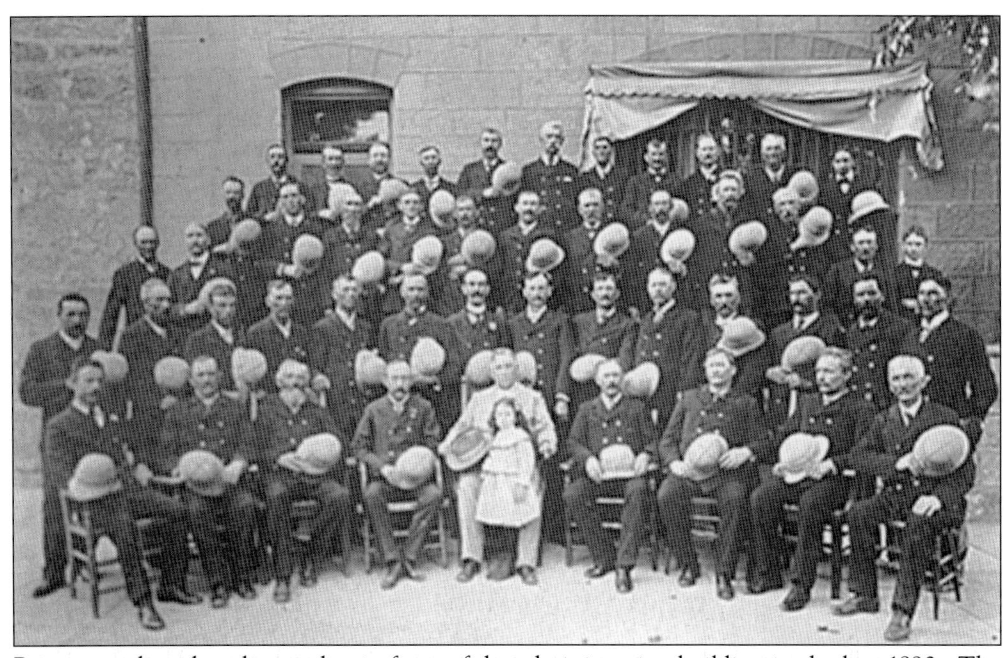

Prison guards and workers gather in front of the administration building in the late 1890s. The man seated in front with the little girl, though not identified, was likely the warden at the time. The warden's family lived in the warden's house on site, and the children were driven to school by prisoners.

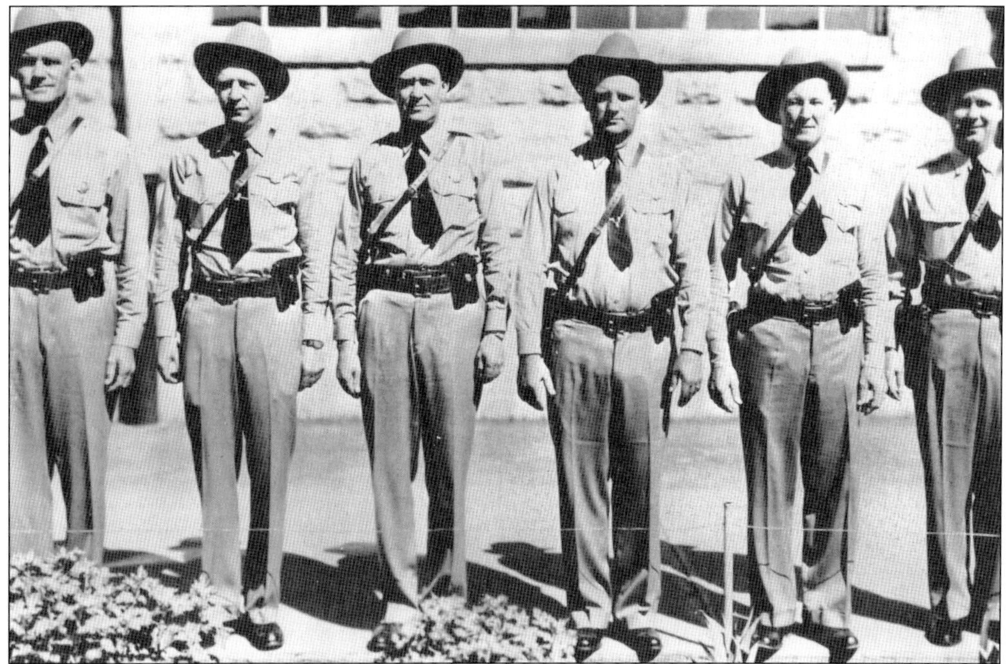

Lining up for inspection, from left to right, are guards Athol Payne, Lawton Anderson, Bob Manley, Gourly Smith, Heteher Madison, and Floyd Rush. Uniforms of the day were tan in color. They have changed over the years to tan shirts and green pants, then light blue shirts and dark blue pants, and now light blue shirts and navy BDUs (battle dress uniforms).

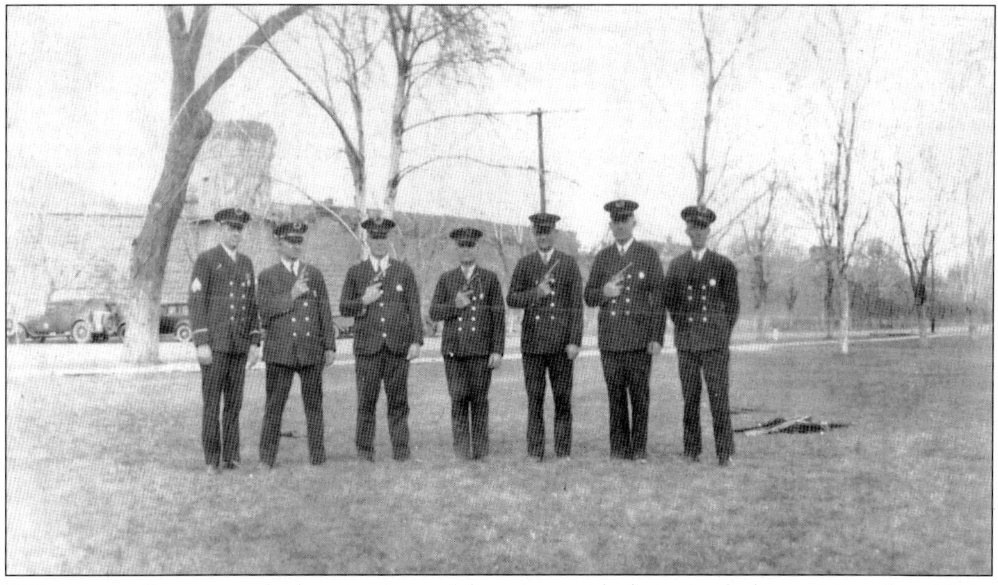

Officers proudly pose on the lawn in front of the prison with their pistols drawn. More than likely, this group was the prison honor guard. An honor guard team is present at all state employee funerals, where members accompany the casket to the grave site, fold the flag, and present it to the family. Upon request, a 21-gun salute is performed and taps is played.

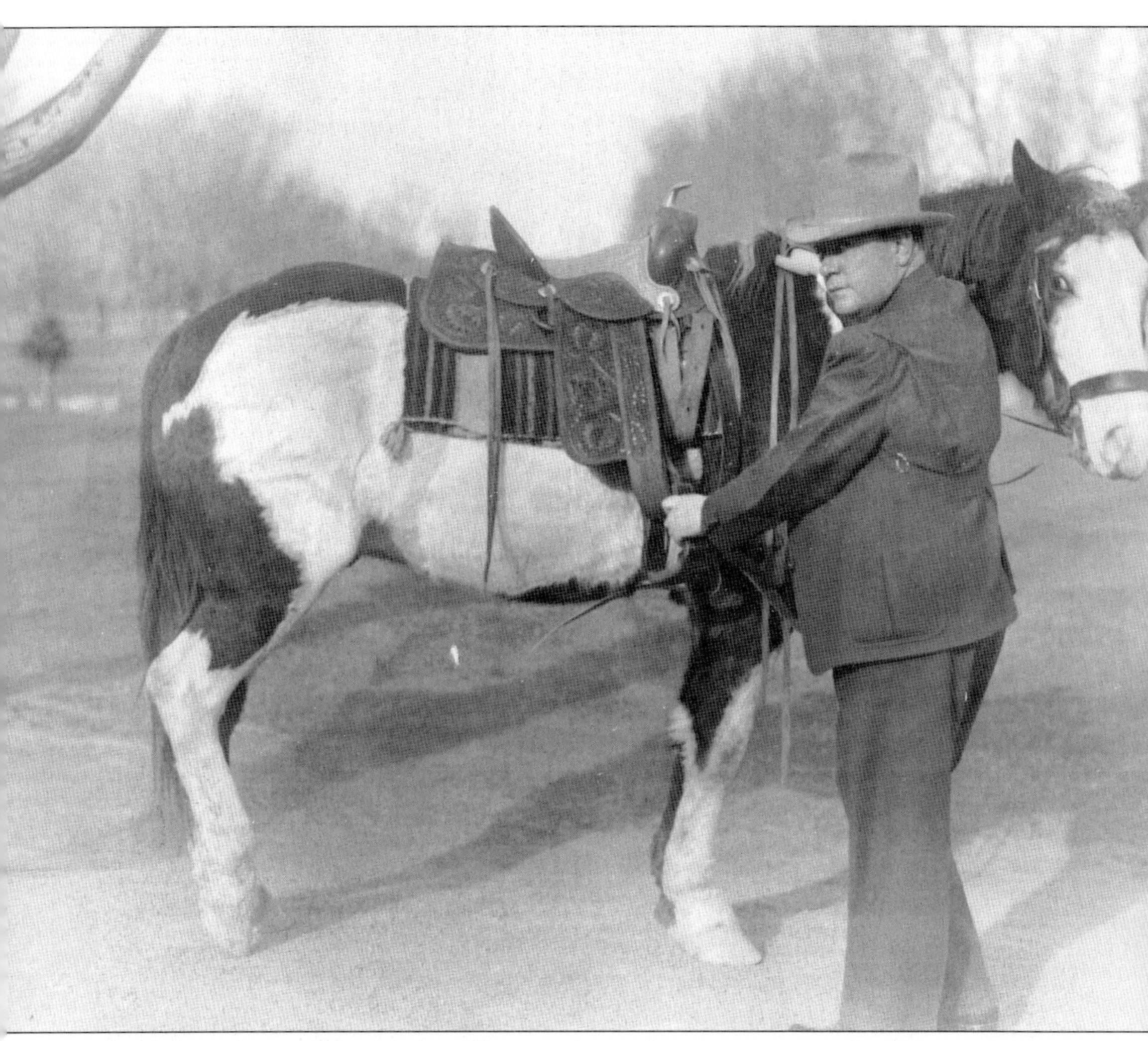

Roy Best served as warden at Colorado State Penitentiary from age 32 in 1932 until his death in 1954. He was a strict disciplinarian who believed that keeping a prisoner busy would keep him out of trouble. During his 20 years of service, construction never stopped. A firm believer in the "Old Gray Mare," the whipping post, Best used it when the crime fit the punishment—not for small infractions. He was well liked by most, but others thought of him as pompous and overbearing. It was said that one either loved him or hated him; there was no in-between. In 1952, Best was indicted for misappropriation of state funds and violation of prisoners' rights and suspended from his job for two years. Two days before he was to return to work, he died of a heart attack.

Warden Roy Best, pictured in front of the original two-seat gas chamber, was known for the good he did the prison but more so for his indictment in 1952. He was suspended for two years but was acquitted of all state charges and allowed to return to work.

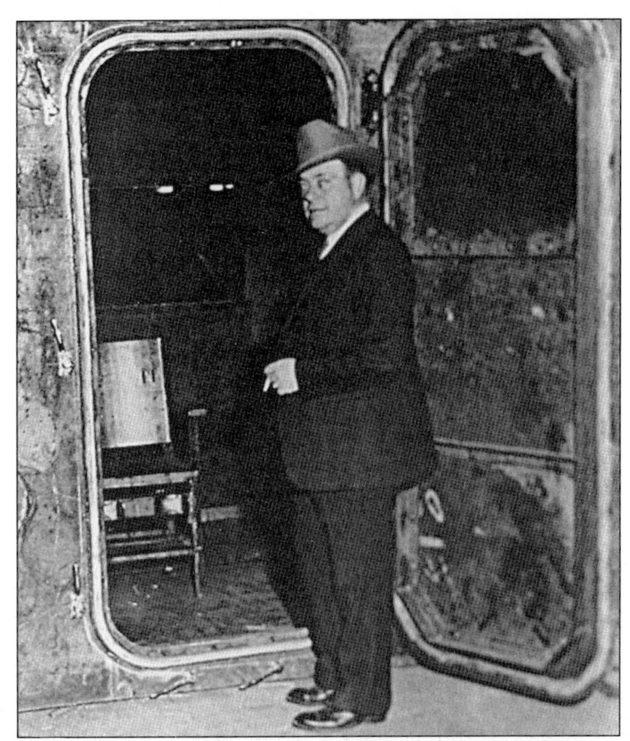

Roy Best loved the limelight, as evidenced by this pose with the 1950 Colorado Rodeo Queen Katy Berry. Every photograph opportunity that occurred at the prison, Roy Best usually took advantage of it. Some describe him as a legend in his own mind.

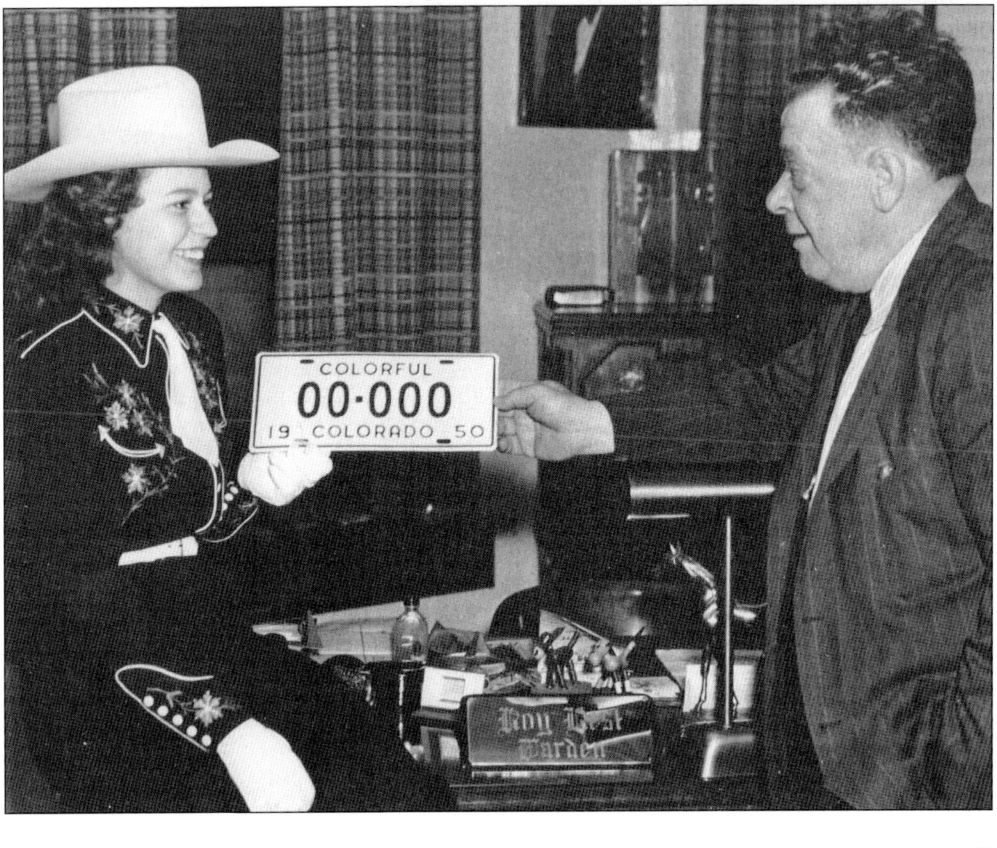

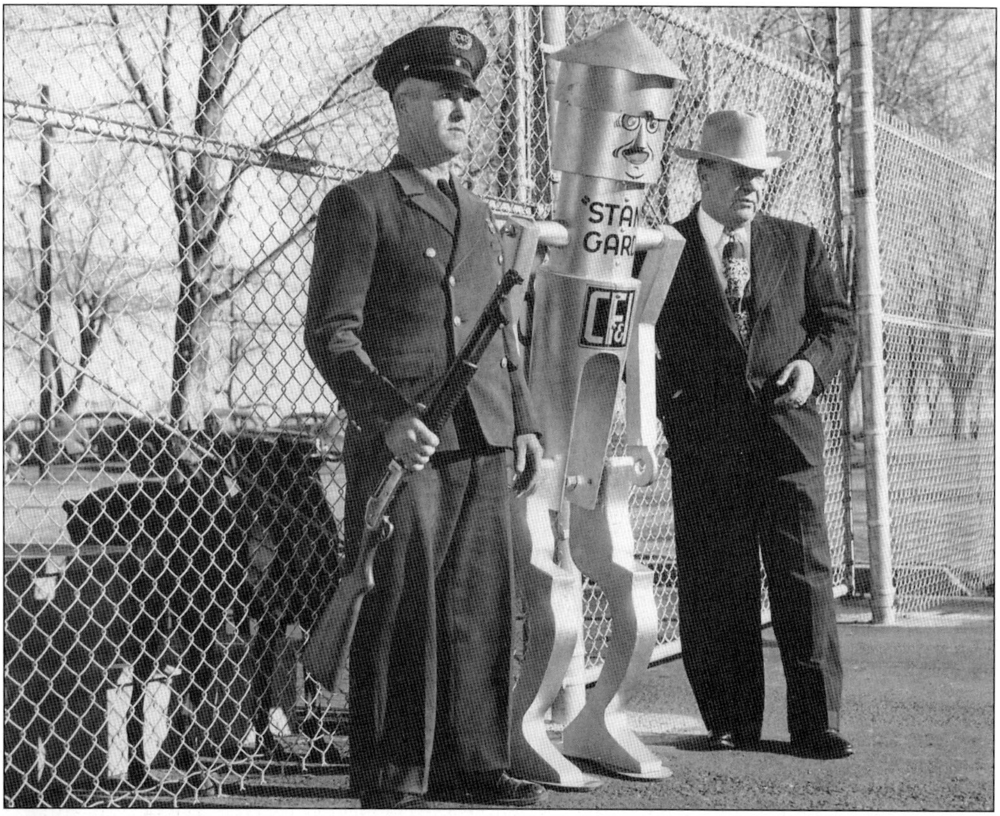

Best (right) and an unidentified guard stand alongside *Stan Guard*, a statue made at Colorado Fuel and Iron in Pueblo. The prison had awarded the company the contract for the prison's steel doors, and in thanks the firm presented the statue.

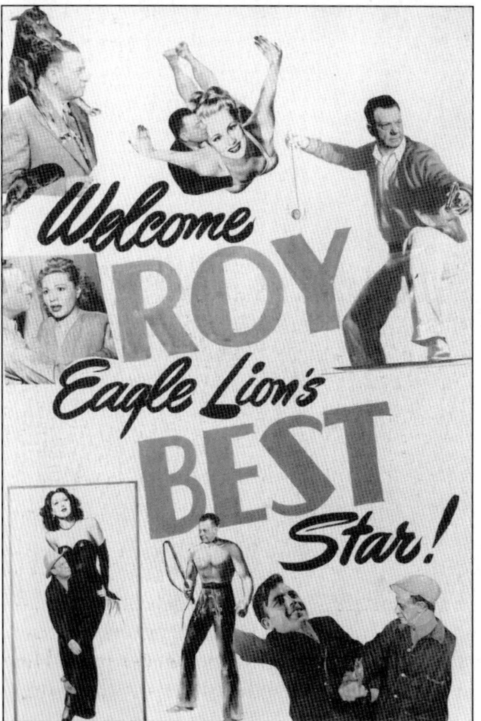

When the movie *Cañon City* was completed in Cañon on July 2, 1948, the city declared it "Roy Best Day." Lions Gate Studio made posters for the occasion, and Roy Best was immortalized in his best poses.

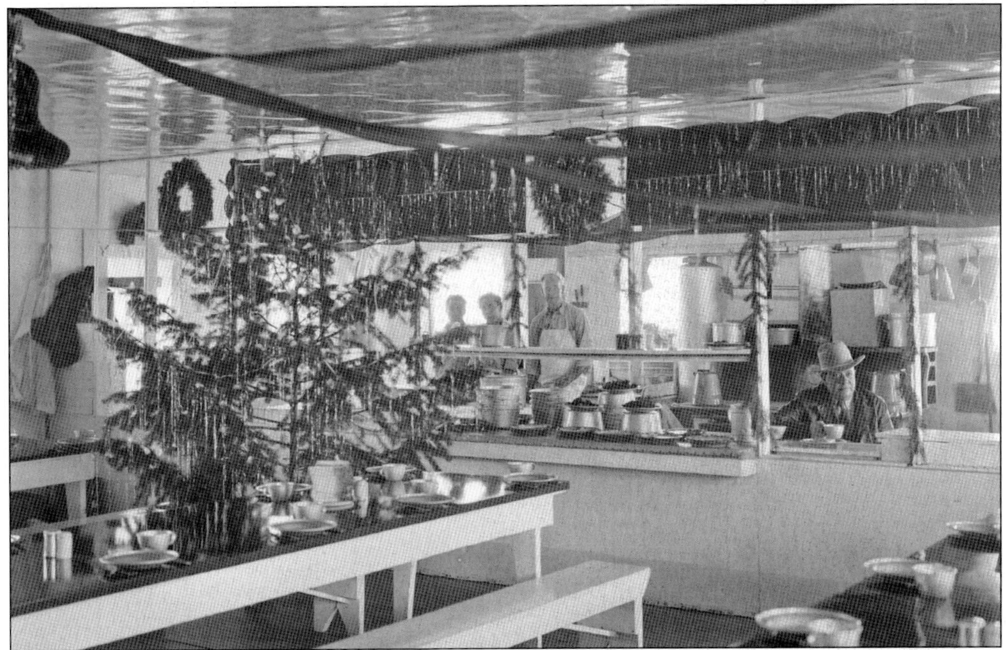

The Ranch 1 dining hall is decorated for Christmas in this 1945 view. Roy Best drinks a cup of coffee in the window. The warden spent much of his time at Ranch 1 ensuring that the construction was up to his standards. He was often seen on the construction site keeping an eye on the activities.

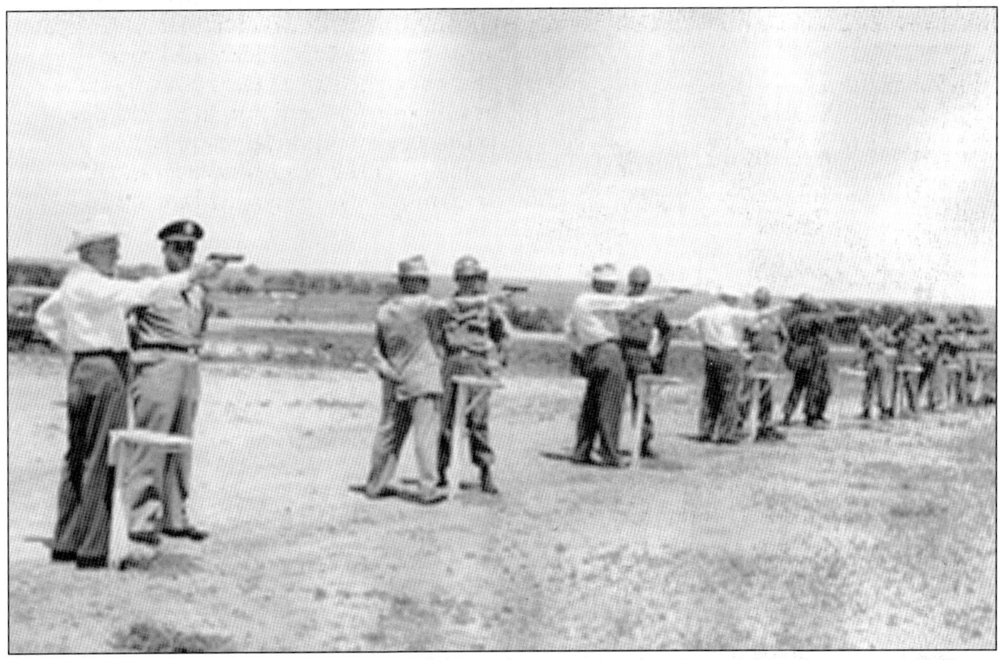

Guards and present-day officers must qualify on the weapons that are used in the prisons. Officers must now qualify twice a year on Ultron stun guns, the 37-millimeter gun, and pepper spray. Here guards line up to perform with handguns, which officers normally carried when making armed transports of prisoners.

NAME: TUTTLE, Harold Richard   TELEPHONE NO.: 275-3879

ADDRESS: 728 North Diamond Canon City, Colo.   DATE EMPLOYED: 7-13-64

COLORADO STATE PENITENTIARY
EMPLOYEE

DATE RETIRED:

DATE RESIGNED:

HEIGHT: 5-11½   WEIGHT: 191

EYES: Hazel   HAIR: Dk. Brown

COMPLEXION: Med-Ruddy

BUILD: Medium

WARDEN'S SIGNATURE:

COMMENTS:

10-A-20

By the 1960s, many locals were working for the prisons in the area. Each staff member was identified by a card bearing his or her personal information. Officer Harold Tuttle (above) worked at Colorado State Penitentiary before serving as the mail room sergeant at Fremont Correctional Facility for many years. William Scutti (below) was employed at Colorado State Penitentiary in 1967 and then moved on to Shadow Mountain as shift commander. When Fremont and Shadow Mountain merged in 1991, Scutti became shift commander at Fremont. He was respected by all who worked under him (the author included) and was missed when he retired in early 2000.

COLORADO STATE PENITENTIARY

NAME ... SCUTTI, William Theodore ...   PAY ROLL TITLE ....

ADDRESS Rt. #1, Florence, Colorado ...   .

TELEPHONE .....784-6220...............   DATE OF BIRTH ......5-8-40.....

SHIFT ....DATE ....   DATE EMPLOYED ....2-6-67......

....   DATE CERTIFIED ....

....

CLASSES ATTENDED:

...............................HRS. ......INSTR.

...............................HRS. ......INSTR.

...............................HRS. ......INSTR.

...............................HRS. ......INSTR.

...............................HRS. ......INSTR.

...............................HRS. ......INSTR.

...............................HRS. ......INSTR.

DATE. ....HRS. ......INSTR.

NAME:	**TINSLEY, Harry C.**		TELEPHONE NO.:	~~1408~~ CR-5-3408
ADDRESS:	Warden's Residence		DATE EMPLOYED:	October 15, 1951

COLORADO STATE PENITENTIARY EMPLOYEE

DATE RETIRED:	
DATE RESIGNED:	
HEIGHT: 6-2"	WEIGHT: 201
EYES: Hazel	HAIR: Lt-Brown
COMPLEXION:	Lt-Ruddy
BUILD:	Medium-Slender
WARDEN'S SIGNATURE:	*Harry C. Tinsley*
COMMENTS:	

Harry Tinsley was appointed warden in the wake of Roy Best's troubles and subsequent death. The prison flourished under the command of this respected leader. His deputy warden, Wayne K. Patterson, had a dream that someday a museum would be built for the prison's history. His dream was realized in 1988 when the Museum of Colorado Prisons opened. Patterson served on the board until his death in 2003.

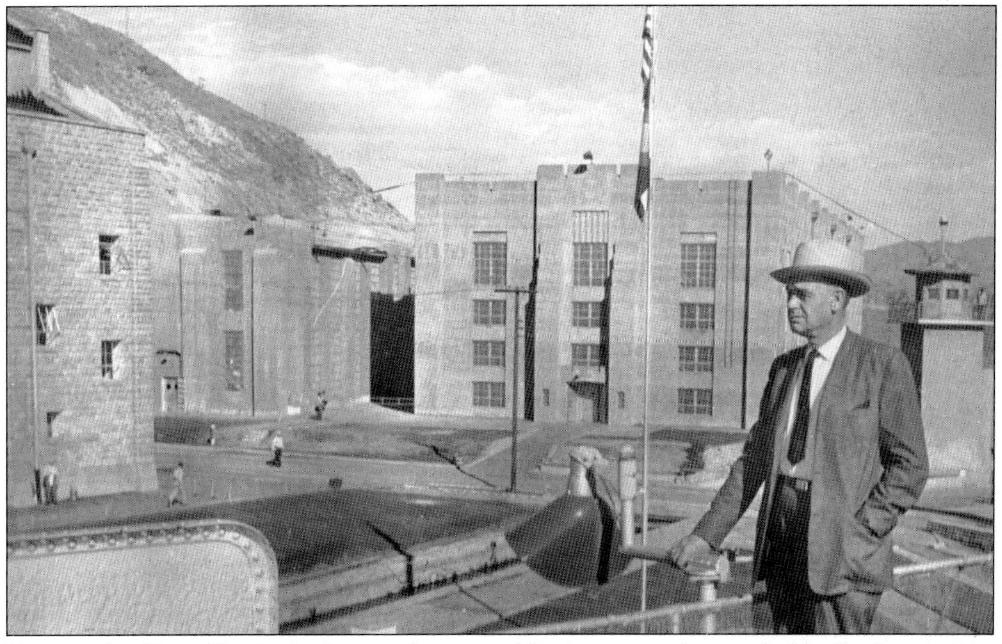

Here warden Harry Tinsley looks over the prison. Tinsley assumed control after the charges were filed against Roy Best. The prison was in turmoil at that time, and it would take a very strong leader to pull things together again. Tinsley was just the man the prison needed.

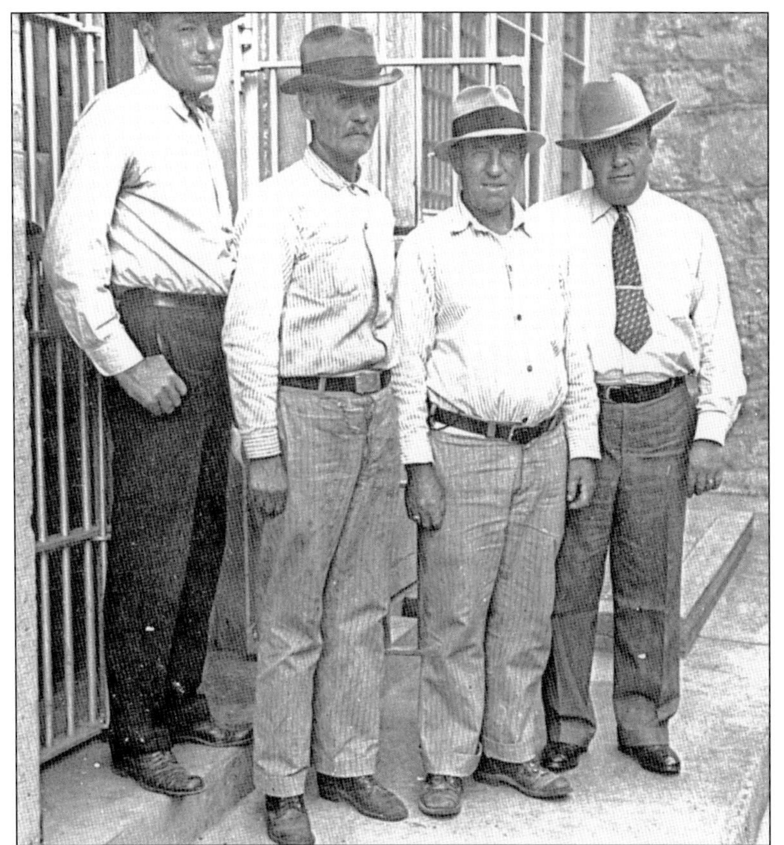

Warden Roy Best (right) stands outside one of the cell houses with a group of unidentified men. A dignitary and a politician, Best welcomed the opportunity to show off what he referred to as "his prison." He was proud of the accomplishments of the inmates he supervised and was often seen leading groups around the prison.

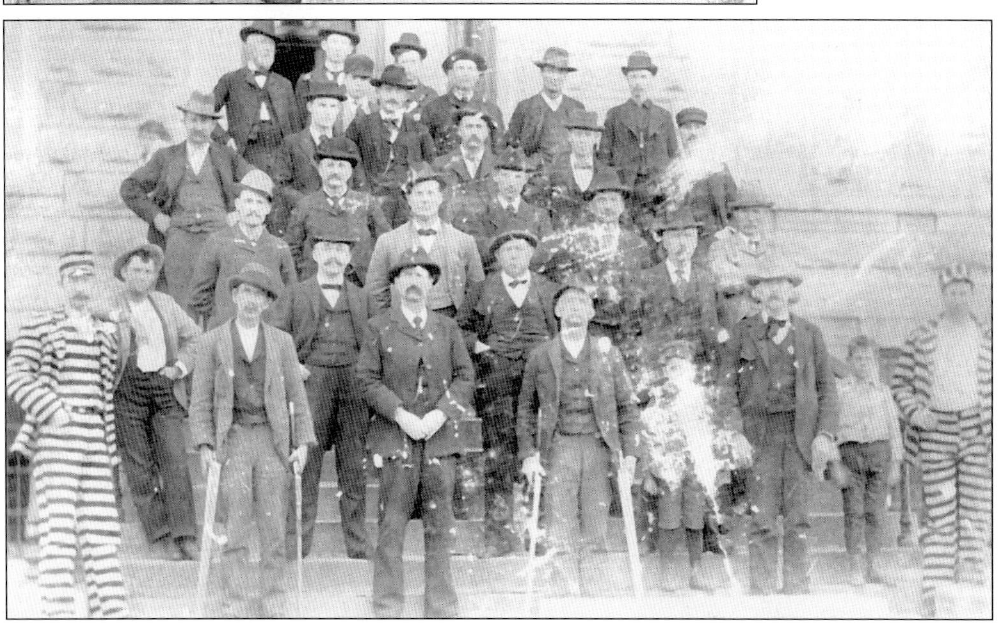

In this late-1800s photograph, employees, some with young children accompanying them, attend a function at the prison, perhaps a minstrel show or a band concert put on for the guards. The prisoners, seen in the striped uniforms, were more than likely trustees escorting the group.

Four

THE INFAMOUS AND THE GAMESTERS

Over the years, the Colorado Department of Corrections has had its share of infamous prisoners. Among them are the legendary Alfred Packer, the only man in history to be imprisoned for cannibalism, and Anton Woode, who at age 11 was the youngest person to be convicted and sent to an adult prison.

Engaging in sports has proven to be a great stress reliever—for the civilian population as well as prisoners. Aggressions can be released by pushing the body to its limits on a playing field, and scores can be settled by point value rather than fisticuffs. The Department of Corrections has allowed many different sports teams to form and compete over the years.

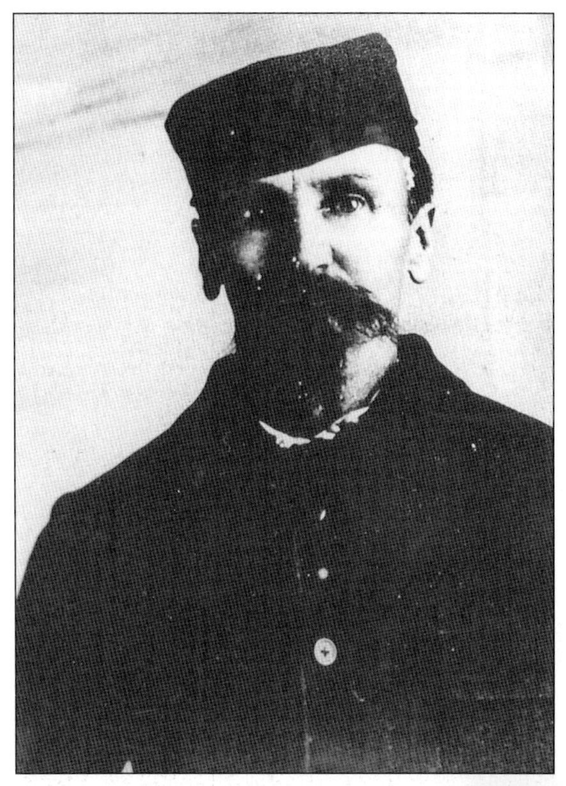

On November 8, 1873, Alfred Packer led a party of 21 from Utah into the mountains of Colorado. In April 1874, he emerged at the Los Pinos Agency in Colorado—alone and healthy. He explained that several of the men had turned back and that he and his party of five continued on their own. He said that the starving men eventually all died. His story seemed unbelievable, and after a search turned up five half-eaten bodies, Packer was charged and sent to prison for cannibalism. When Judge M. B. Gerry passed down his sentence, he reportedly stated, "Packer, they was seven Democrats in Hinsdale County, but you, you voracious, man-eating beast, you ate five of them and I therefore order you hung by the neck till you are dead." His sentence later commuted, Packer was released in 1901.

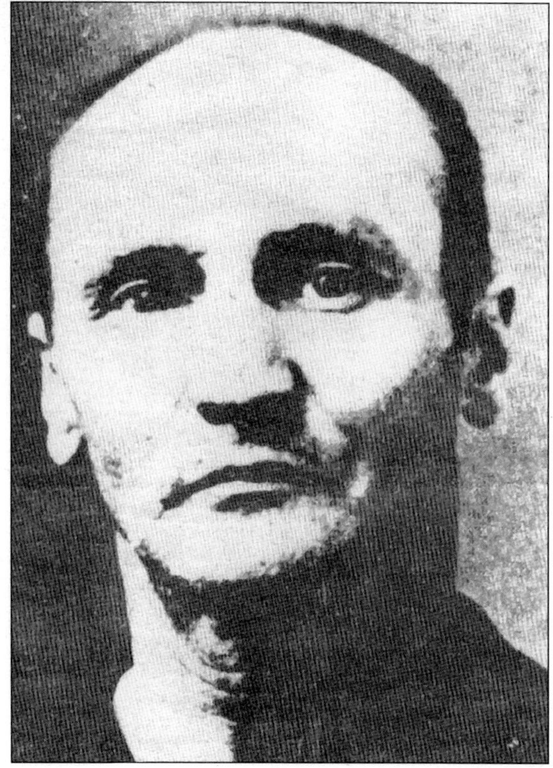

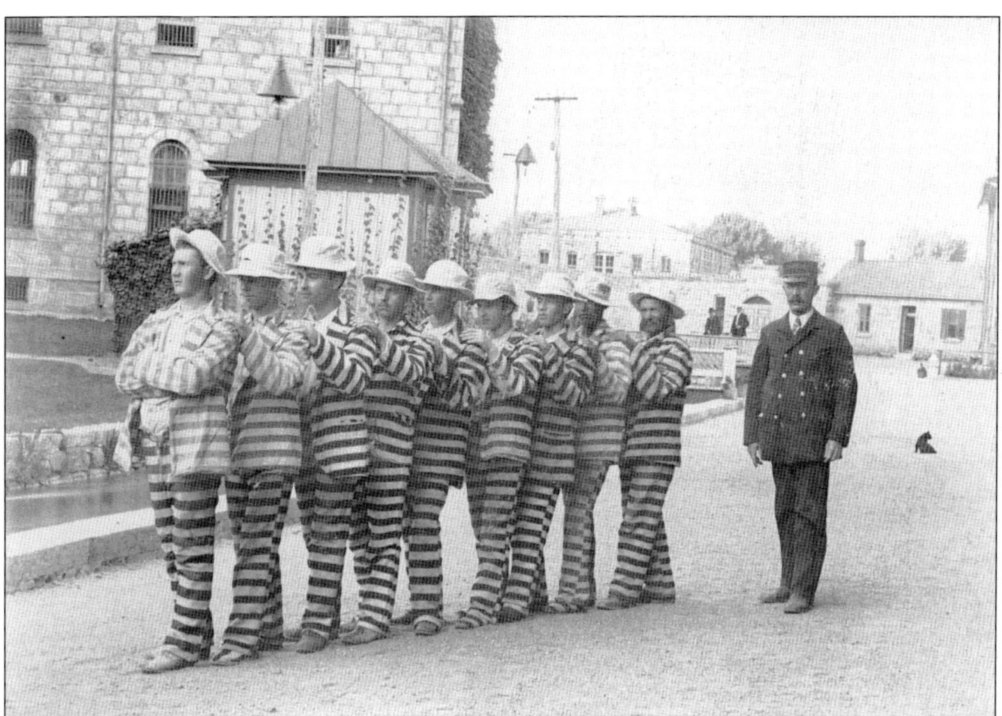

In the 1870s, prisoners wore black-and-white striped uniforms and hats resembling sailor caps. The formation seen here was called the lockstep, and all prisoners were required to walk this way when outside their living quarters.

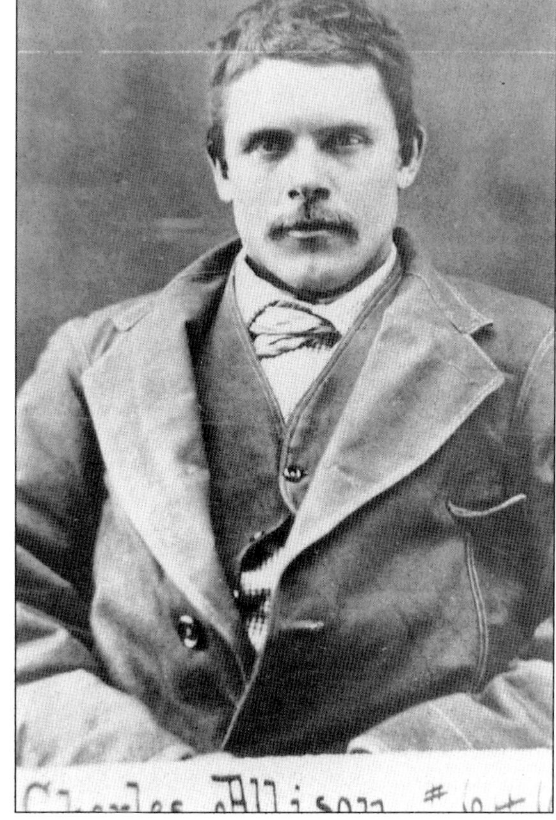

Charles Allison, No. 646, belonged to the infamous Allison Gang. Allison and his four-member gang terrorized New Mexico and Colorado Territory in the late 1800s. Finally caught in 1886, Allison, Henry Watts, and Louis Perkins were given sentences of 25 years to life, while W. A. Belcher received only three years in exchange for ratting on the rest. Allison served from 1881 until his release in 1890.

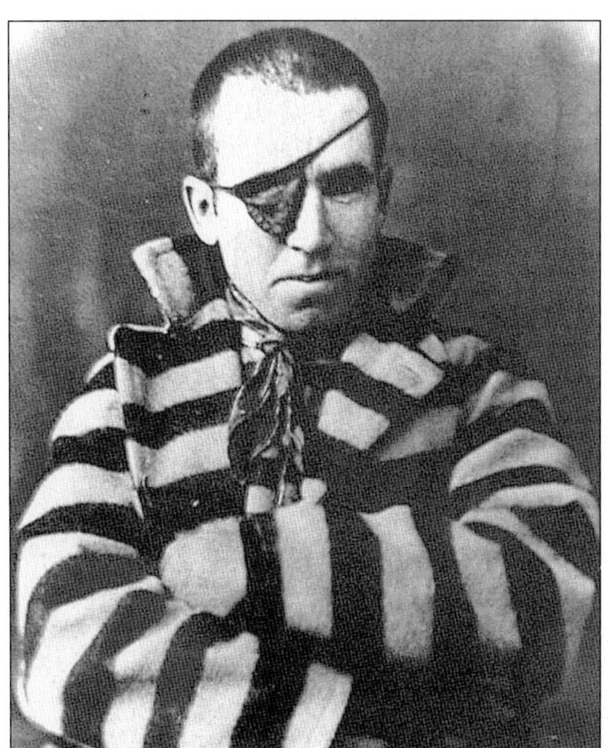

The first person to be tried and convicted as an abortionist in Colorado was John Douherty, No. 792. He arrived at the prison on October 4, 1882, and was released on December 29, 1883, serving just 14 months for manslaughter. It is not noted if the death was the mother or that of the fetus.

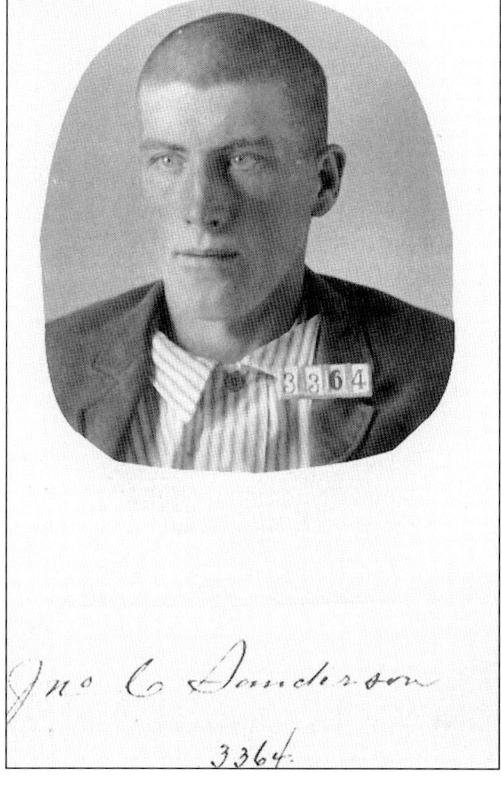

J. Anderson, No. 3364, became a prisoner in 1893. These earlier mug shots were taken on glass negatives and reworked into photographs. The Museum of Colorado Prisons holds hundreds of the glass negatives in its archives. Anderson served a year and a half for burglary.

John Cox, No. 4307, had been in prison for 40 years when this photograph was taken. He was used on a float for the Blossom Festival in the 1930s. A few prisoners made bits and spurs for the prison teams and also for the staff to buy. John Cox crafted several that are very valuable today.

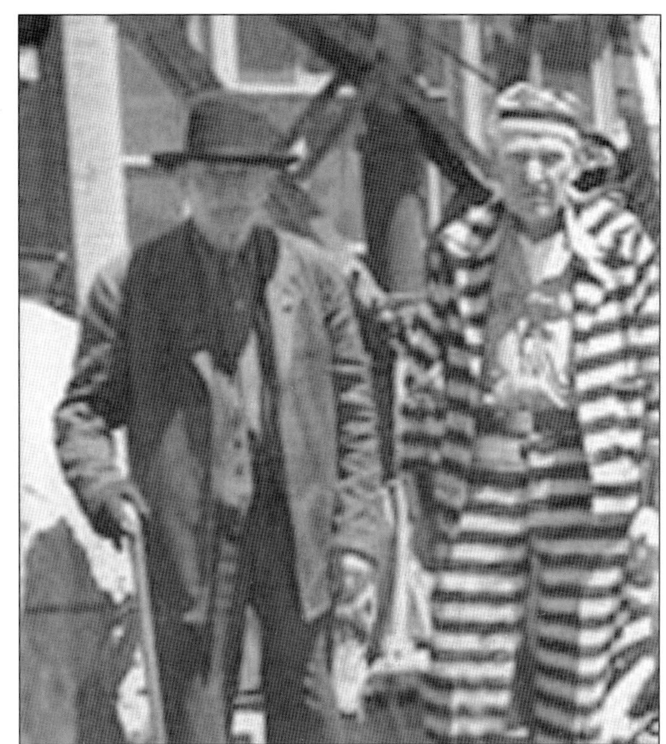

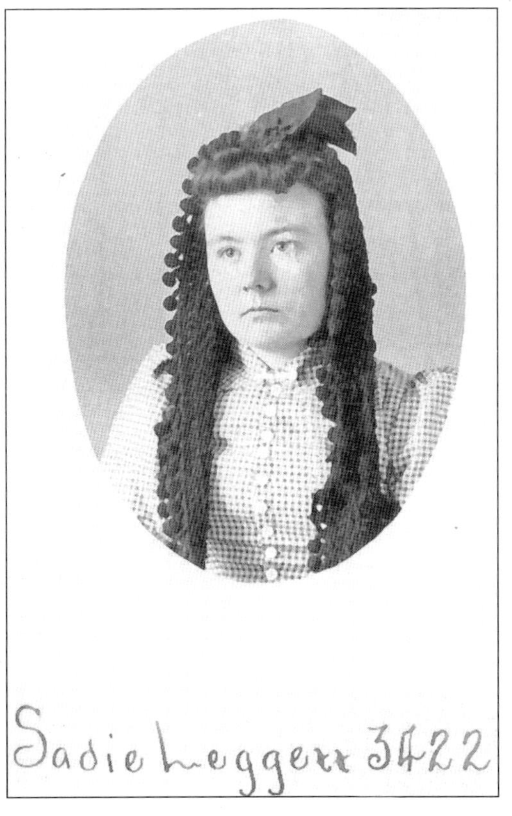

Sadie Leggett, No. 3422, was the first woman to occupy the new cell house inside the walls, built separate from the men. She was serving time for infanticide (the killing of a child) but was only sentenced to three years. She was released in 1895 after just 15 months.

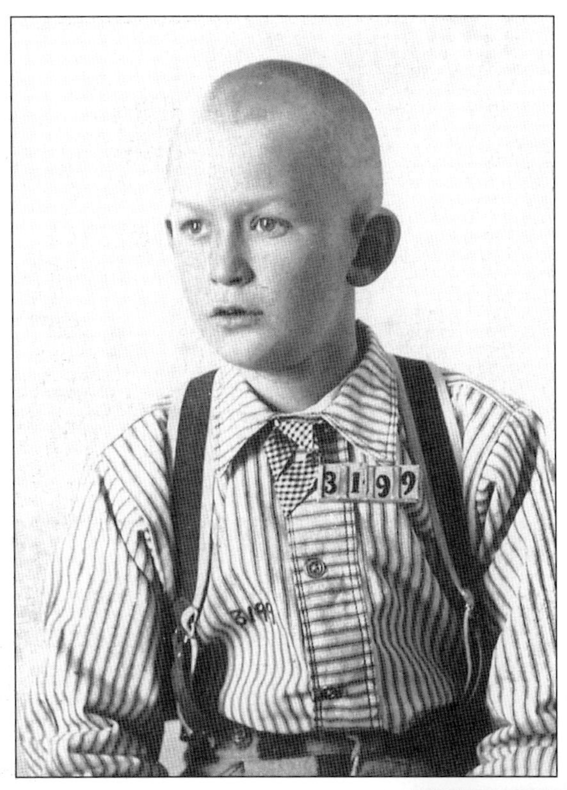

Anton Woode, No. 3199, was the youngest person in history to be sentenced to an adult prison. He was 11 at the time of his crime. A group of Denver businessmen set out on a day of hunting rabbits. They met a young boy also hunting, Anton Woode, and asked where the best place would be to spot rabbits. When Woode led Joseph Smith away from his party, it was the last time his friends saw Smith alive. The boy had admired a gold pocket watch Smith had pulled from his pocket and wanted it. Smith's friends reported hearing a shot and simply figured that the two had found a rabbit. When Smith failed to return that evening, several people were sent out to find him, and that they did—with a shot in his back. Woode was discovered hiding under his bed at home with the watch in his pocket. He received 25 years in 1893 (left) and was released in 1905 (below).

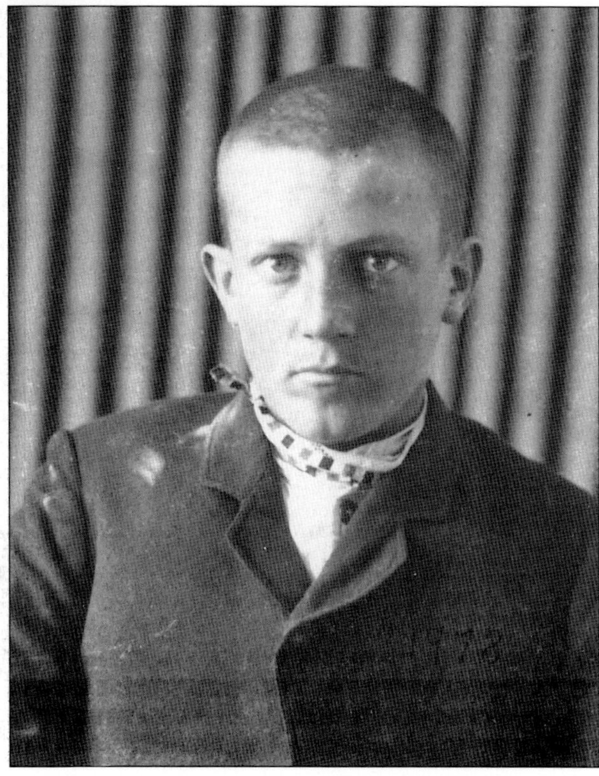

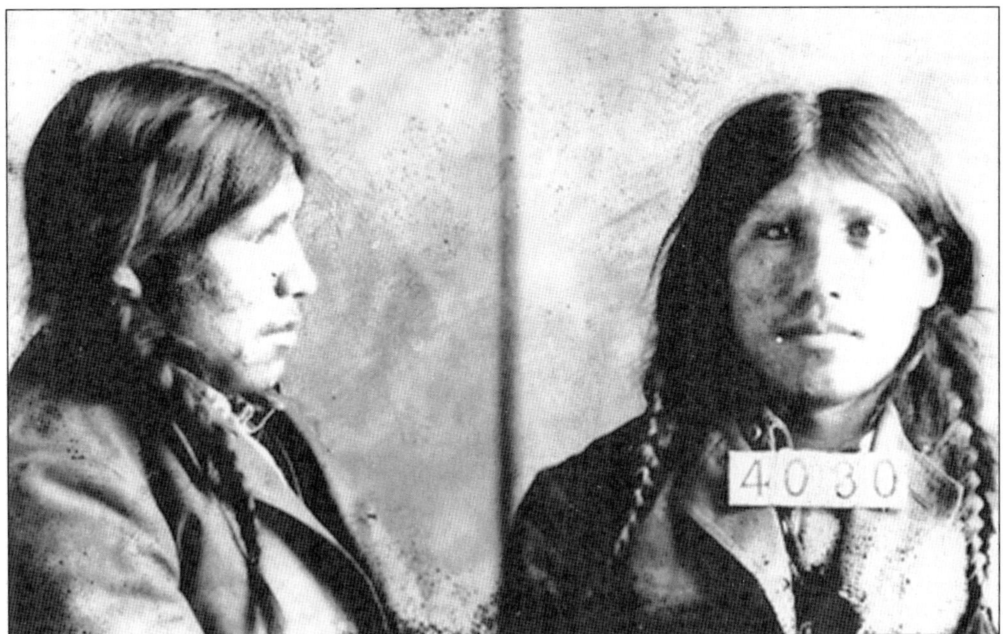

Pablo Hatch, No. 4030, was listed as an American Indian when he entered the prison in May 1896. He was placed on death row for murder and was taken to the death house the last week of October to await his fate. Before he could be hung, however, Hatch died of consumption.

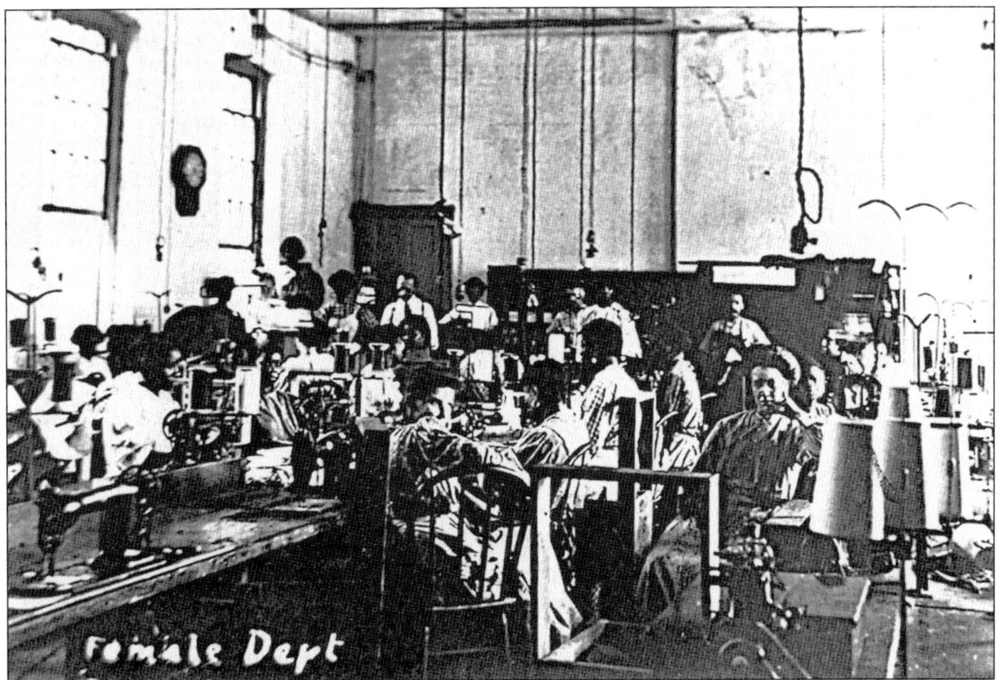

In the early years, women were scarce in the prison system since most were mothers, and many jurors felt they were needed at home. By the 1900s, incarcerated women were put to work in the sewing shop, as seen here. They made anything from uniforms to linen for the tables and curtains.

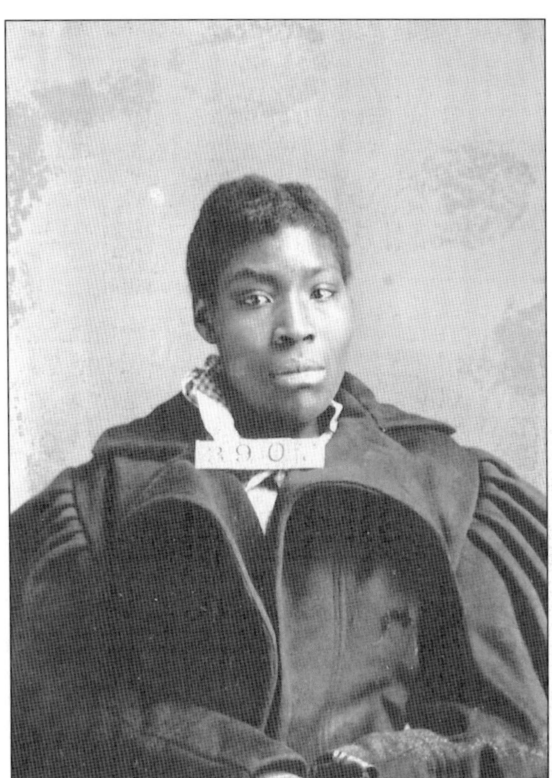

Annie Thompson, No. 2907, entered the prison in 1895 for larceny and was released in 1896. Just 29 years old, she was listed as an "American Negress" from Kentucky.

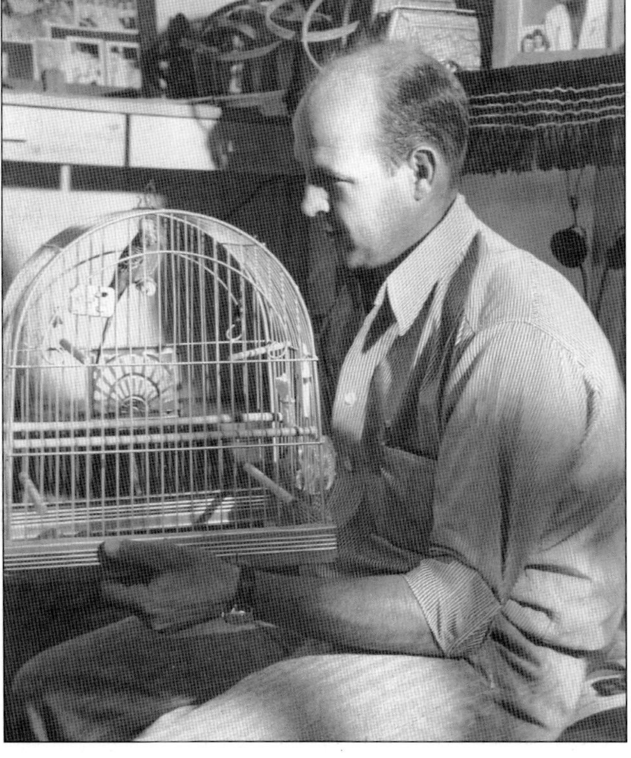

An unidentified prisoner sits in his cell visiting with his pet bird. Prisoners could possess personal items, including pet birds if approved by the cell house. Many inmates made pets of stray cats and the litters of kittens they subsequently produced. A cat was often seen walking the tiers of the cell houses.

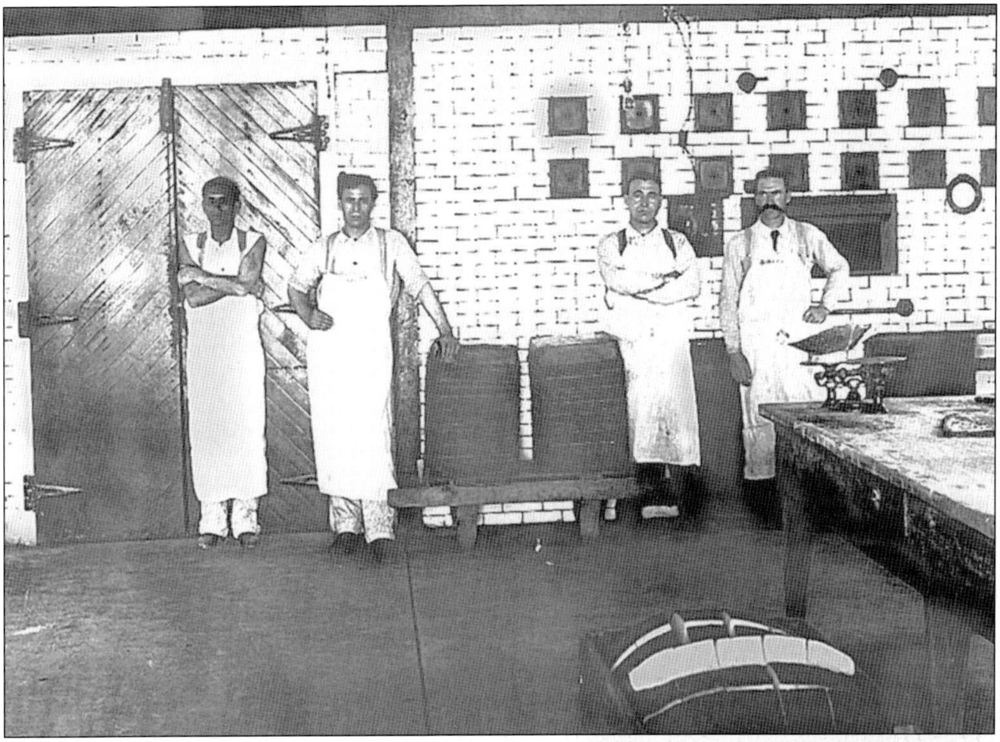

Early risers stand proudly by their creations in the bakery in the early 1900s. Bread and rolls were to be baked by the time that chow was called—as early as 5:00 a.m.—to get the prisoners fed and to work on time. Some bakers were on the job by 12:00 a.m. to get things rolling.

Over the years, prisoners worked as housekeepers and cooks in the warden's house. Here is a group of such men in 1890. These inmates were used as housemen, taking care of the chores around the home and assisting with the special gatherings held by the warden.

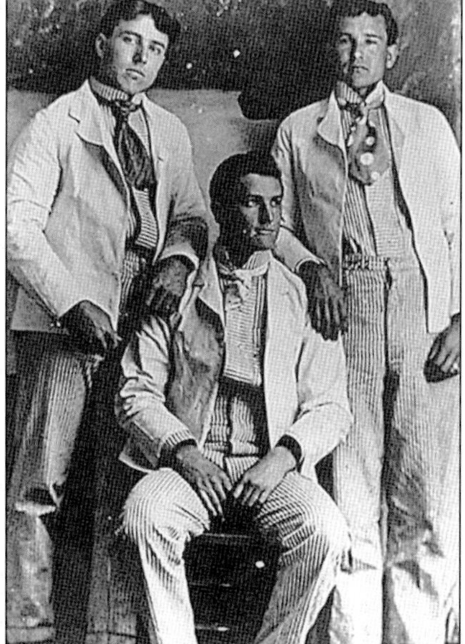

These prisoners are dressed up for some occasion and from their clothing this was taken sometime during the 1890's. Prisoners were used to help serve at the Warden's home and were used in various places around town and when some special occasion warranted.

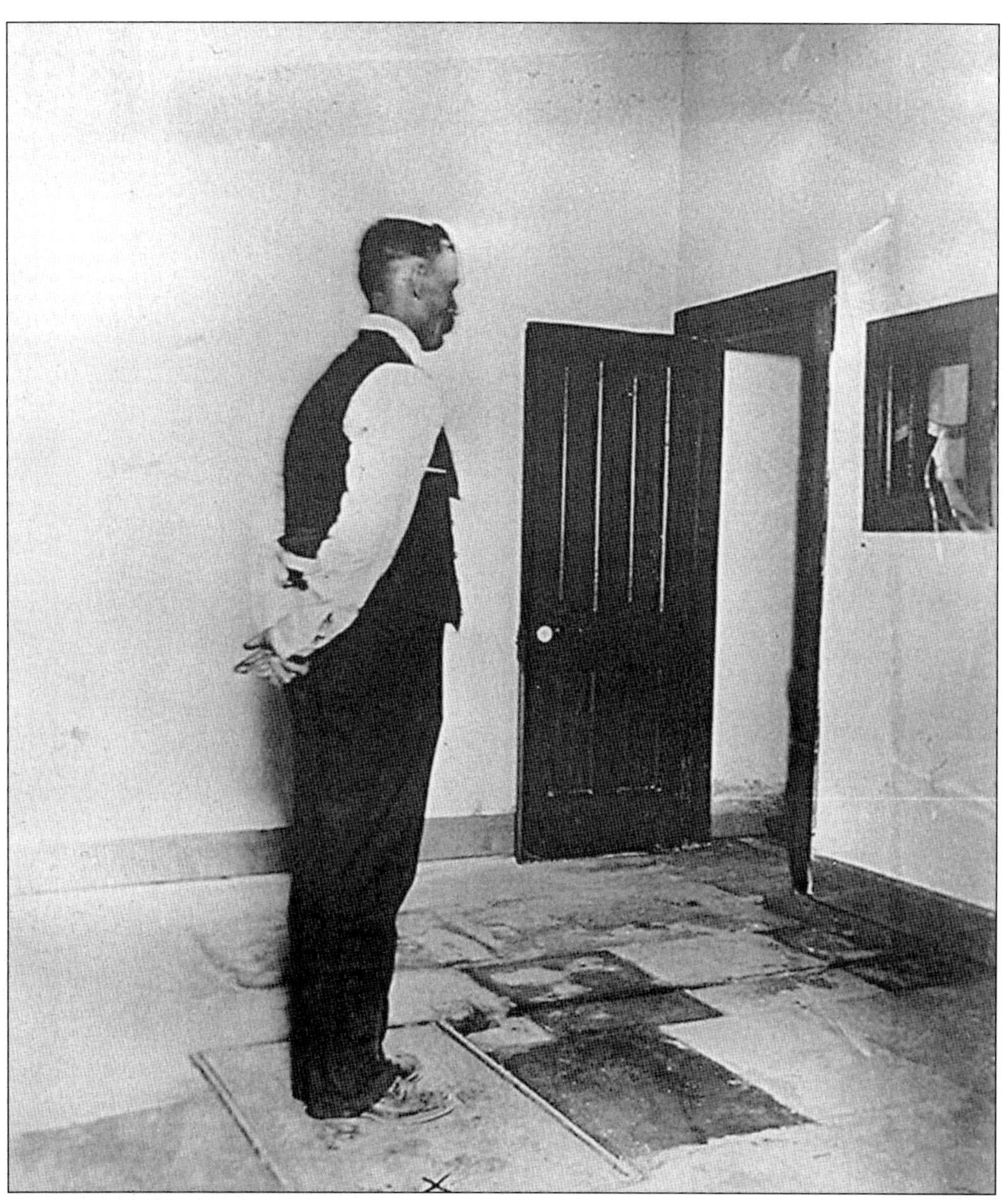

From the beginning in 1872, the method of execution was hanging. Executions were scheduled for a weeklong period instead of a set date, and the prisoners were taken to the death house to await their fate. Most were hanged within a year of the conviction and some in a matter of months, unlike today, when some sit on death row for 10 years or more. In the early 1900s, a hanging machine was implemented to eliminate the risk of a rope breaking or a person's neck not snapping and thus leaving the condemned to dangle for as long as 24 minutes, as one report stated, before death. The prisoner stepped on the platform seen here, at which point his weight would start a self-hanging apparatus that would jerk the person three feet into the air and instantly break his neck. It did not work as well as expected, and the gas chamber was initiated in 1933.

Searches in prisons
are a necessary evil
for the prisoners and
the staff. Inmates
are searched coming
to and from work
assignments, before
and after visits,
or anytime a staff
member deems
appropriate. Their
cells are searched
routinely and job
sites are checked
daily, along with the
chow hall because
of the likelihood of
stolen food.

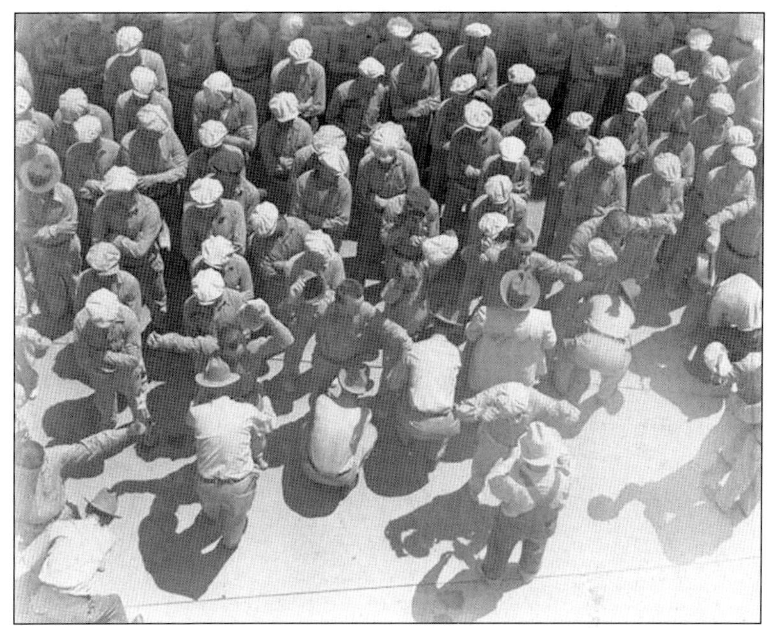

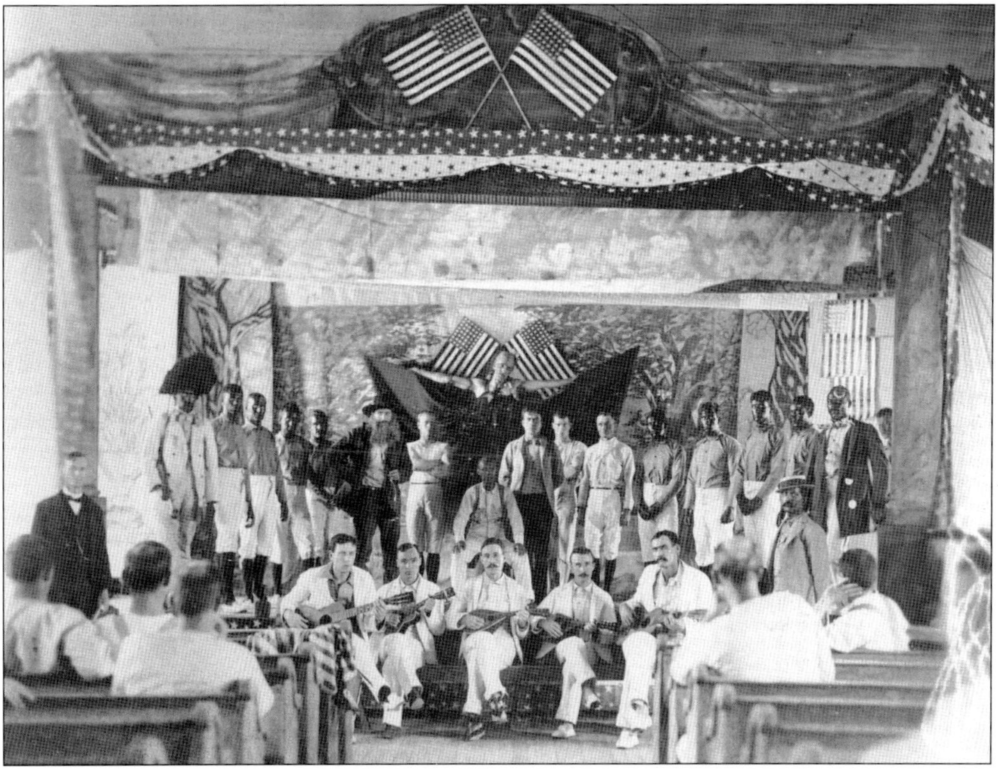

In the early 1900s, talented traveling troupes visited prisons across the country. Many were of
a religious nature, but others were like the one pictured: a minstrel show with actors dressed in
blackface. Now it would be politically incorrect, but then it was accepted talent.

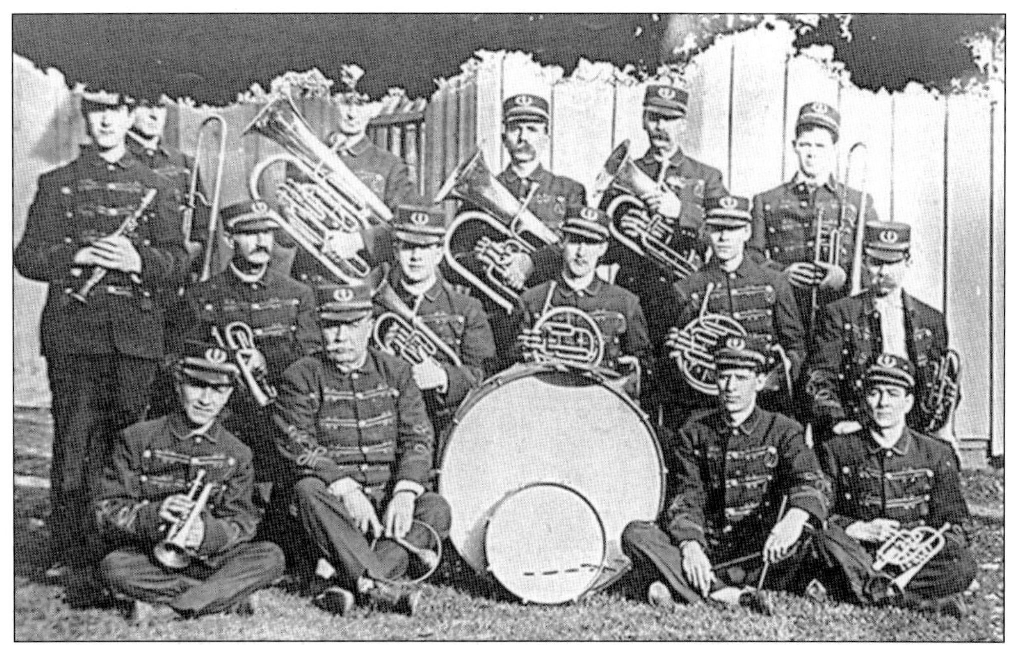

A prison band is decked out in finery, probably for a parade, in 1891. Inmates can still form bands with the instruments usually kept in the gym or music room. Concerts are often held in the yards on special occasions such as Independence Day.

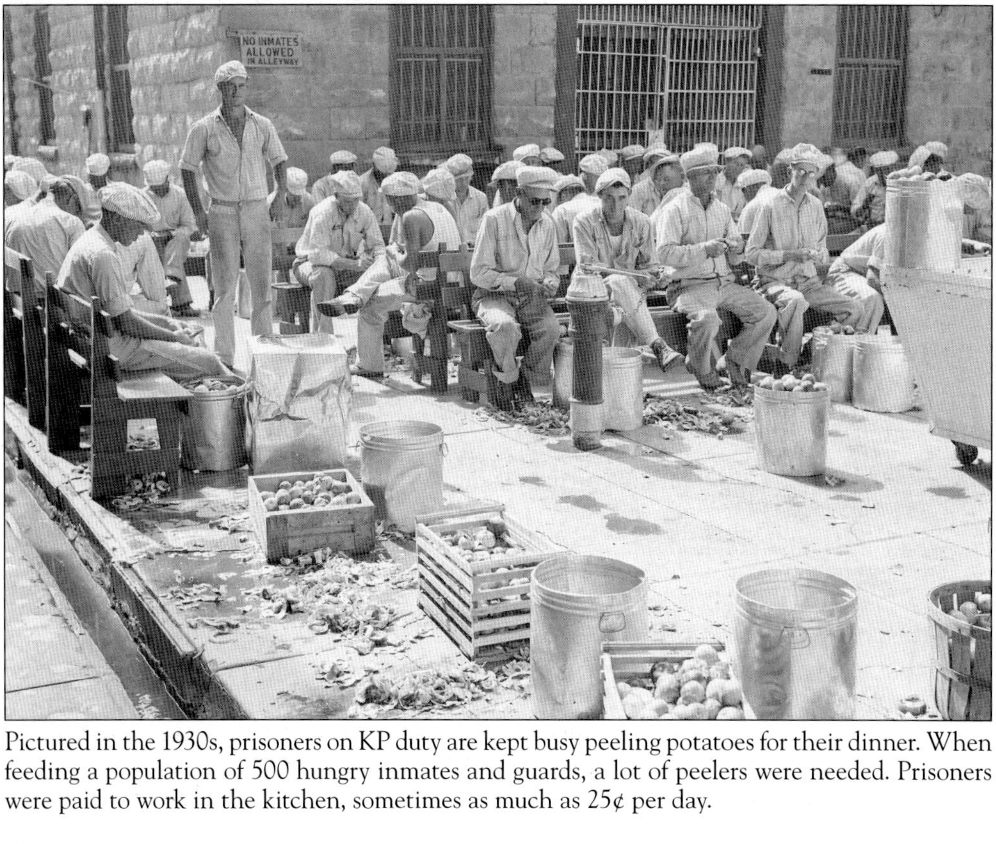

Pictured in the 1930s, prisoners on KP duty are kept busy peeling potatoes for their dinner. When feeding a population of 500 hungry inmates and guards, a lot of peelers were needed. Prisoners were paid to work in the kitchen, sometimes as much as 25¢ per day.

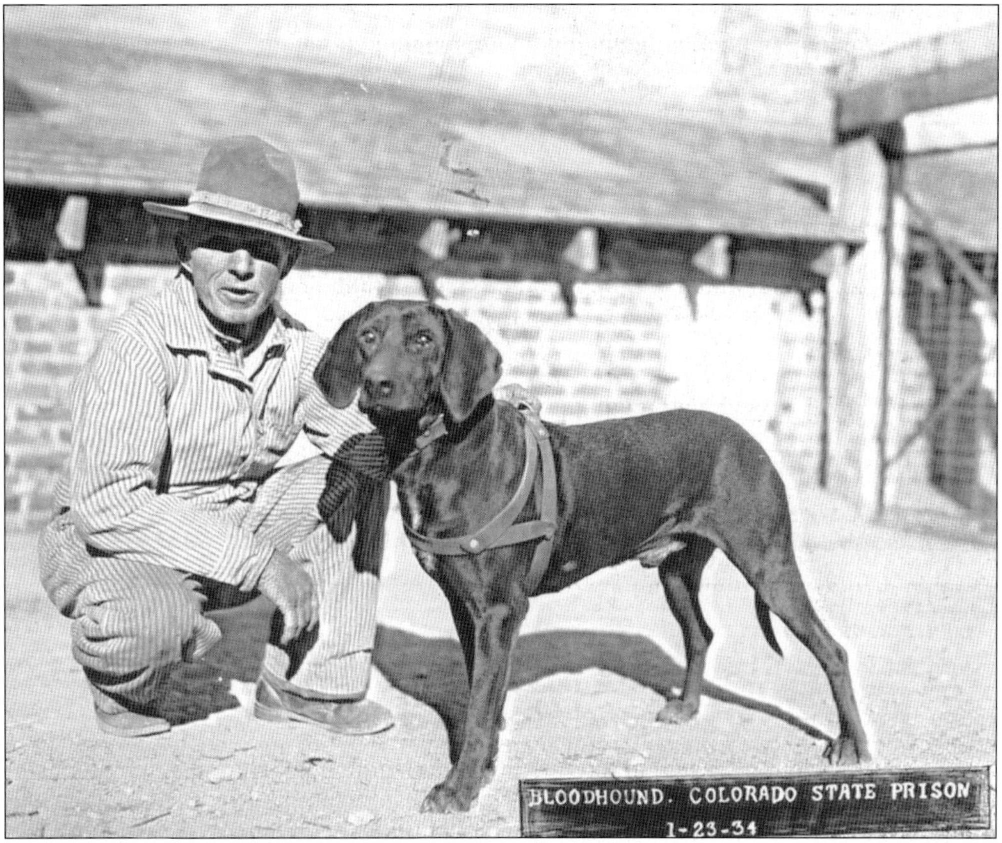

Bloodhounds and other breeds of dogs were housed at the prison for use in the event of an escape. In 1934, the dogs were trained and cared for by a prisoner who served as their handler. Today the dogs are imported from Germany, and the handlers are highly trained staff members who live with the dogs.

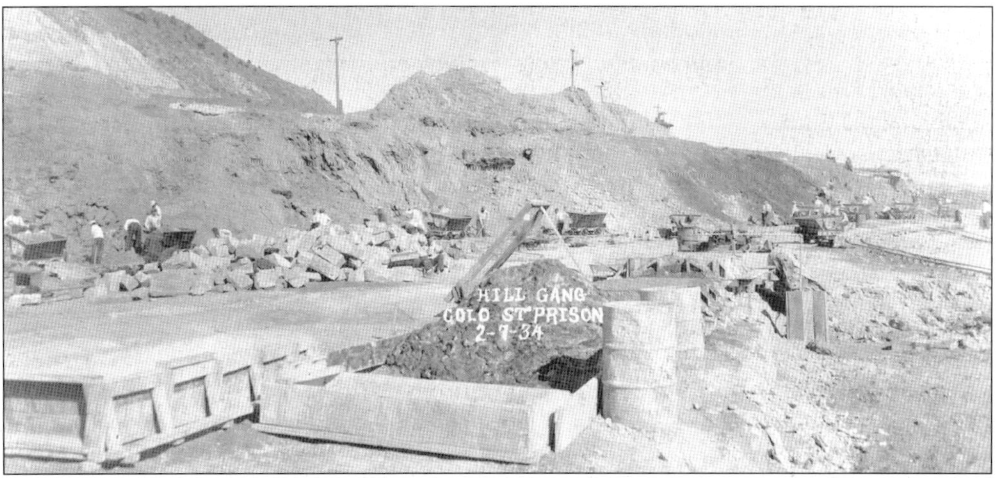

In the 1930s, the construction of a new cell house was ongoing. Prison labor was cheap and kept the inmates busy and out of trouble—for the most part. Warden Roy Best believed in keeping prisoners working in the daylight hours so that they were too tired at night to do anything but sleep.

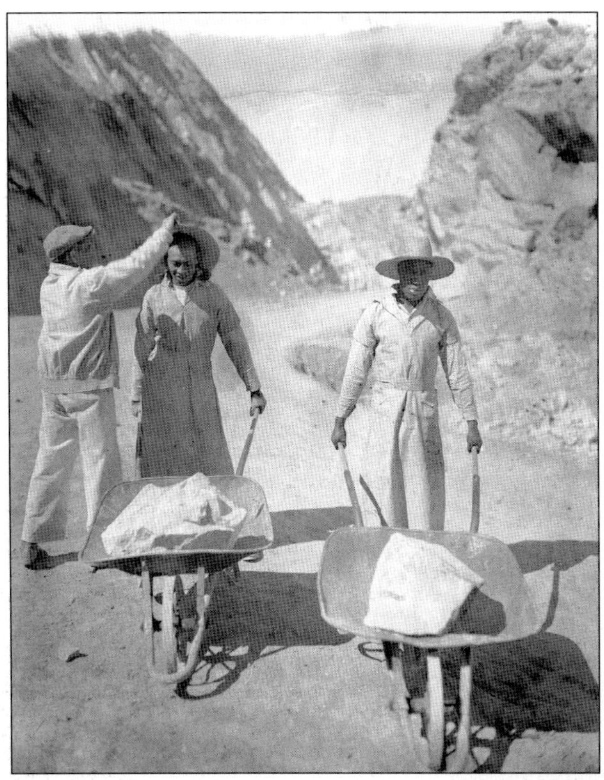

In the 1930s, homosexuality was believed to be sinful and was in violation of prison rules. Prisoners who were caught engaging in homosexual activity were forced to wear dresses, as seen here. This pair, part of the Skyline Drive crew, had to endure humiliation while on the job.

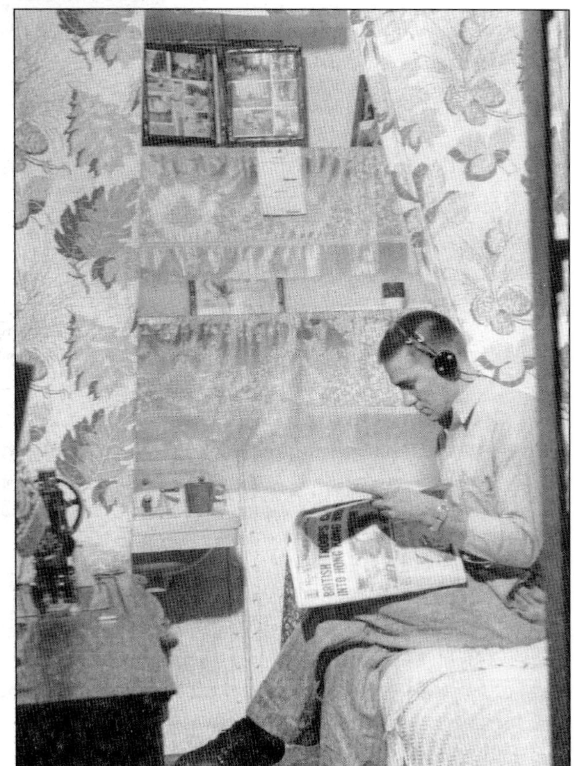

This 1930s prisoner seems to have all the comforts of home. He can listen to music on his radio, read up on the happenings of the world, and decorate his room.

Marching to and from work was a prison practice of the early 1900s. A guard accompanied the inmates everywhere they went in groups: to work and home and to chow and home. These prisoners are marching with their arms crossed on their chests, a standard practice.

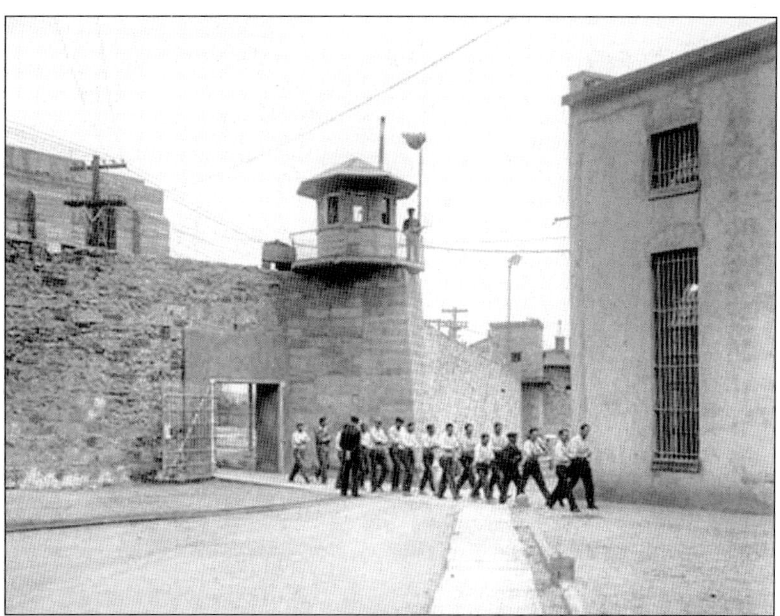

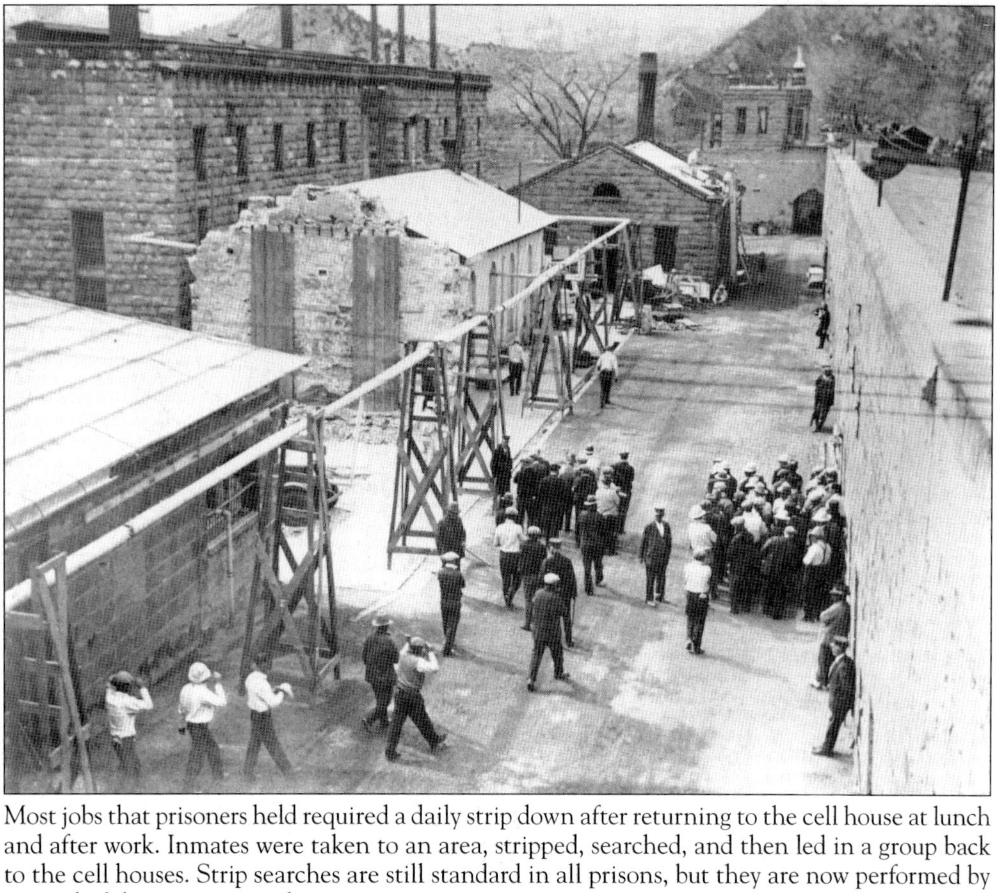

Most jobs that prisoners held required a daily strip down after returning to the cell house at lunch and after work. Inmates were taken to an area, stripped, searched, and then led in a group back to the cell houses. Strip searches are still standard in all prisons, but they are now performed by a guard of the same sex as the prisoner.

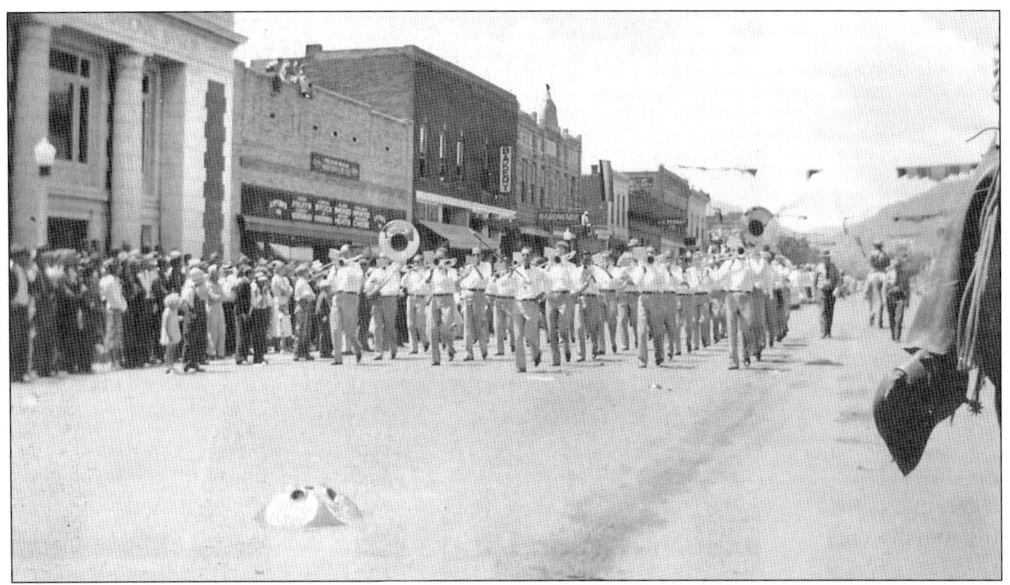

The prison band plays during the 1935 Music and Blossom Parade in Cañon City, held every year on the first weekend of May. Because of the likelihood of escape, band members were heavily guarded during events that were off grounds.

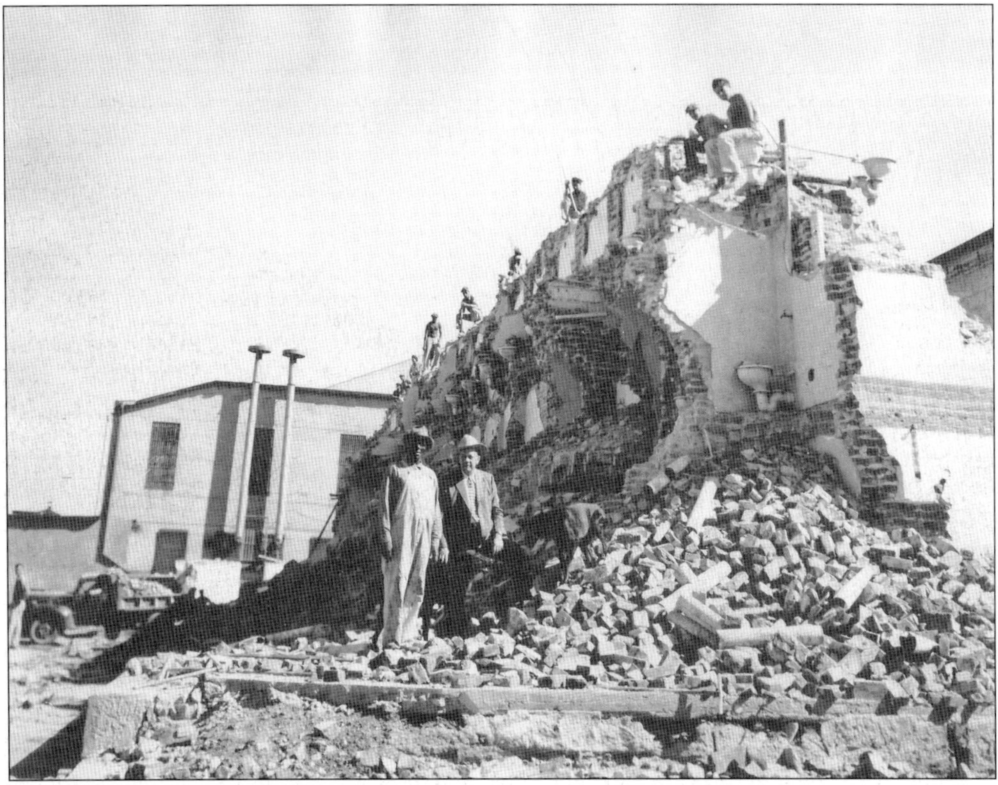

Roy Best was usually present to get his photograph taken when a building went up or came down, as in this view. "Out with the old, in with the new" was his motto, and this cell house had become obsolete. During his 30-year reign, construction never ceased.

Inmates were kept busy plucking and preparing turkeys for the oven on the prison's two turkey farms in the 1930s. The poultry was sent to the Colorado State Hospital in Pueblo for holidays and to other state agencies. Fremont Correctional Facility, with 1,471 men, still cooks fresh turkeys for the inmates on Christmas Day.

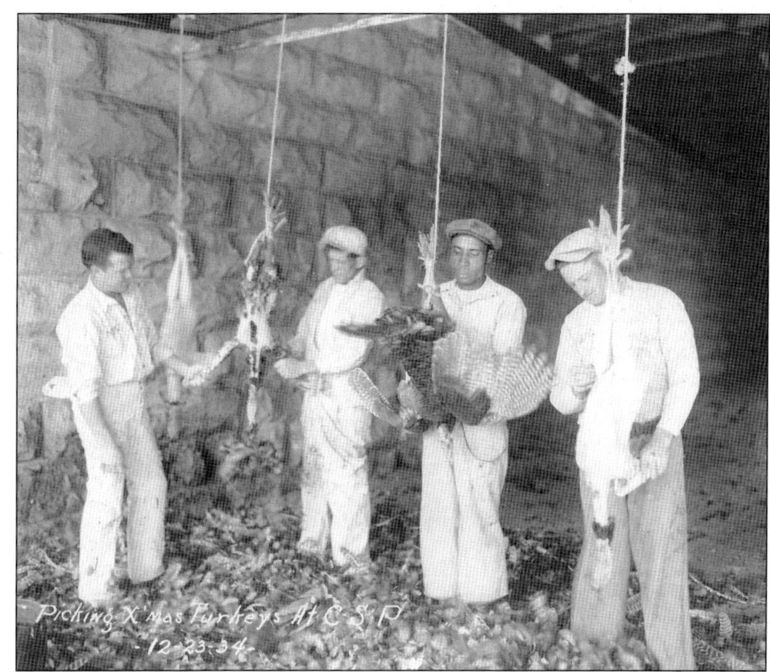

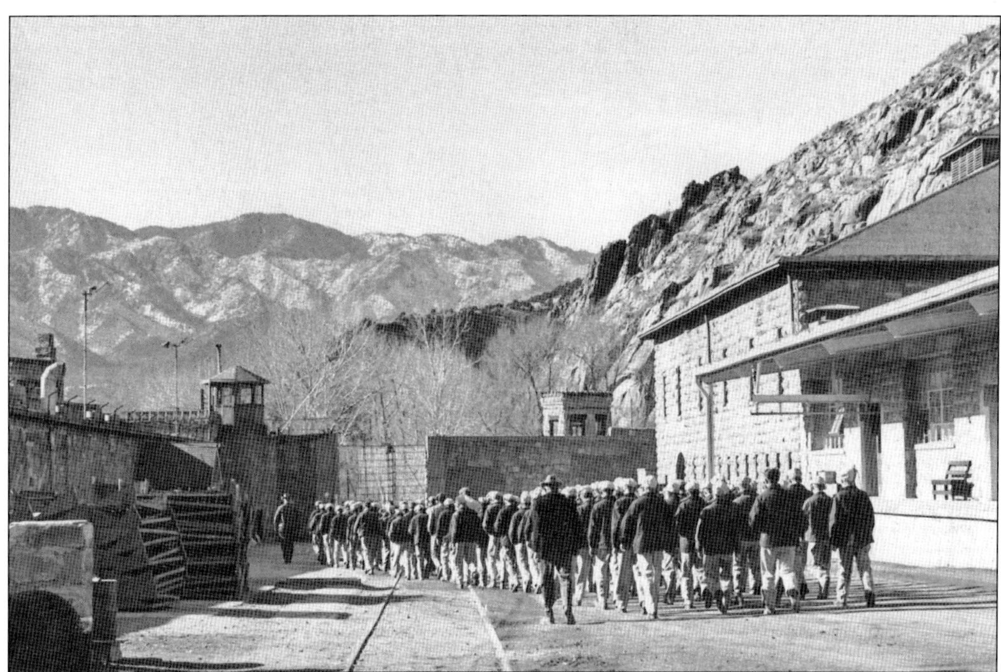

The ridge to the right in this view is Skyline Drive, and those who are brave enough to drive it can look down into the Territorial Facility. Prisoners have escaped only to get lost in the treacherous terrain and surrounding mountains. One even gave himself up to area hunters because he was cold and starving after being lost for five days without food or warm clothing.

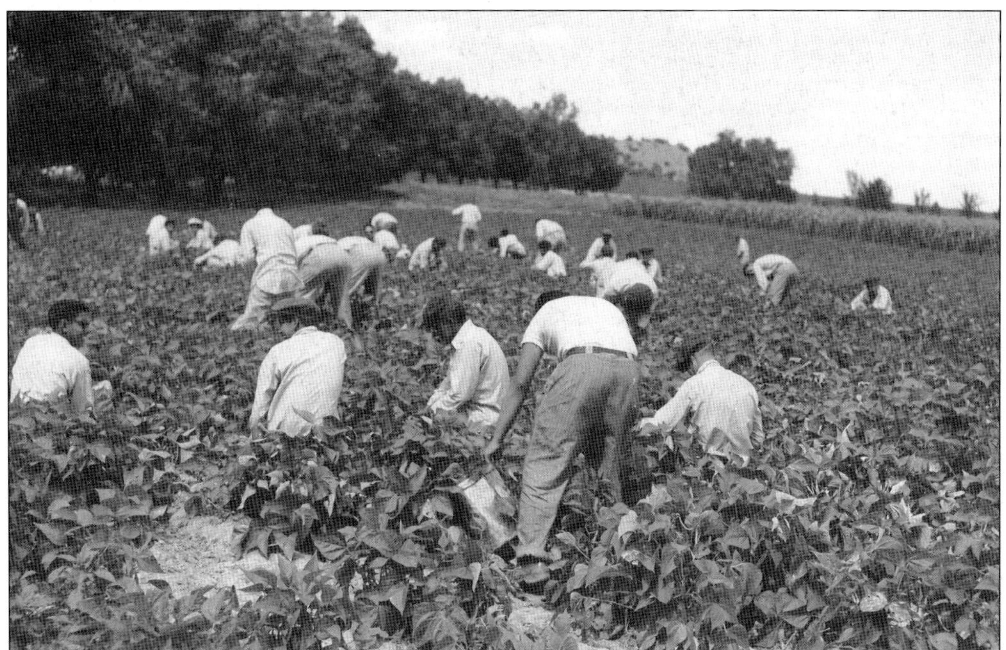

During the early years, the prison boasted beautiful flower and vegetable gardens. Prisoners tended them when harvest time arrived, picking the products for canning that later fed the prison population. A dairy run by inmates provided their source of milk and cheese, and livestock were raised for meat. The prison was self-sufficient.

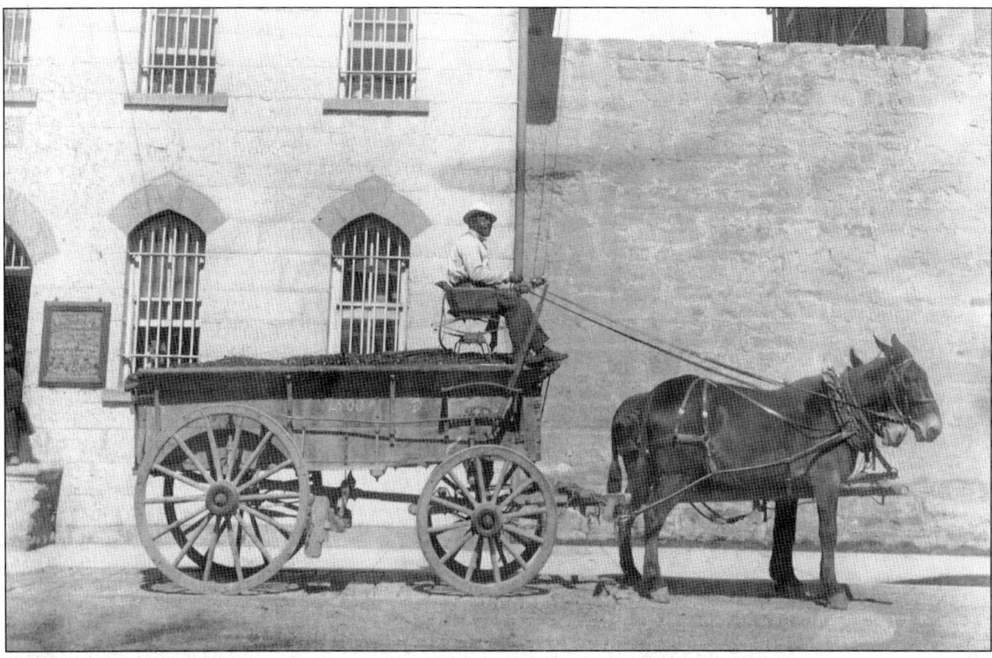

Coal heated the prisons until the 1980s, when most of the boilers were converted to gas. Here a prisoner takes a load of coal through the prison on one of the horse-drawn carts. The carts were also used to haul coffins to the Greenwood Cemetery's Woodpecker Hill section, where prisoners were laid to rest. This wagon is on exhibit in the prison museum yard.

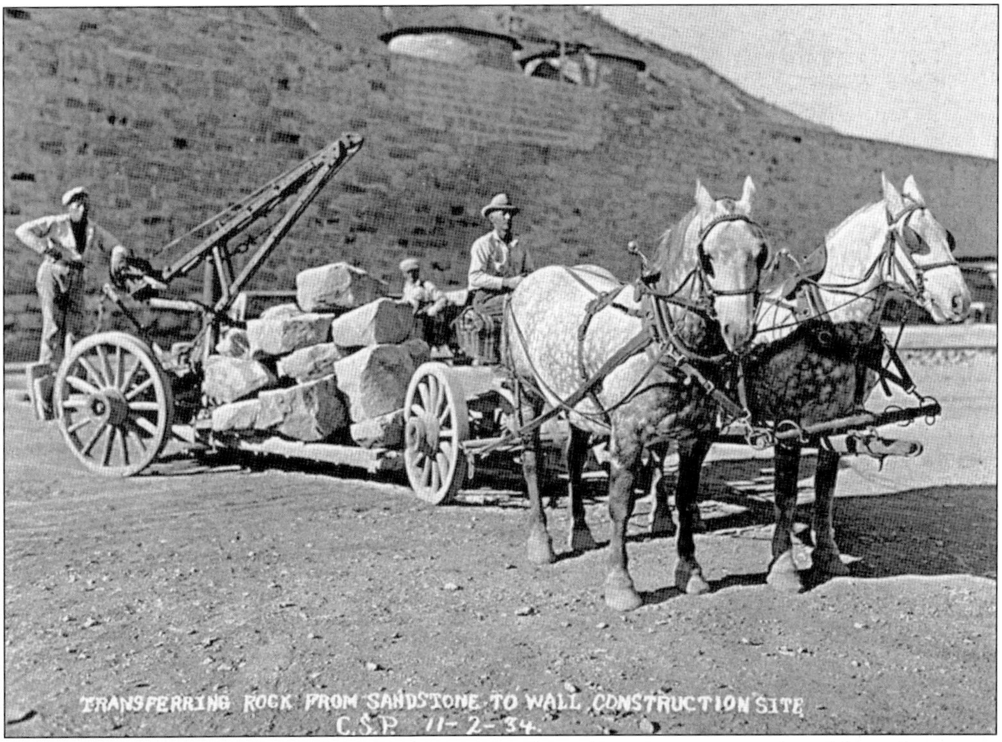

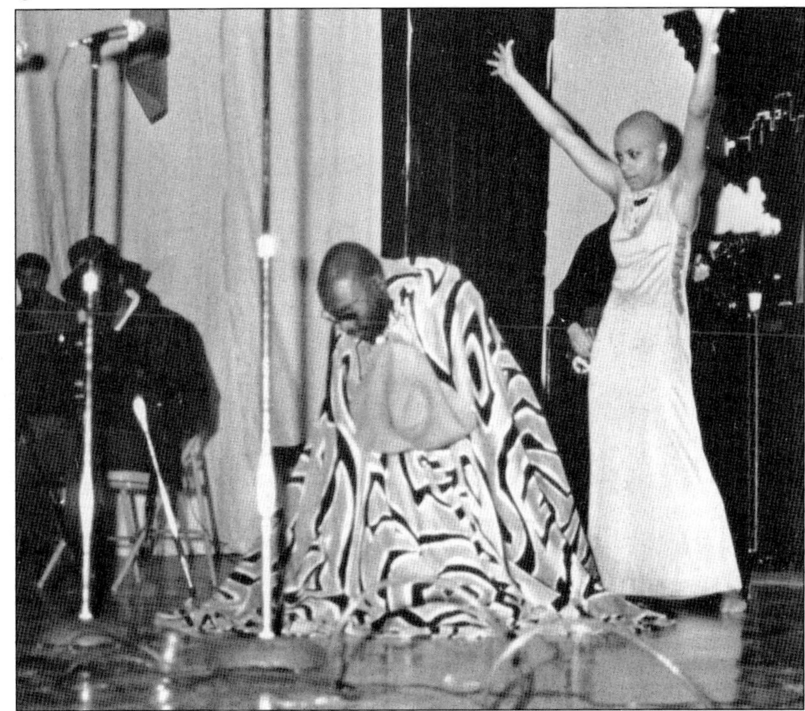

During wall construction, which took years to complete, the stone was transferred from the quarry to the job site by sturdy plow horses. The wench in the back was used to pick up the rocks and put them on the wagon.

Many famous people have entered the walls of the prison over the years. In the 1970s, Isaac Hayes and his band came to perform for the prison population at Territorial. He and his group also toured the facility and talked with inmates along the way.

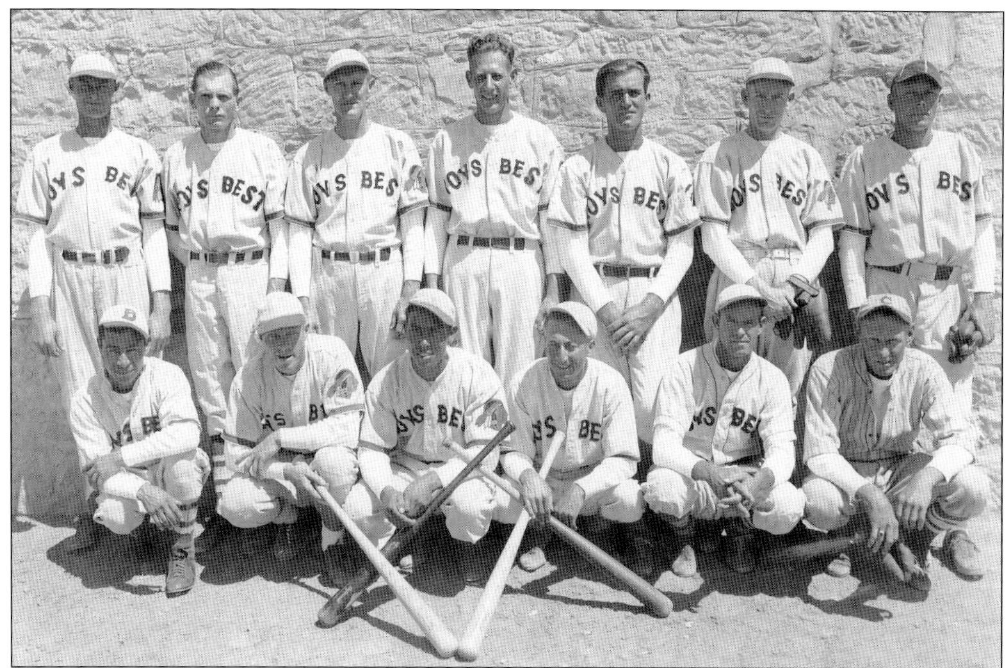

Over the years, sports have played a big part in the recreation aspect of the prison. In the 1930s and 1940s, the baseball team was named Roys Best, after the warden. The team often played other area civilian teams on prison grounds. The games were taken very seriously, with the scores printed in the local newspaper.

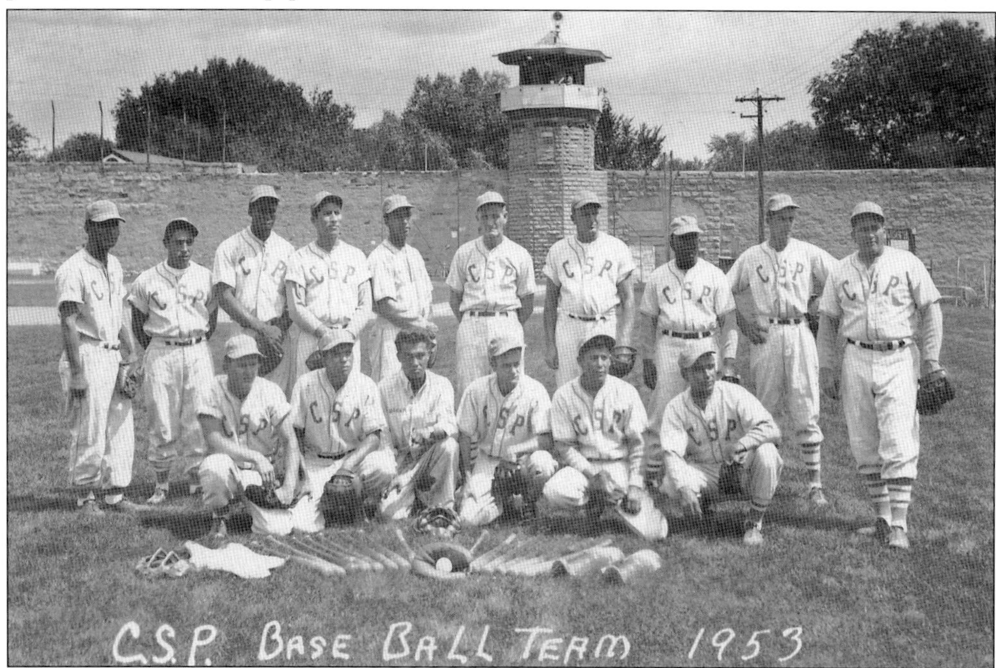

In 1953, following Roy Best's suspension, the baseball team's name was changed to CSP. This photograph was taken in the big yard with Tower 5 in the background. The team was allowed to travel outside the prison to play other teams in different towns—under supervision, of course.

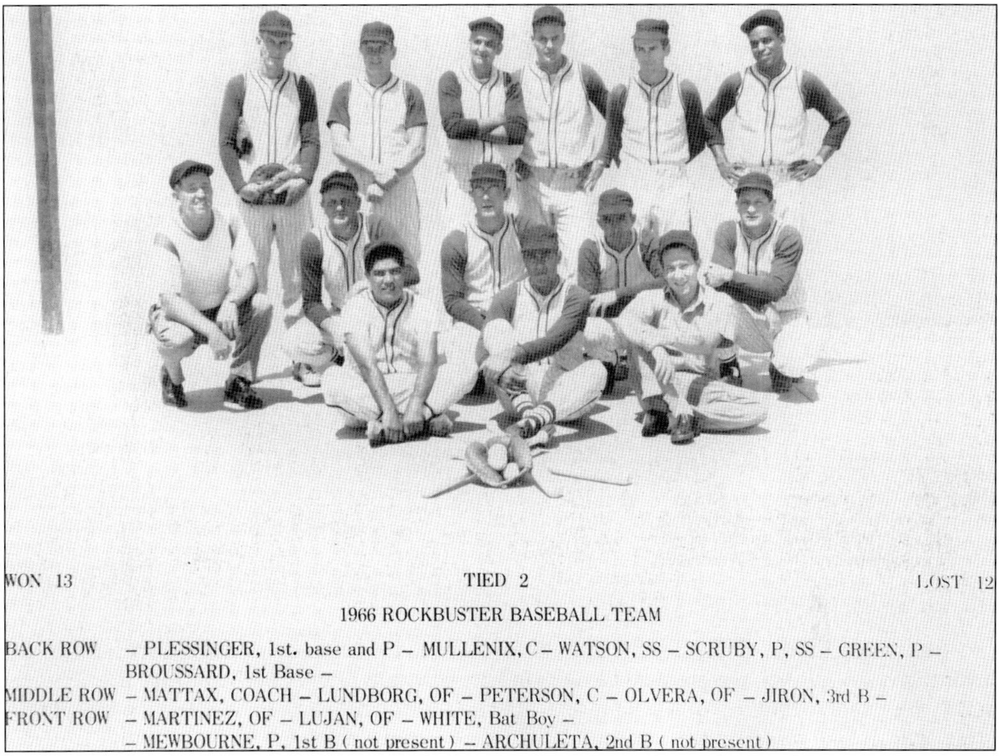

By 1966, the baseball team's name had changed again, this time to the Rockbuster. As one can see, the group had a pretty good season consisting of 13 wins and 12 losses. Ronald Plessinger (back row, left), a pitcher for the team, pitched against the Greeley Grays for three years running when on the road.

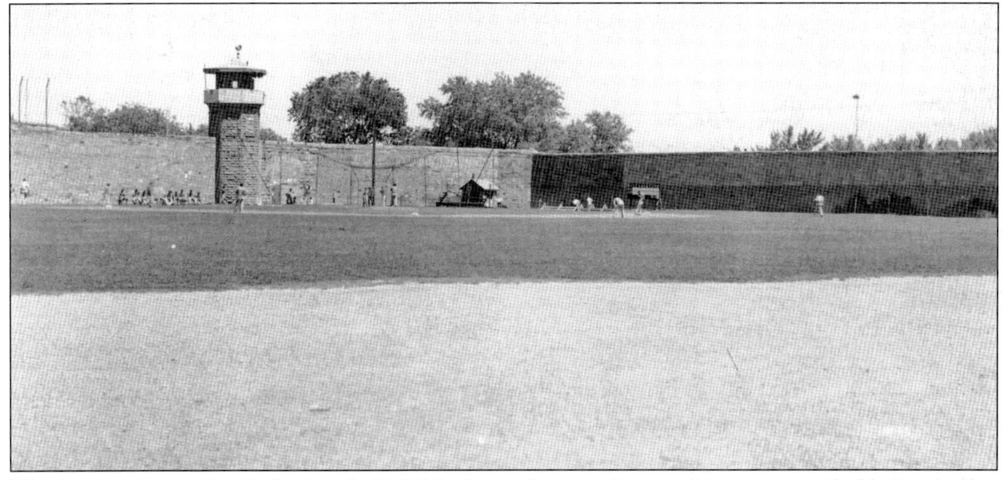

The big yard contained the baseball field where the practices and games were held. Baseball is still a good pastime for inmates, although prison-sponsored teams are no longer in existence. From the museum front yard, one can hear the prisoners playing baseball on the weekends.

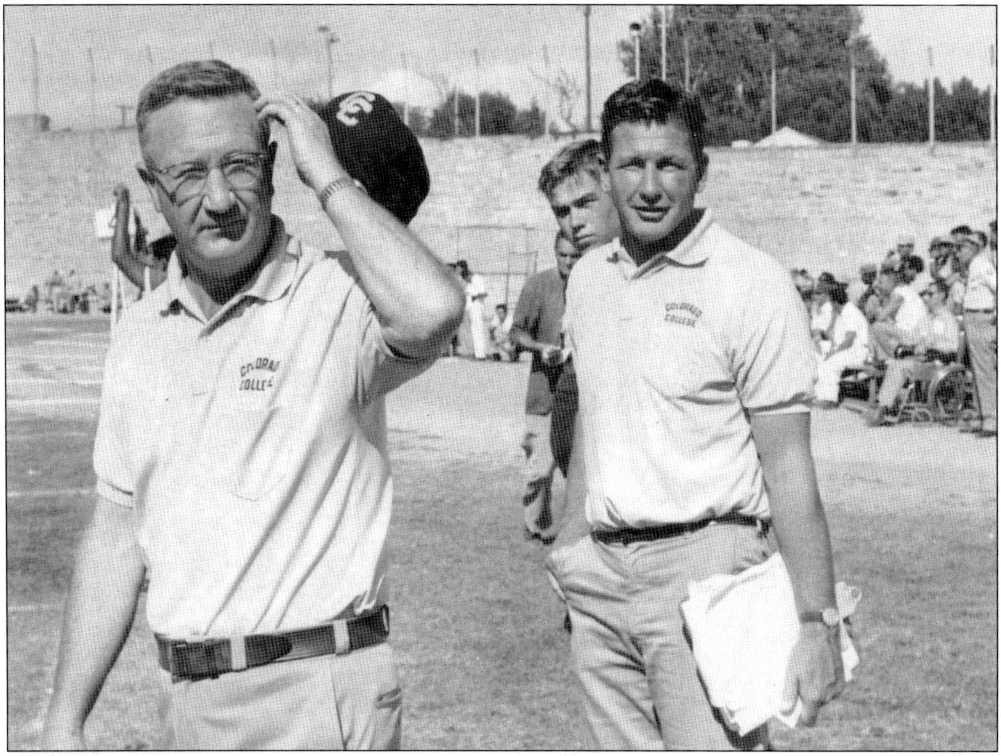

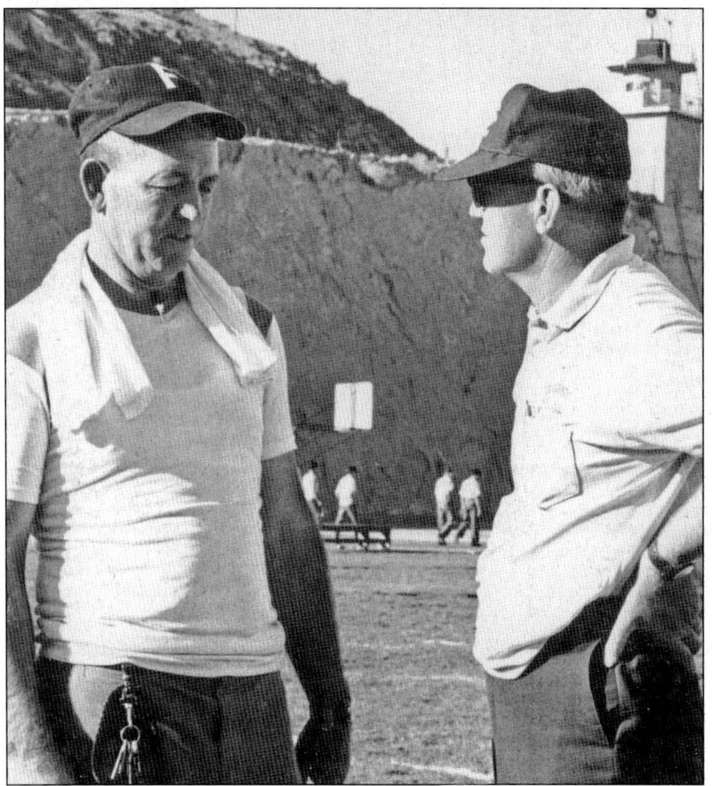

Colorado College was a guest team to the prison during the 1960s, as the games provided good practice. Coaches from the college, one looking confused, pose for the above photograph on the baseball field behind the walls. At left, two coaches from the prison confer, possibly during the same game. Coaches of the prison teams were normally guards who volunteered their time for the sport. At times, the guards held games against the prisoners, and those games could be wild to say the least.

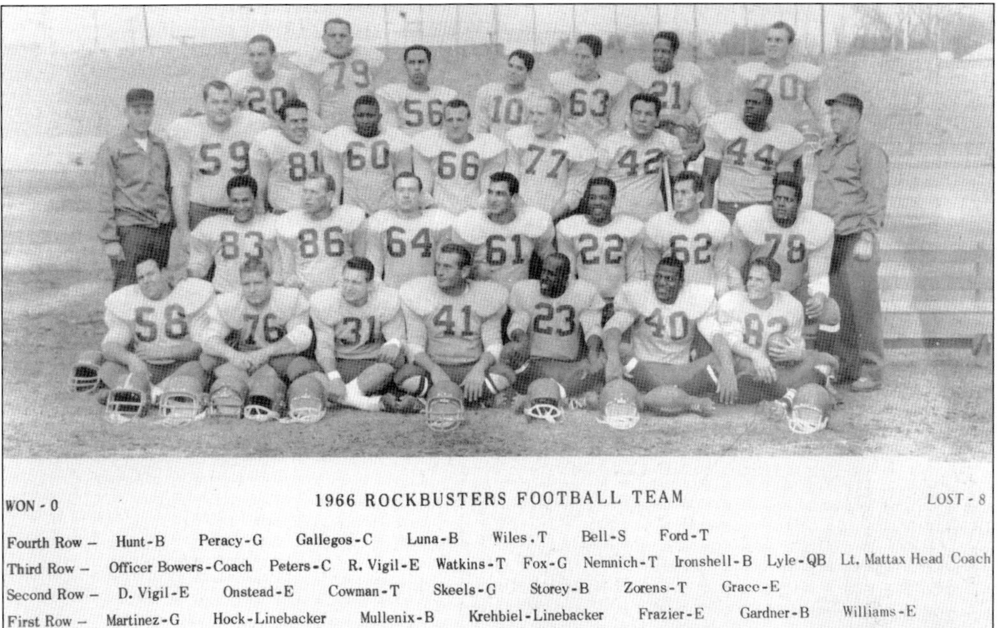

WON - 0 — **1966 ROCKBUSTERS FOOTBALL TEAM** — **LOST - 8**

Fourth Row — Hunt-B   Peracy-G   Gallegos-C   Luna-B   Wiles-T   Bell-S   Ford-T

Third Row — Officer Bowers-Coach   Peters-C   R. Vigil-E   Watkins-T   Fox-G   Nemnich-T   Ironshell-B   Lyle-QB   Lt. Mattax Head Coach

Second Row — D. Vigil-E   Onstead-E   Cowman-T   Skeels-G   Storey-B   Zorens-T   Grace-E

First Row — Martinez-G   Hock-Linebacker   Mullenix-B   Krehbiel-Linebacker   Frazier-E   Gardner-B   Williams-E

Along with baseball there was football. In 1966, the Rockbusters football players pose for a team photograph. Their season did not seem to be going too well, with no wins and eight losses. Guards were also coaches for the football teams.

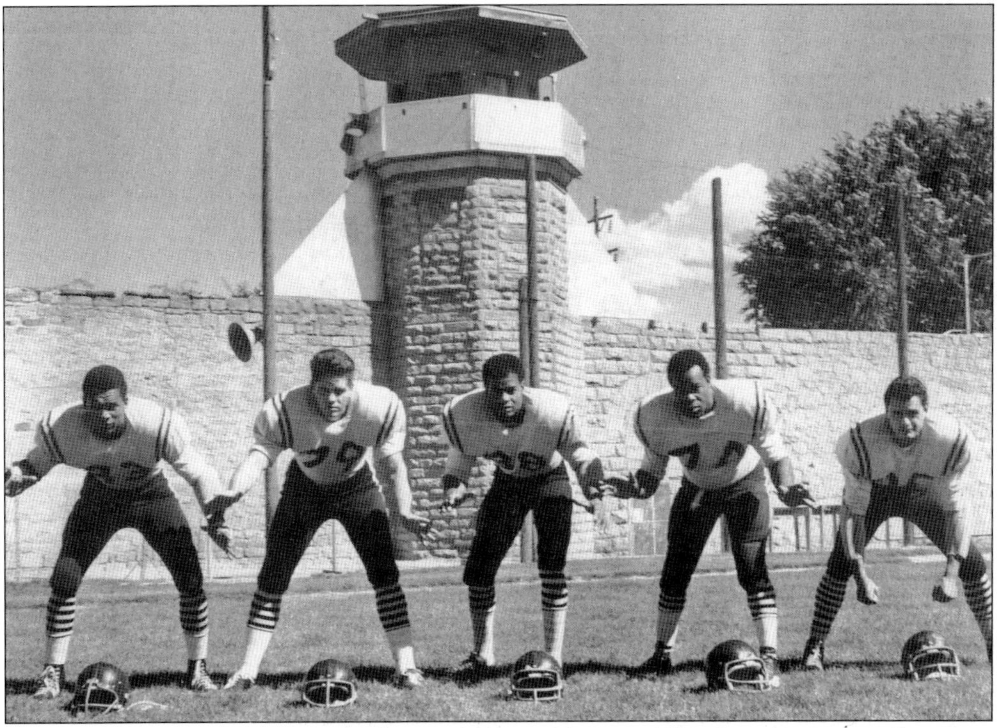

If not for the tower looming in the background, these athletes could be players from any college team preparing for a big game. This 1960s team lineup displays the star players. One, prisoner Nicholas John Cowman (far right), later escaped and was gone for a year before his remains were found.

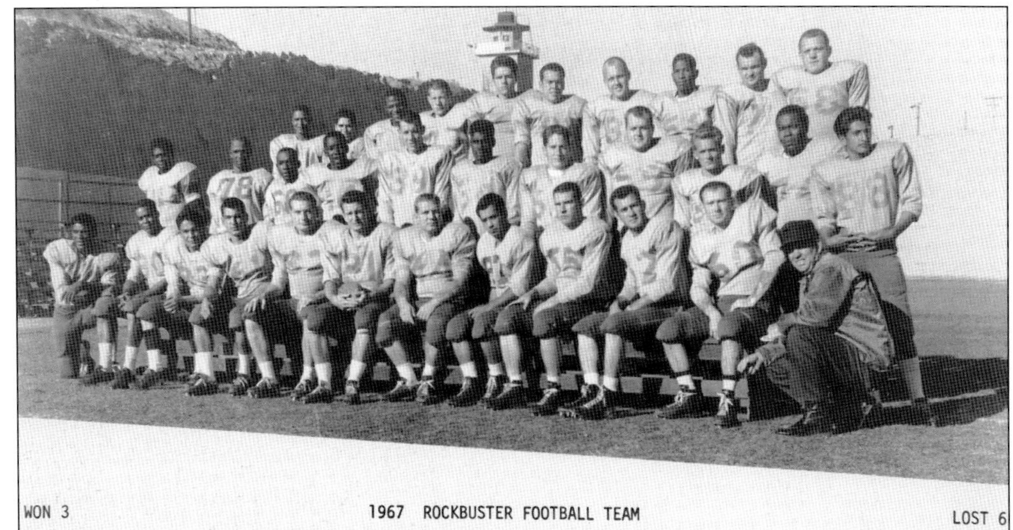

Back Row: Jordan, HB; Luna, Safety; Gardner, FB; Novosad, T; Anderson, Def T; R. Vigil, E; Randall, Def E; Lee, MG; Geary, Def T; Piercy, T.
Middle Row: Lyle, Slotback; Arthur, T; Whitney, Punter; Williams, Def B; Boes, E; Brown, Tailback; Wiles, G; Peters, C; Herod, Def HB; Holsey, Def T; Cervantes, E.
Front Row: Mitchell, Tailback; Broussard, E; D. Vigil, Def E; Skeels, G; Krehbiel, Def LB; Mullenix, QB; Hock, FB; Casias, Def HB; Wammack, G & C; Zorens, Def LB; Cowman, G; Lt. Mattax, Coach.

The 1967 Rockbusters photograph (above) was taken in the big yard on the football field (also used as the baseball field). This season seems to be going better for the team, with three wins and six losses. The 1968 team photograph (below), taken in front of Cell House 3, does not include the wins and losses but reveals that the group has grown considerably in size. Local businesses occasionally helped sponsor the teams to offset the costs of uniforms and equipment. Prisoners received no special treatment or compensation for playing. Most did it for the fun and freedom, as the sport allowed them to go out in public at times and break the monotony of the everyday prison routine.

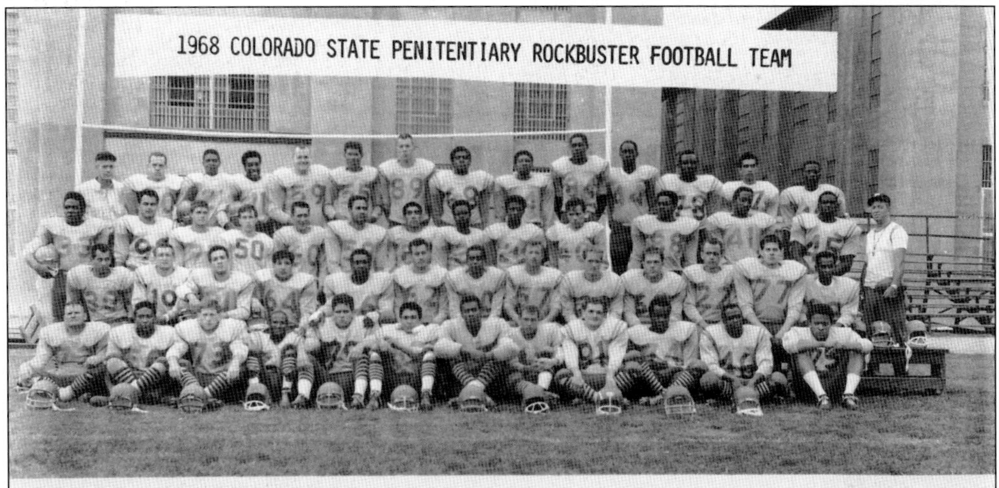

Back Row: Beckstead-Assist, Vermillion-T, Jordan-DH, Britton-LB, Peters-C, Larkin-C, Boes-E, Whittley-T, Mathis-S, Knight-E, Swinton-LB, Armstead-T, Cortinaz-LB, Rodgers-QB;
Third Row: Mitchell-LB, Sandoval-DE, Martin-DT, Beeman-DHB, Ruark-G, Castro-LB, Rael-E, Stinner-Flanker, Miller-HB, Hixon-HB, Smith-DE, Jones-FB, Lyle-FB, Mattax-Head Coach;
Second Row: Casias-DHB, Mullenix-QB, Strock-Running Back, Martinez-G, Bishop-G, Zorens-LB, Broussard-E, Gilmore-LB, Herod-DHB, Gillespie-G, Murray-S, Puckett-T, Ferrell-E;
Front Row: Shumaker-T, Madison-C, Novosad-T, Clark-G, Anderson-DT, Vigil-G, Watts-DE, Martin-LB, Simons-T, Holsey-DT, Hardiman-Running Back, Manual-Flanker.

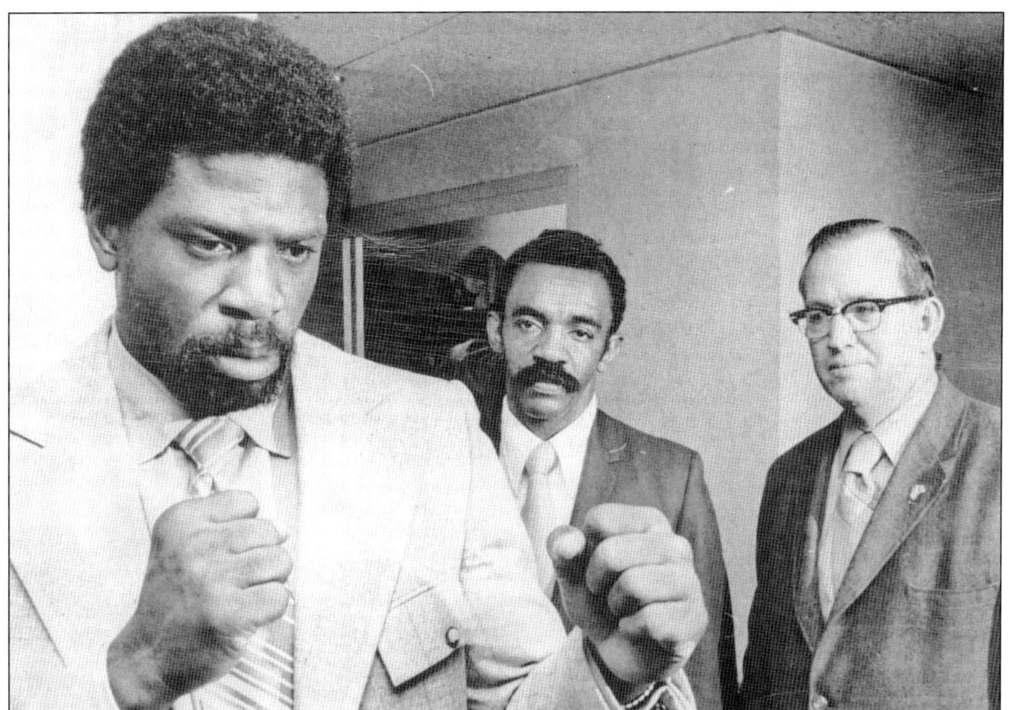

Ron Lyle, a contender for heavyweight champion of the world, spent time at Colorado State Penitentiary before his boxing career took off. He entered the prison in June 1962 and was paroled in November 1969 after serving 7 years of a 15-to-20-year sentence for second-degree murder. While in prison, Lyle was written up for fighting and using foul language with the guards. He took part in the boxing program while incarcerated and won most of the matches. It is said that Lyle spent his time in prison preparing for his run at the heavyweight championship.

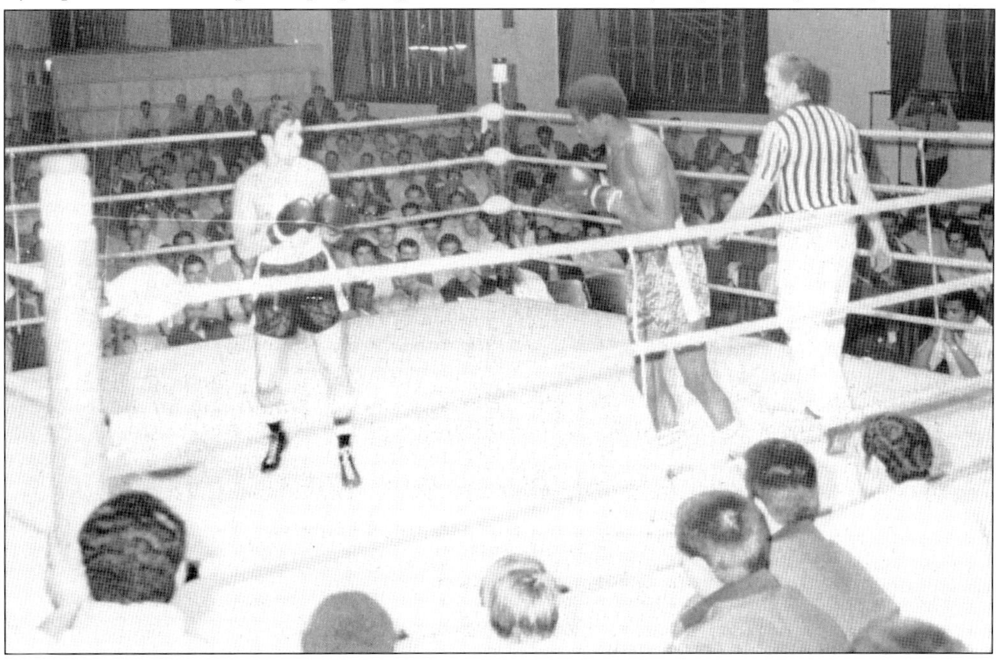

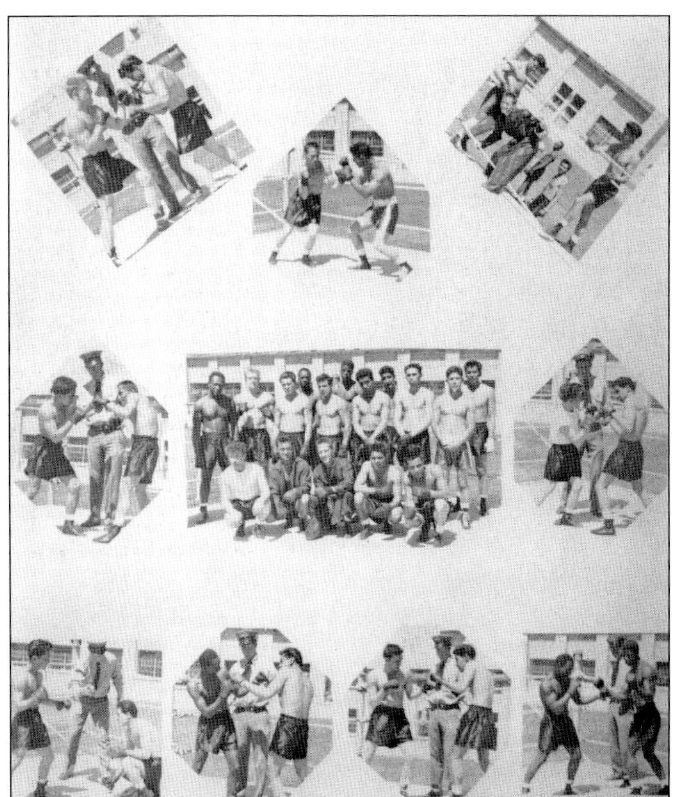

The prison also sponsored a boxing team that held matches against outside teams. Team members traveled to other towns for boxing matches and often boxed against law enforcement agencies. Ron Lyle came back into the prison after his release to give pointers to those in the boxing program.

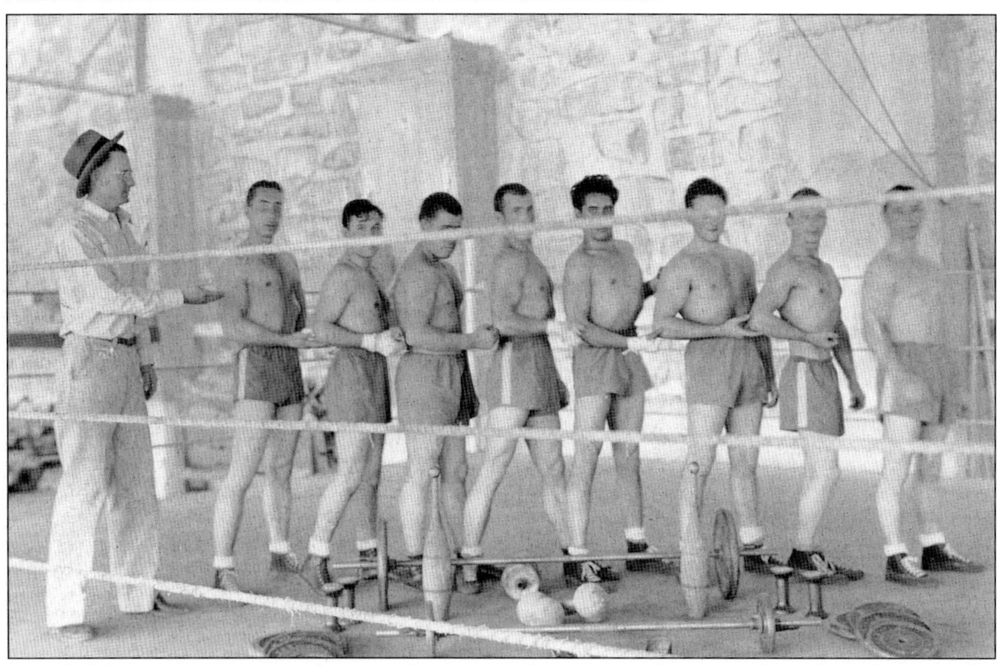

Weightlifters pose, some sucking in their guts, for a team photograph in the 1930s. Today weightlifting is huge in prisons. Many inmates use the equipment, and some even have muscles that would rival today's world champions.

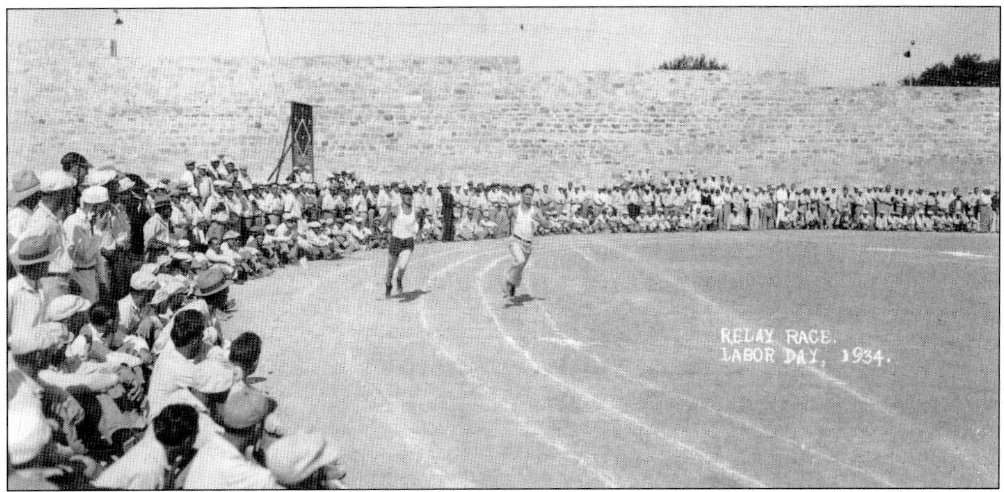

On Labor Day, bands entertained and games were played. On the holiday in 1934, two prisoners made a run for it—for the finish in a relay race, that is. From the look of the crowd, the games had a fine turnout.

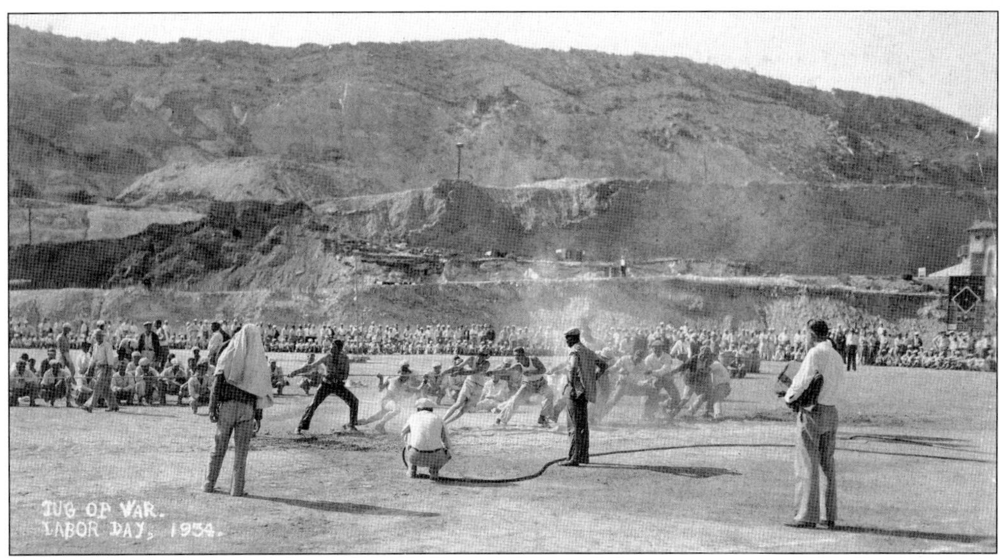

Many times on the holidays, games were staged between prisoners and staff. Unfortunately the group on the other end of the tug-of-war rope cannot be seen. This view from Labor Day in 1934 shows the back side of the prison, where the site of the rock quarry and a dirt berm are depicted instead of the stone wall.

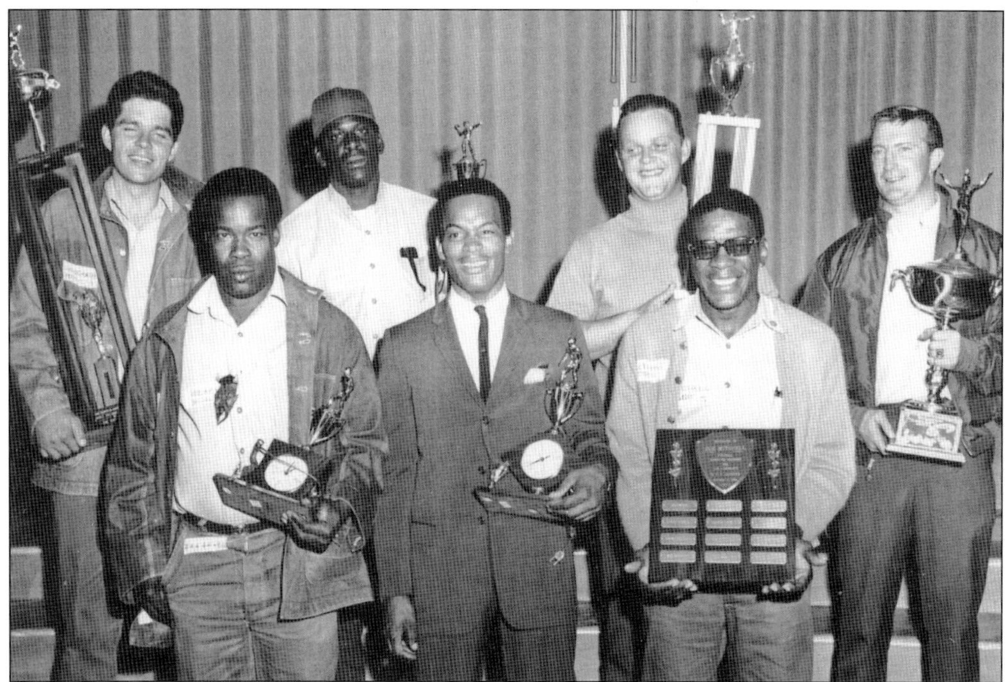

Winners pose with the trophies they received for different sports. Ribbons, medals, and a trophy were handed out to the different athletes for their excellence. Prisoners were very proud to win an award from sports.

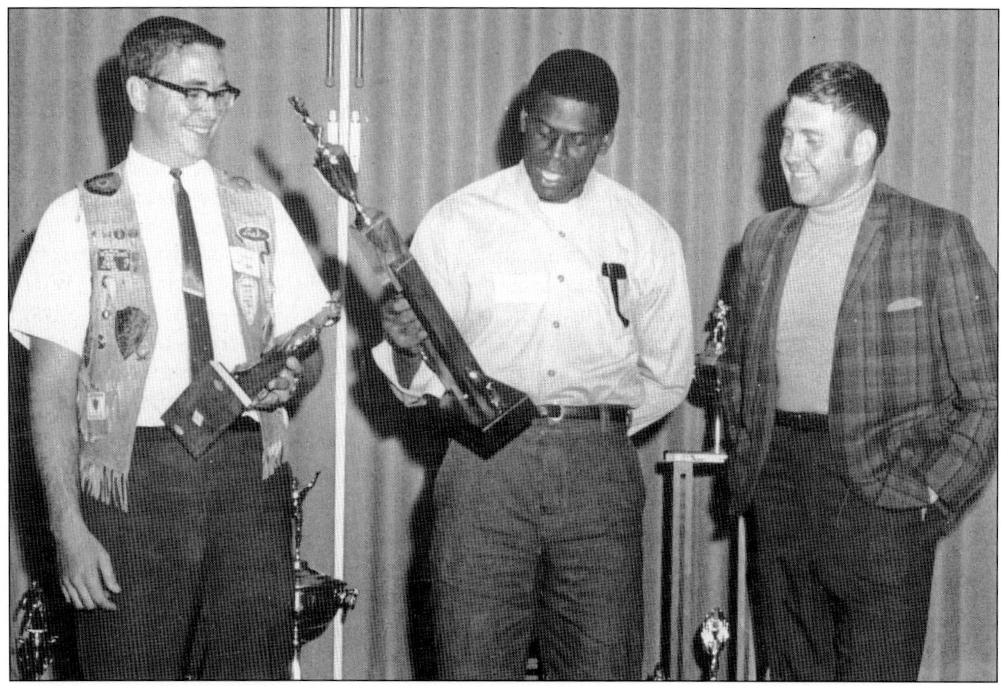

A local organization from Cañon City often sponsored a prison team, and when the season was over, trophies were handed out to those whose achievements excelled. Here a local group, possibly the Boy Scouts or the Jaycees, presents an unidentified prisoner with his prize.

Five

GOING TO THE MOVIES

The Cañon City area has always been a hot spot for Hollywood to come calling. Many movies have been filmed in the mountains and plains. Buckskin Joe, an Old West town 12 miles west of Cañon, has been featured in such films as *White Buffalo, Cat Ballou, The Sackettes, Cactus Flower,* and more. Tom Mix owned a movie company at one time in Cañon and filmed many westerns there himself.

The prison has had its share of movie productions as well, including *The Big House, Scarecrow, The Women of San Quentin, In Cold Blood,* and the most famous of them all: *Cañon City.* When the prison had an auditorium—from the early 1930s up until the 1980s—movies were a good pastime for prisoners. The inmates could spend a Sunday afternoon watching newsreels and a feature film acquired by the prison. When *Cañon City* was finished, the prison showed it to the inmates who were involved in the actual escape. They loved what Hollywood drama added to the tale and used the embellishment of their stories to reap sympathy for their acts.

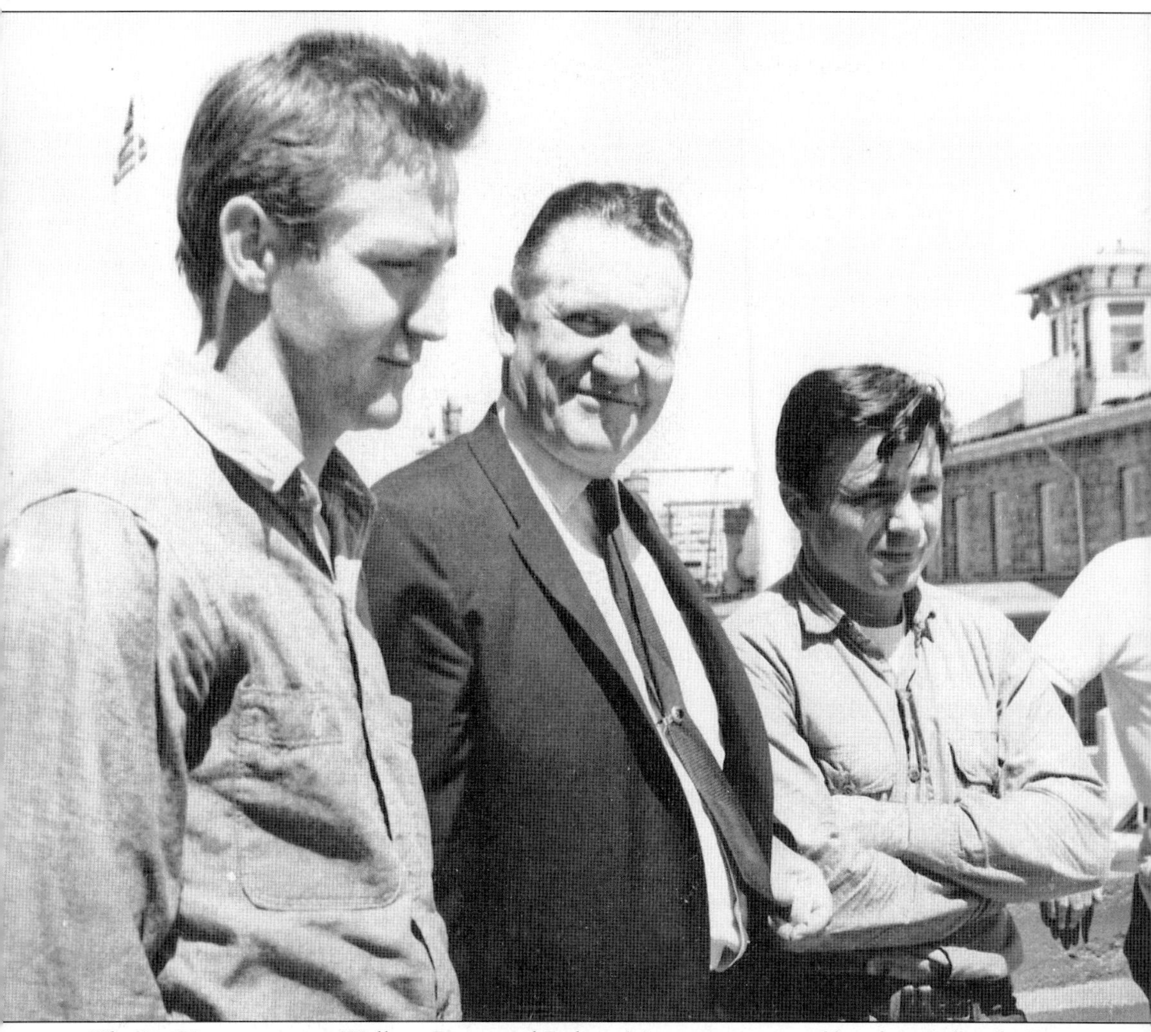

The Big House, starring Wallace Berry and Robert Montgomery, was filmed at Colorado State Penitentiary in 1930. It earned two Oscars and was one of the most realistic prison movies of all time. *Scarecrow*, starring Gene Hackman and Al Pacino, and *The Women of San Quentin*, starring Hector Elizondo, Ernie Hudson, and Stella Stevens, were filmed in part at the prison. In 1967, the prison was used for the death house and hanging scene in Truman Capote's *In Cold Blood*. It starred a very young and good-looking actor, Robert Blake (right), as Perry Smith, and Scott Wilson (left) as Richard Hickock. Standing with the two actors in the prison yard is warden Wayne K. Patterson. The movie is now a cult classic.

Warden Wayne Patterson (left) is presented with an autographed photograph from John Forsyth (right), who played the detective in the movie *In Cold Blood*. Many of the actors from the movies filmed in the area would stay for months to finish filming and intermingle with the locals, who then had a story to tell about meeting a star.

Prisoner Richard Heilman was the one who made it outside the walls on a cold night in 1947. He had only traveled a few miles down the road when he was shot in the head and hand and hauled back to the prison. When asked about the escape while on the mend, he stated, "It wasn't worth it." That night he was half-frozen and stumbling around in the dark and snow. These events were the inspiration for the movie *Canon City*.

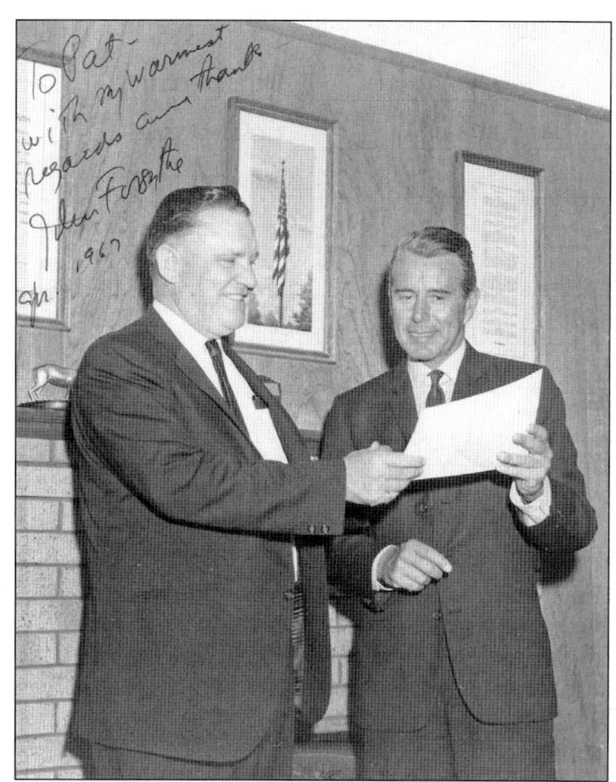

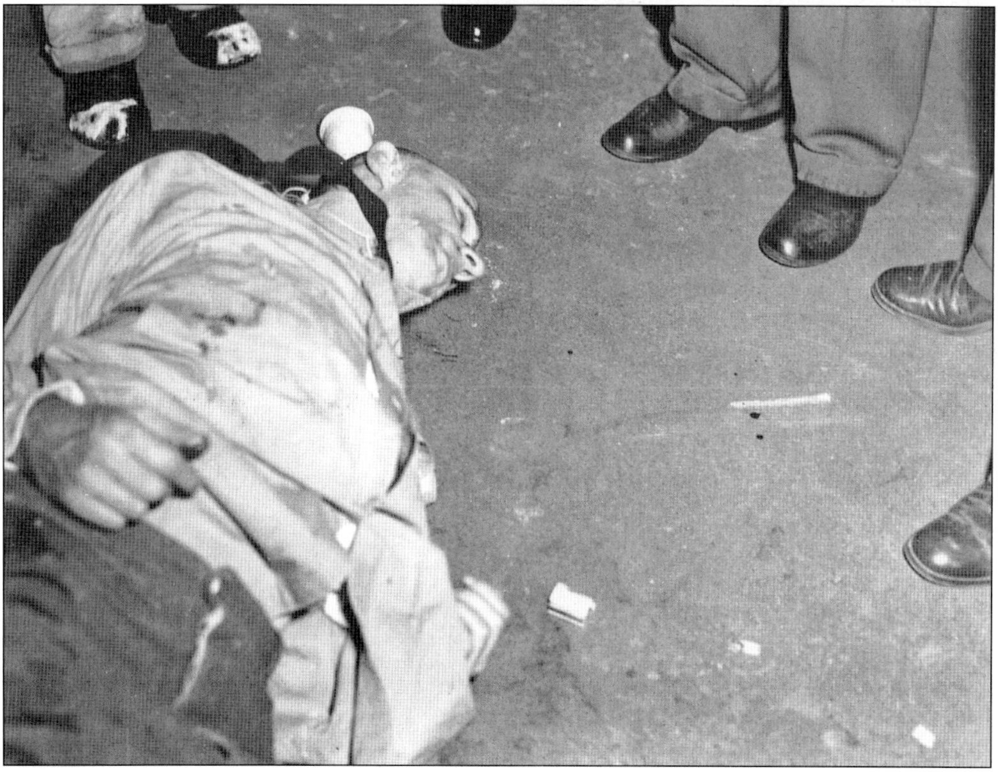

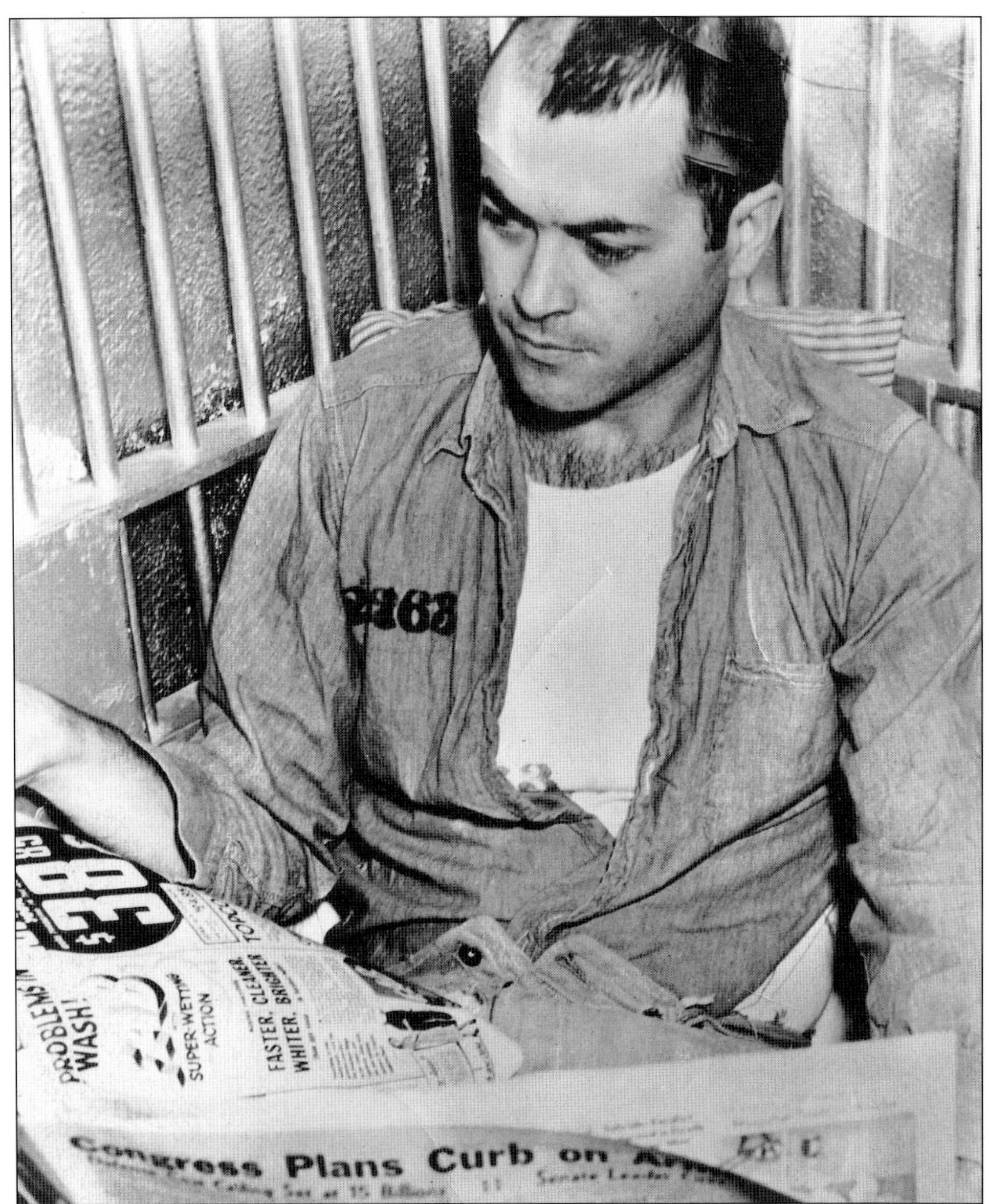

James Sherbondy was a petty thief his whole life in the small town of Redcliff until one night in 1937, when sheriff's deputy Oscar Meyer tried to stop him and his family while they were leaving town with all their belongings piled high on a truck. Sherbondy pulled a gun on Meyer and killed him. He was sentenced to life in prison for the murder. In 1947, Sherbondy was involved in an escape that made national headlines and later became a movie. A fugitive, he went into a home and held the family hostage. During the night, one of the children became ill and so Sherbondy allowed the mother to take the child to the area hospital. He was captured the next day. He visited the Old Gray Mare and then spent 18 months in solitary for his part in the escape. In the 1960s, while free legitimately but having broken parole, Sherbondy was gunned down on a Denver street while fleeing from a police officer who had recognized him in an adjacent car. The officer was seriously wounded.

The Colorado National Guard was called out for the search in 1947. When the whistle blew, many people from Cañon came to the prison to help. Living in a prison town, most residents had weapons and were more than willing to assist when needed.

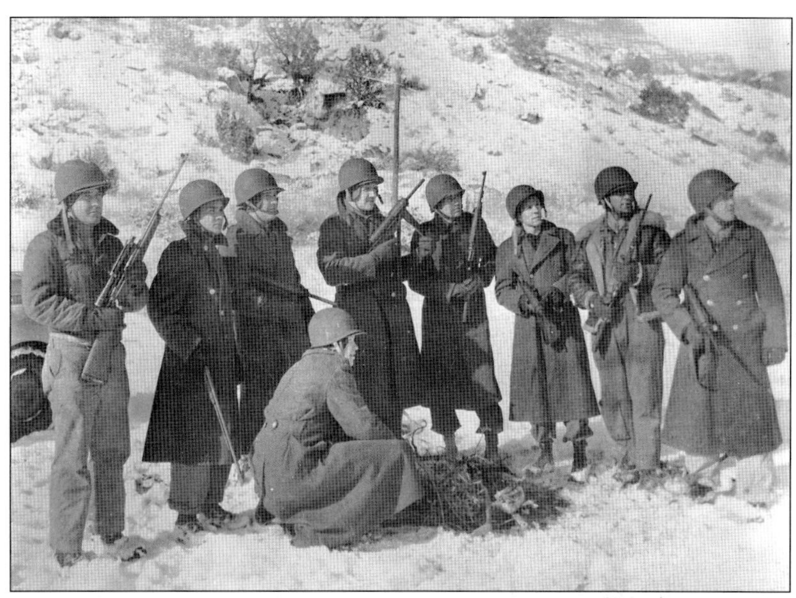

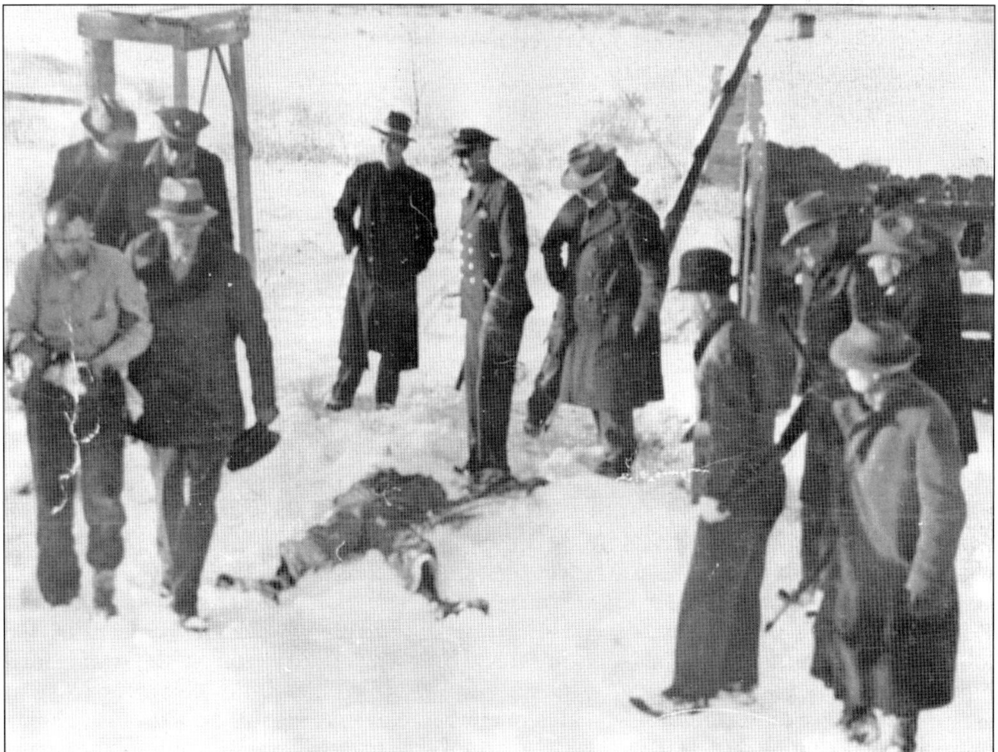

It was the end of the road for prisoner Orville Turley upon his capture following the 1947 escape. As guards led prisoner John Smalley away in cuffs, Turley lay on the ground dead from gunshot wounds to the head. Because Turley's family did not claim his body, he lies in the pauper's section at Lakewood Cemetery in Cañon City.

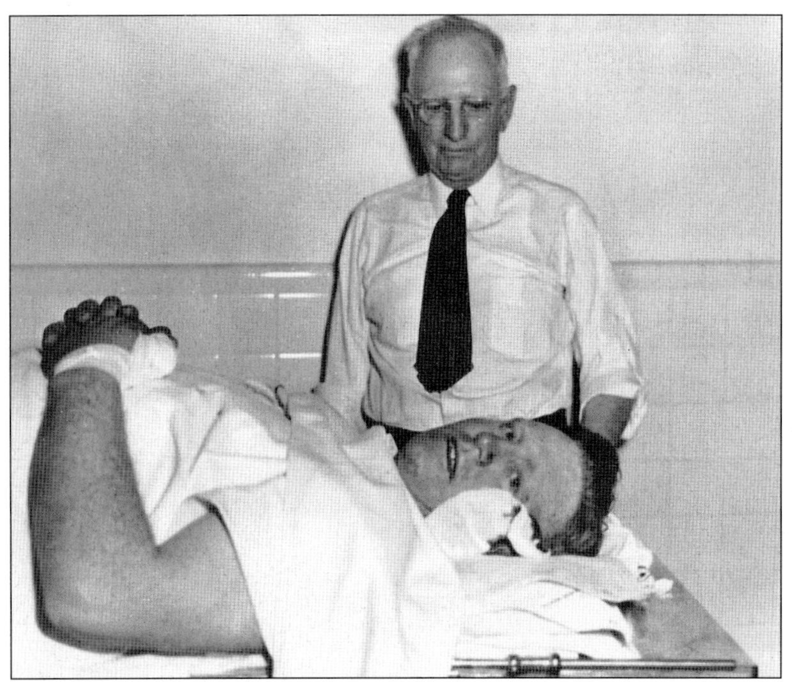

Lt. Chet Yeo, a guard at the prison during the 1947 ruckus, lies wounded on the operating table at St. Thomas More Hospital in Cañon City as Dr. Shoun looks on. He suffered a head injury during the escape but lived, continuing to work at the prison for many years.

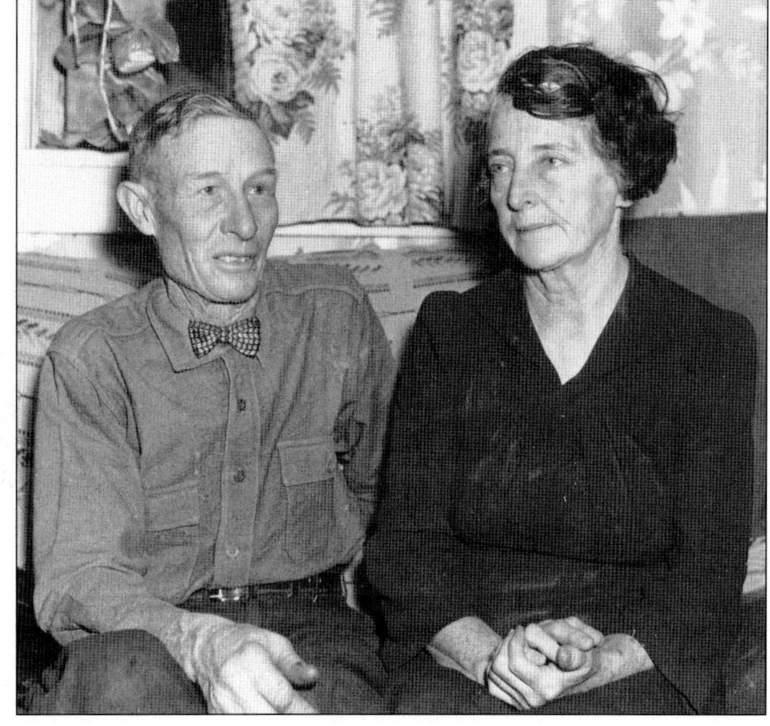

Laurence and Oda Oliver were spending a quiet night at home when prisoner Wilbur Schwartmiller came busting in and held them captive for several hours. Schwartmiller demanded that Oda "cook him food and lots of it." Later she snuck up behind him and hit him in the head with a hammer. He was seriously wounded but lived to serve out his sentence at the prison.

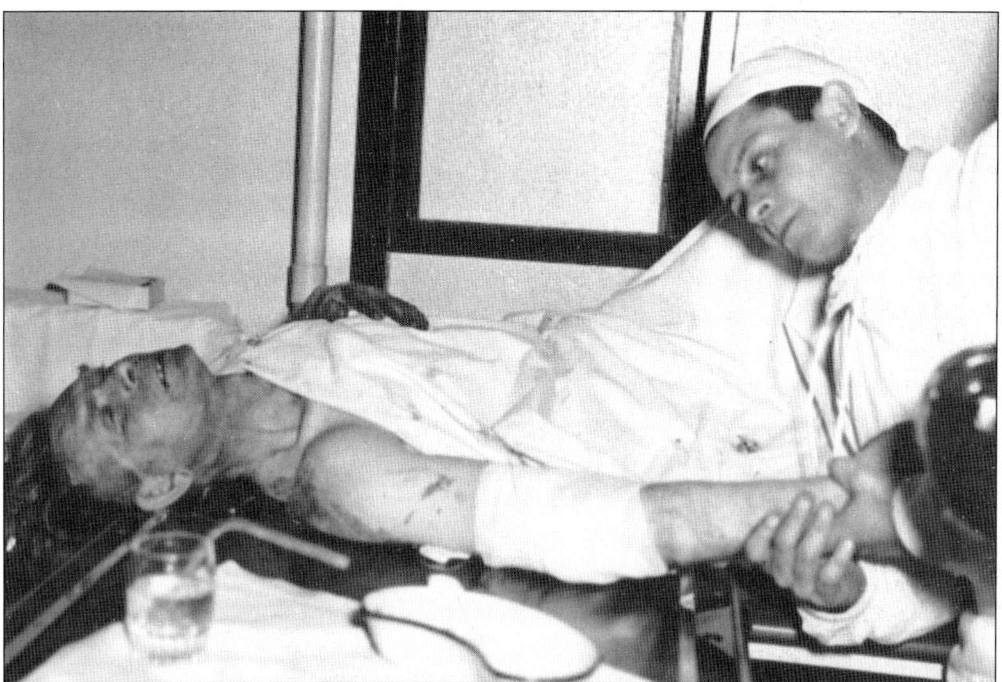

Oak Creek Grade rancher A. M. Smith lies on the table at St. Thomas More Hospital after being shot in the arm while helping in the search. Thankfully no one was seriously injured or killed among those in the search parties that night.

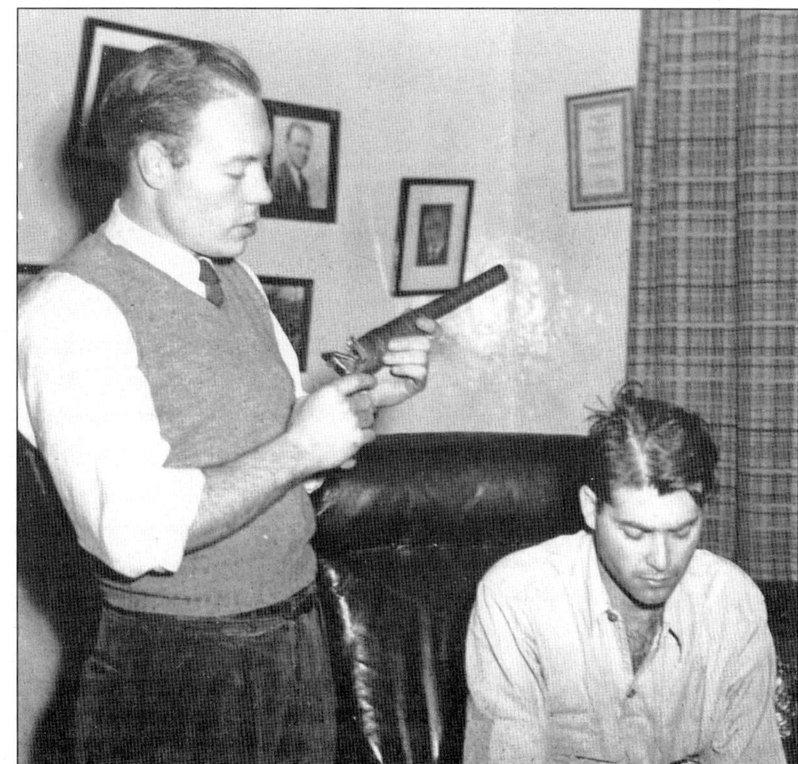

Following his capture, an uninjured James Sherbondy (right) is questioned about the escape by an unidentified man. The man holds one of two homemade guns used by prisoners during the escape. This one was found under a bridge in the Cañon area.

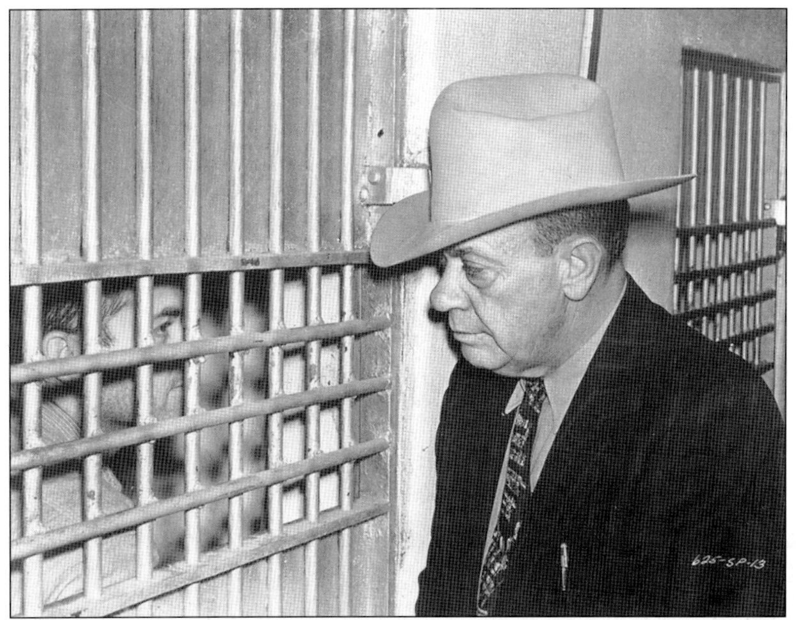

Warden Roy Best visits with Sherbondy in his cell in the solitary section. Sherbondy would take a double dose of the Old Gray Mare for an injured prisoner who was in the infirmary. He would stay in solitary for 18 months after the escape.

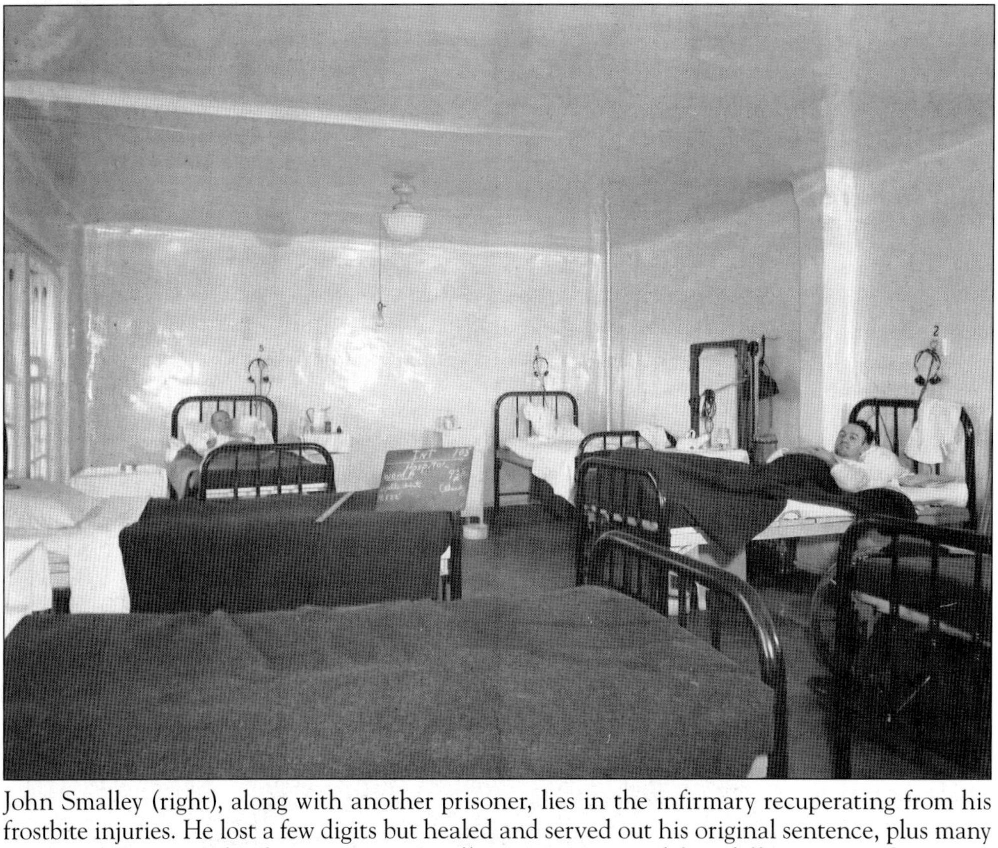

John Smalley (right), along with another prisoner, lies in the infirmary recuperating from his frostbite injuries. He lost a few digits but healed and served out his original sentence, plus many more for his part in the daring escape. Smalley was imprisoned four different times from 1937 until his release in 1967.

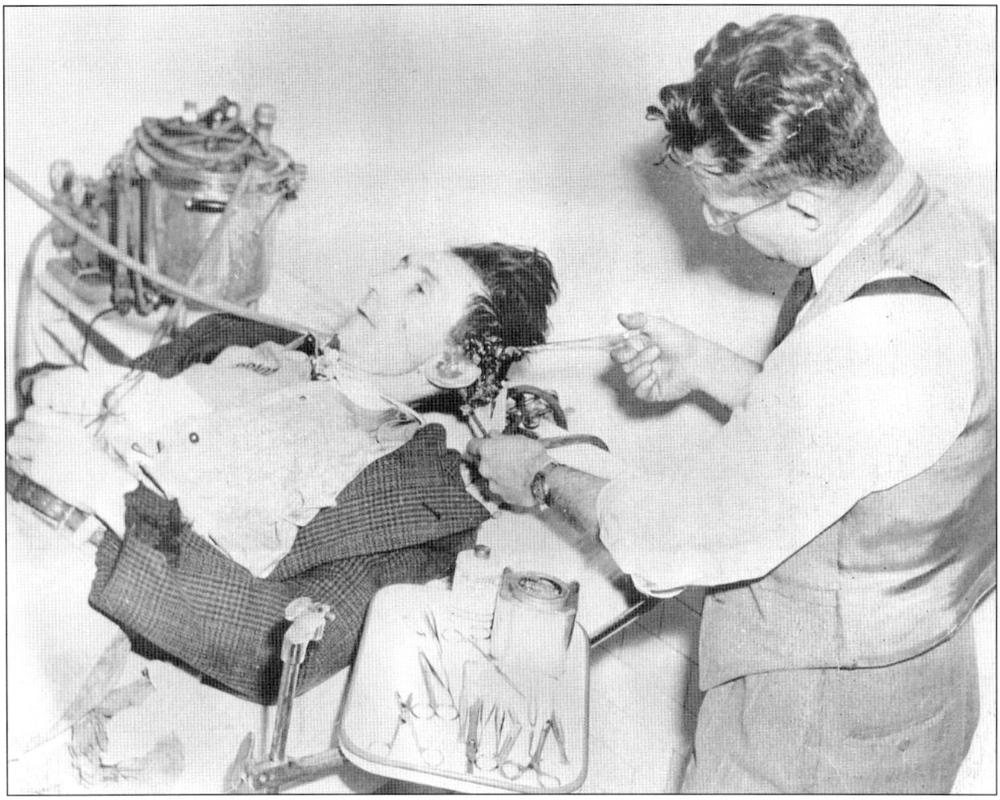

On the morgue table is prisoner Orville Klinger. Still wrapped around his hands is the wire with which he tried to kill his captors. Deputy coroner William A. Wilson stitches Klinger's head wound to prepare the body for burial.

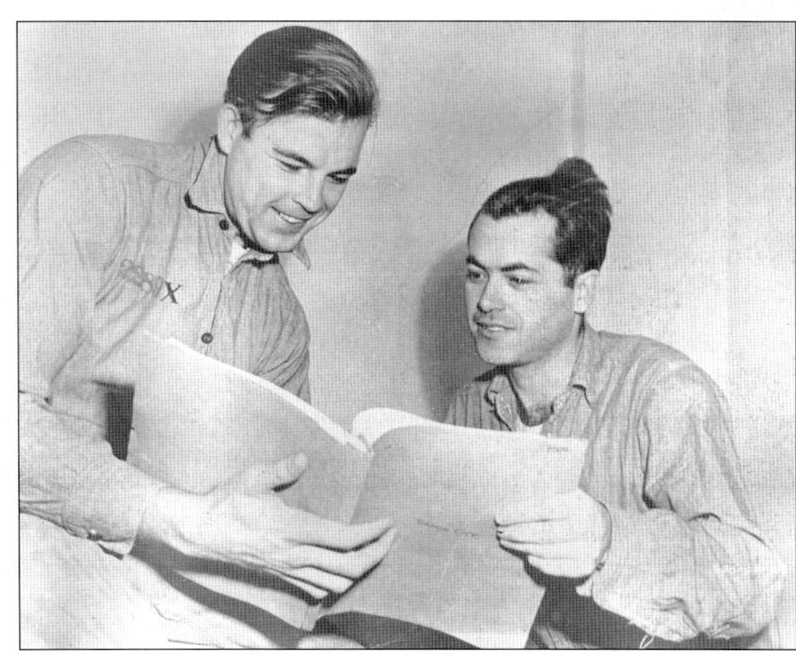

Film star Scott Brady (left) played prisoner James Sherbondy (right) in the 1948 movie about the famous escape, aptly named *Cañon City*. Lions Gate Studio filmed the movie in its entirety here in Cañon City and inside the prison, using prisoners and guards for many parts.

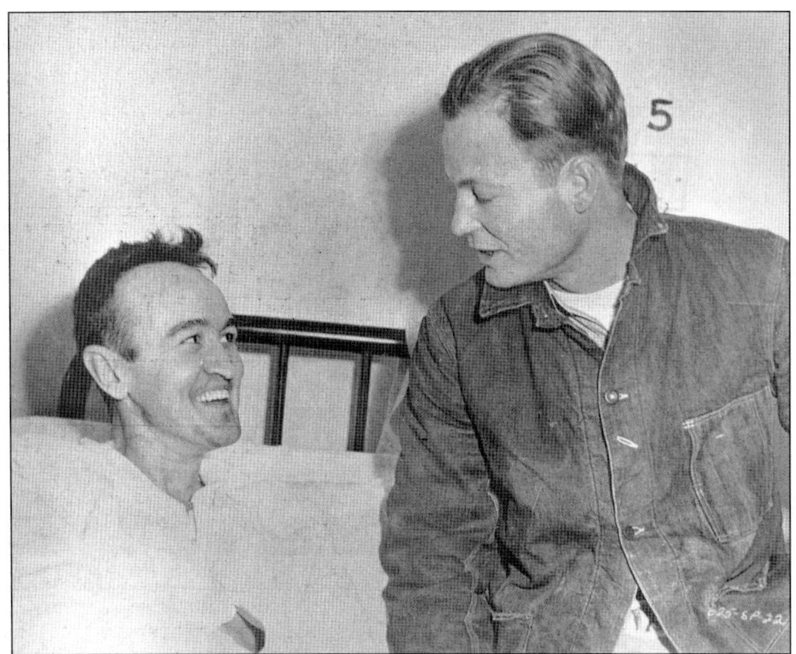

Deforest Kelly (right), who played John Smalley, goes over the script with Smalley while in the infirmary. Kelly was known for many movies, but his claim to fame was his portrayal of "Bones" in the *Star Trek* series.

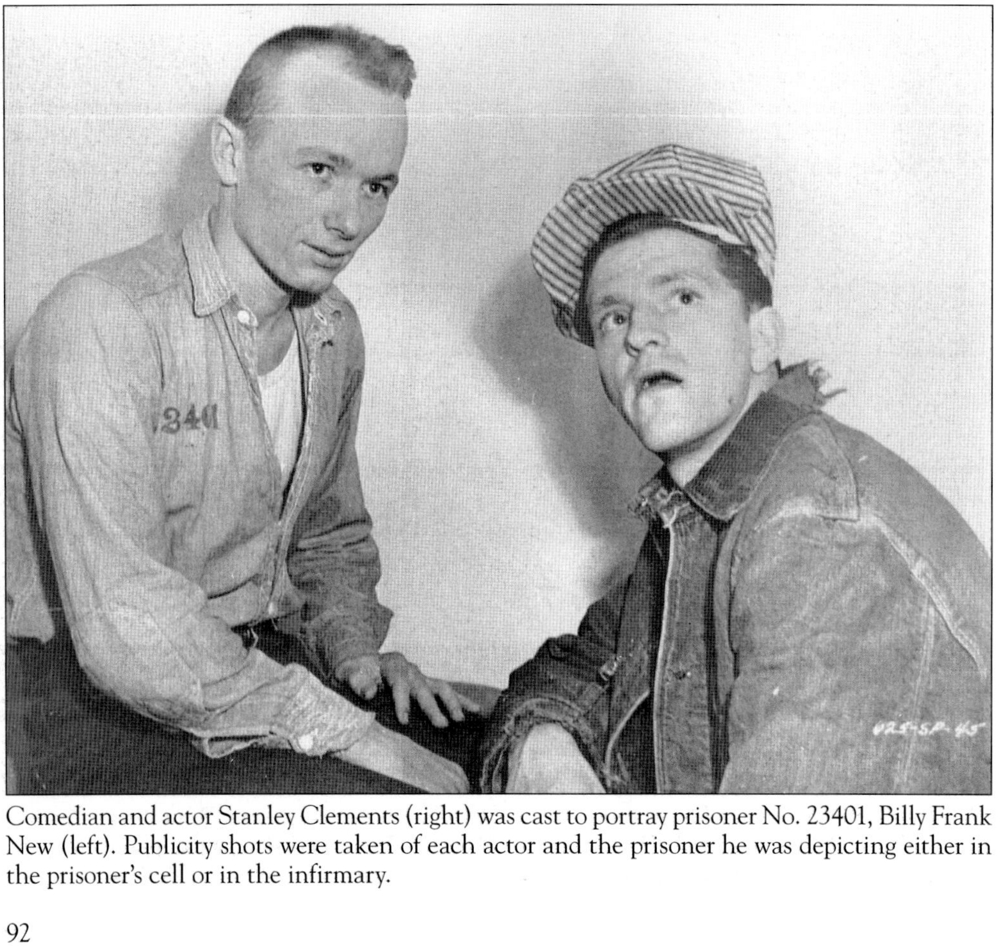

Comedian and actor Stanley Clements (right) was cast to portray prisoner No. 23401, Billy Frank New (left). Publicity shots were taken of each actor and the prisoner he was depicting either in the prisoner's cell or in the infirmary.

Guards and prisoners were used as players in the movie; actual guards are seen here during the film's escape scene. Now a classic, *Cañon City* can be rented at video stores or purchased from the Museum of Colorado Prisons. It has also been known to show up on late-night television stations.

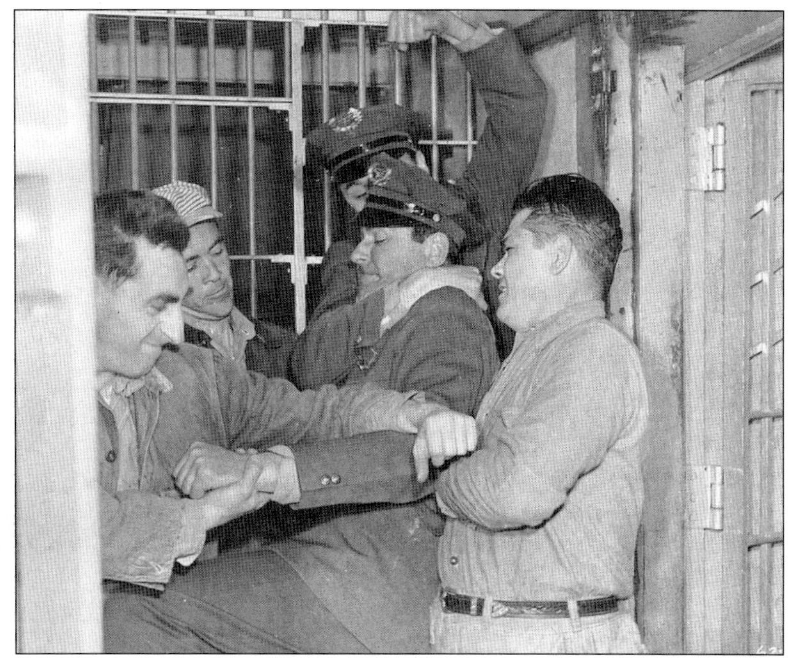

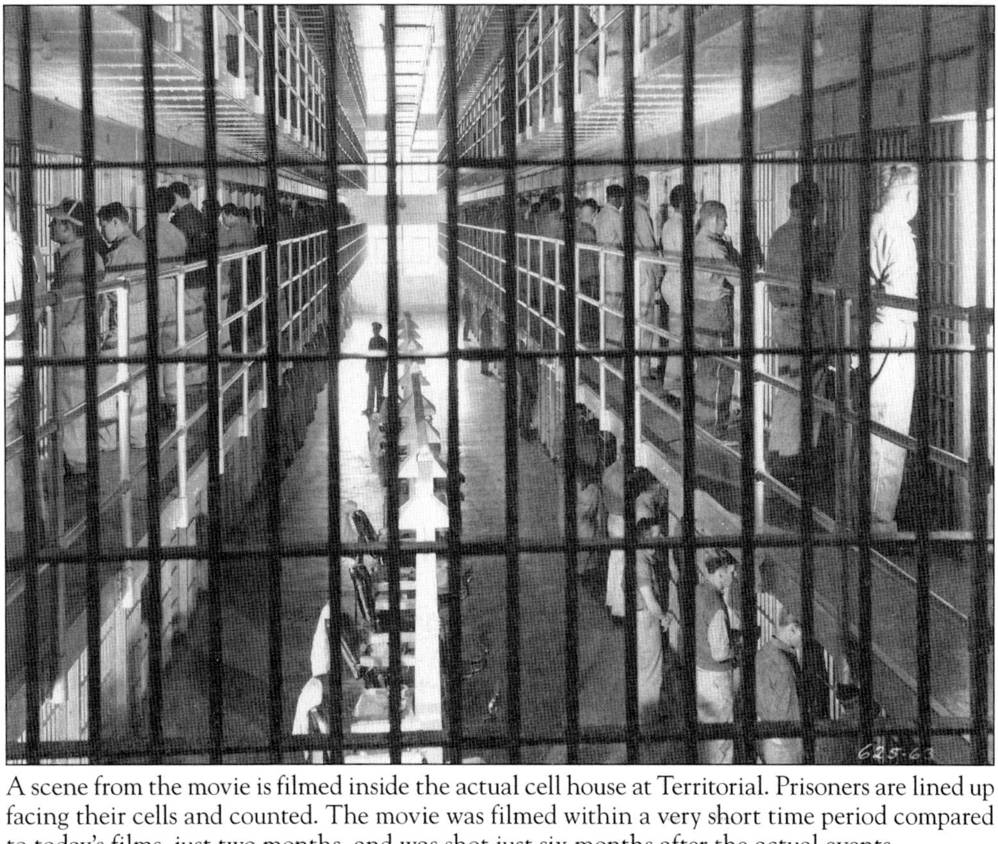

A scene from the movie is filmed inside the actual cell house at Territorial. Prisoners are lined up facing their cells and counted. The movie was filmed within a very short time period compared to today's films, just two months, and was shot just six months after the actual events.

The dining area was filmed during an actual meal for the prisoners. The cage hanging above the tables had an armed guard in it in case of trouble in the chow hall. No talking was allowed while eating, and eye contact was restricted to food only.

This scene from the movie was shot inside. Looking at the original stills, one can make out the backdrop. The filming of the movie occurred in winter to keep the authenticity of the escape intact. Scott Brady said of the movie shoot, "It is beautiful country but you can freeze your parts off out here."

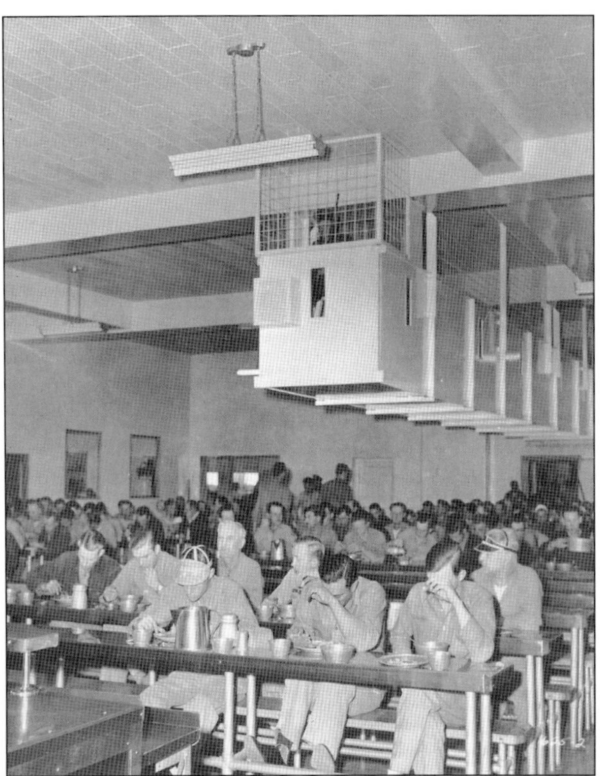

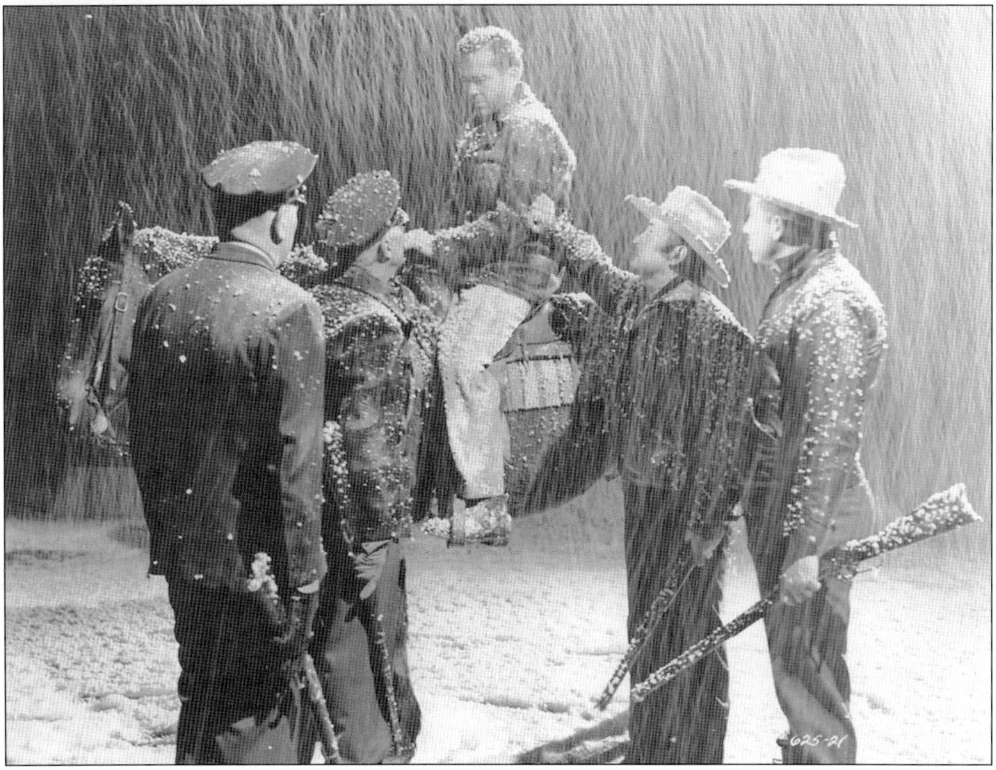

Six

Dirty Deeds

Inside the prison walls and fences is a world no one on the outside can fathom. Escape plans are often found in cell searches, the makings of bombs confiscated, death threats to staff and other prisoners often uncovered, and seemingly innocent arguments can escalate to a full-blown riot in seconds. It is said that staff are paid for what might happen, not for what normally happens. Employees deal with many levels of anxiety—from the belligerent prisoners to the sometimes belligerent staff who have been pushed too far. Stress runs high in a prison, and anything can happen in the blink of an eye. The old saying goes, "Idle hands are the devil's workshop," and that is true in this type of setting. The prisons have held abortionists, pyromaniacs, bank robbers, and heinous murderers. Guards and officers have ended up on the wrong side of the law and landed in prison themselves. Former police officers, FBI agents, and political officials—no one is immune to the draw of crime.

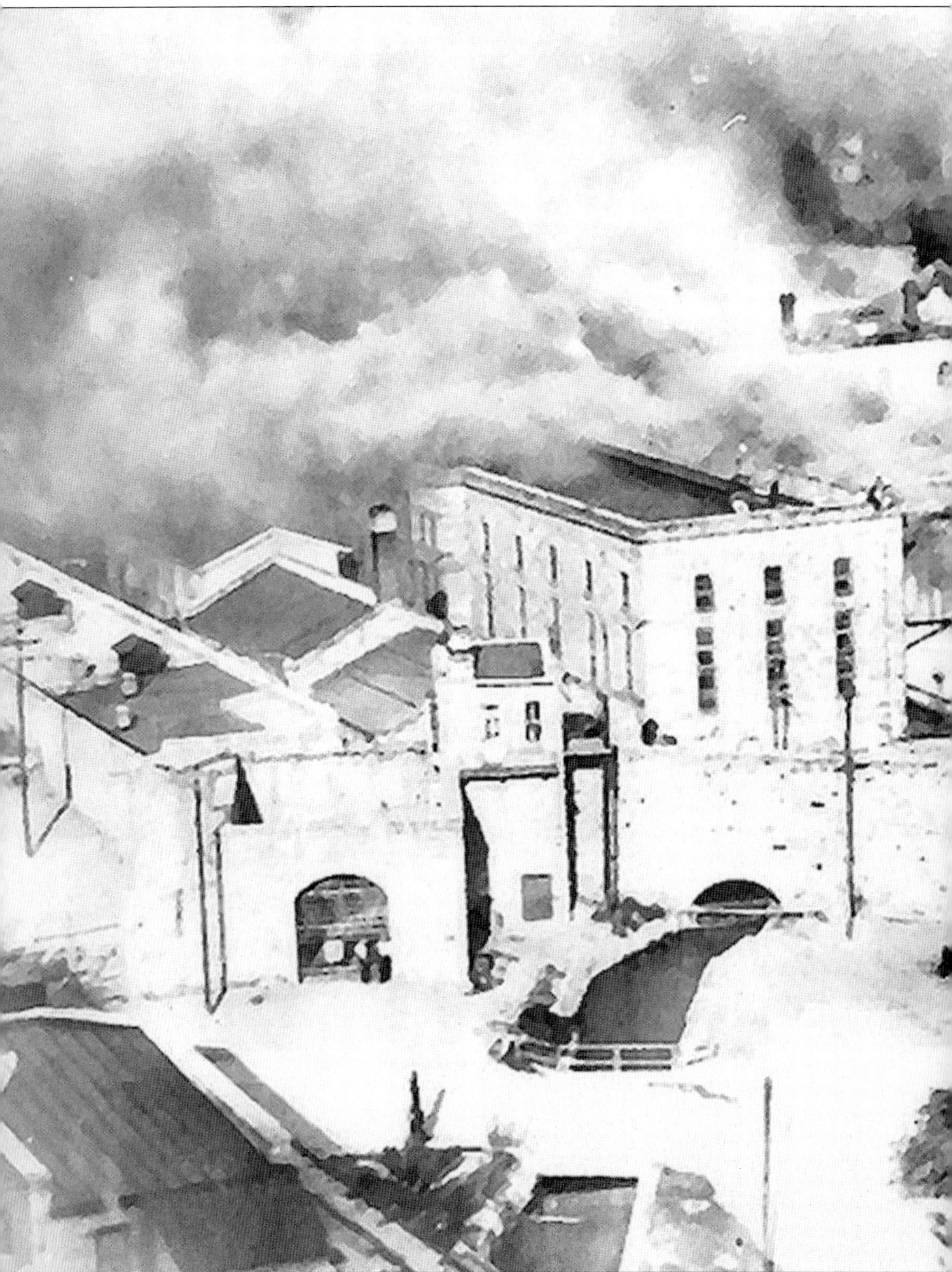

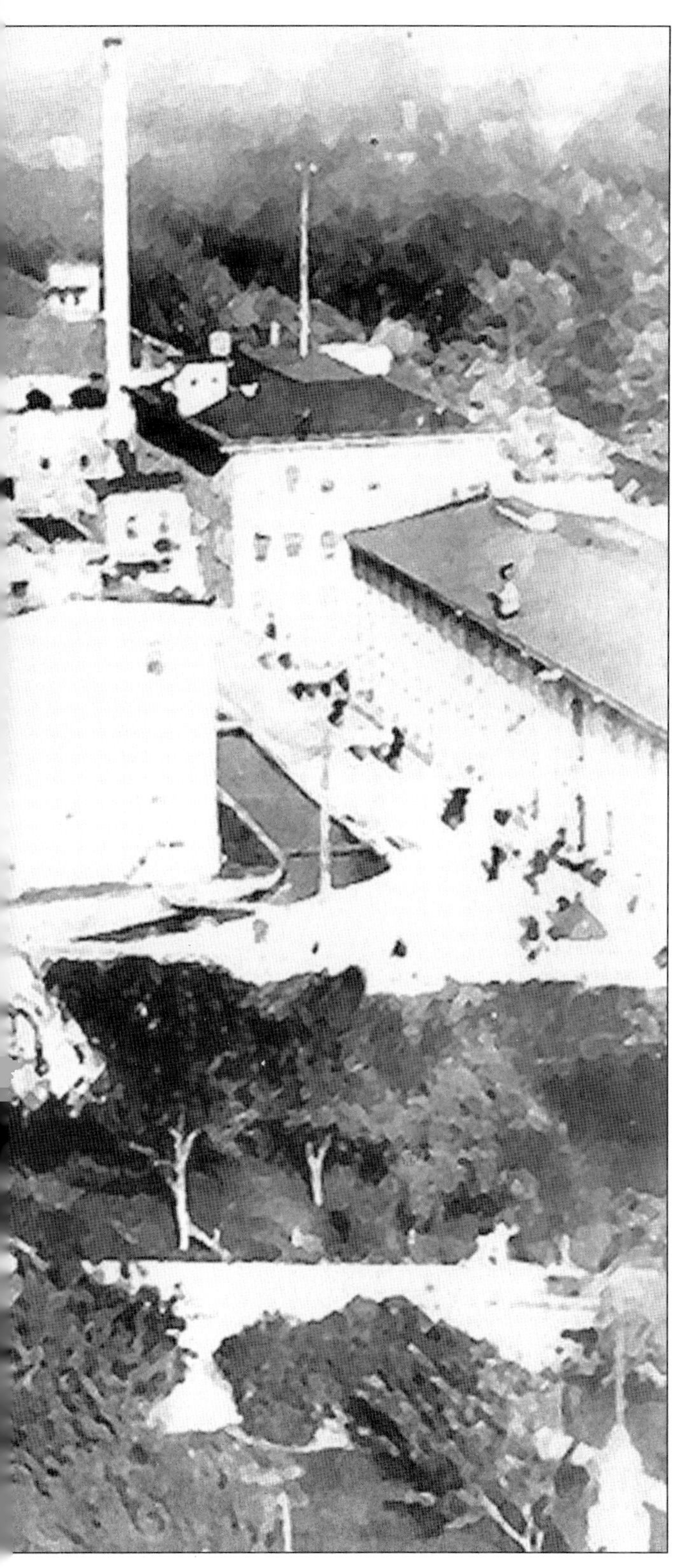

In 1929, the unthinkable happened on a day that will always be remembered as one of the darkest in the prison's history. The prison whistle alerted facility employees and Cañon City citizens that there was trouble: an escape plot had gone wrong, and a riot was now underway. Thirteen guards were being held hostage by five key prisoners. Over the course of three days, the prisoners demanded cars and money for their escape again and again, and each request was denied. When the riot ended, eight guards had been murdered and several severely injured; buildings had been burned to the ground and cell houses destroyed; and the five prisoners and one jail snitch lay dead in the cell house by their own hands.

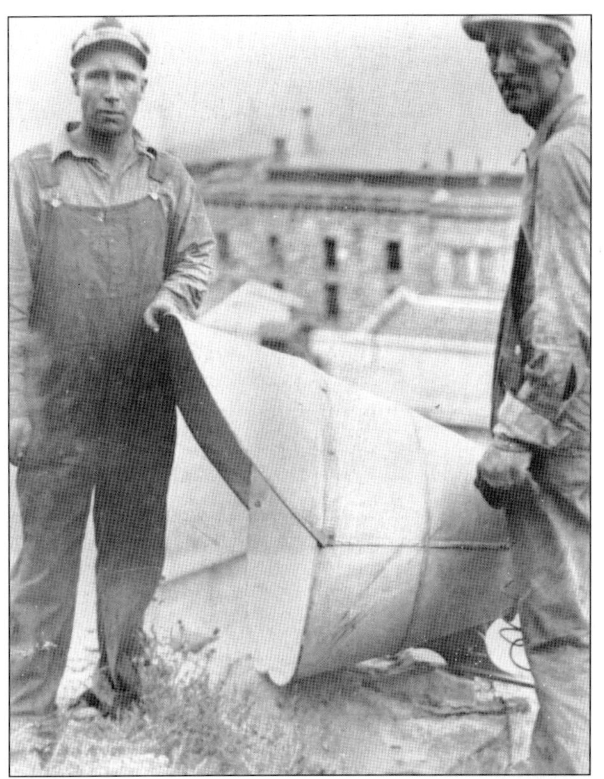

Two unidentified people ready the lights to illuminate the prison once night sets in. Negotiations went on for the lives of the 13 guards held hostage, but in the end all 8 were shot in the head. Three more were shot and simply acted dead, thus saving their own lives.

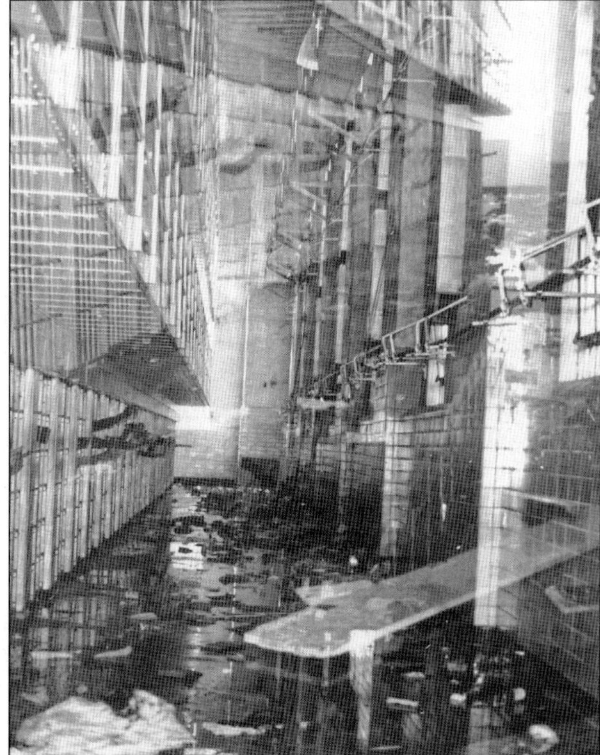

Pictured here is one of the cell houses after the riot. The structure was later determined to be a total loss and had to be rebuilt. Fires had been set, toilets and sinks flooded, and toilets and sinks ripped off the wall and used as weapons.

One ringleader died early from gunshot wounds. When the other prisoner ringleaders—Daniels, Reilley, Pardue, and Davis—decided to end it, they shot and killed themselves, taking prisoner Albert Morgariedge with them because he had proved to be a jailhouse snitch. Their bodies were laid out after the riot for all to see. All but Davis were buried the next day in a mass grave at Woodpecker Hill.

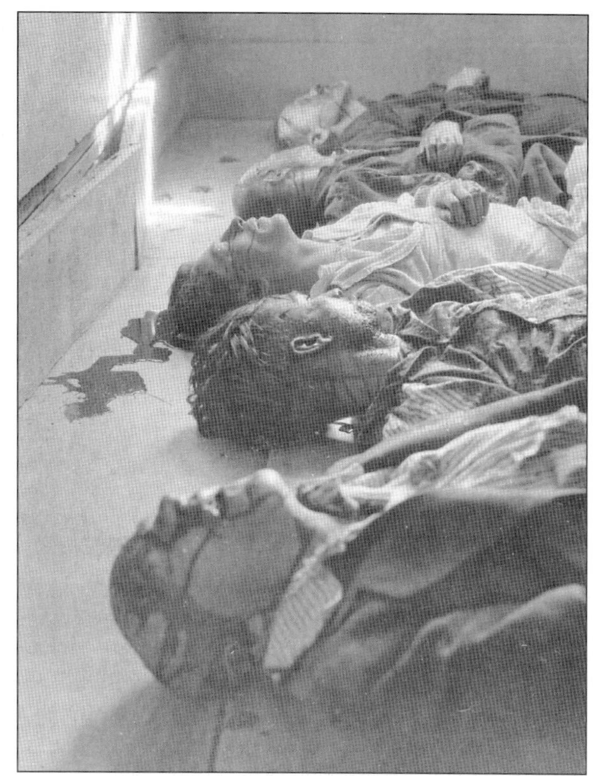

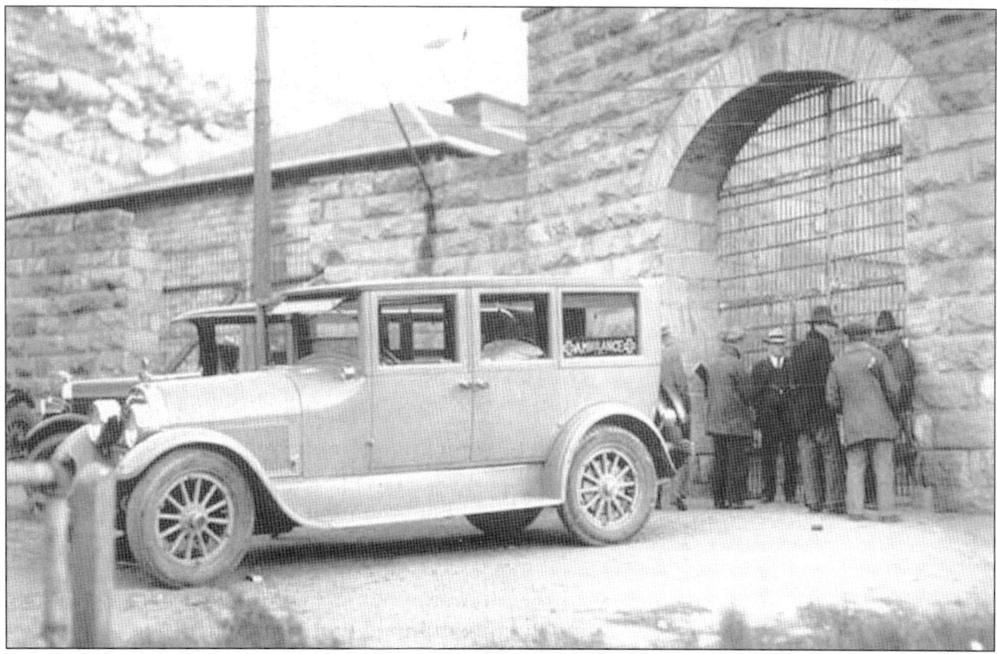

After the 1929 riot, the murdered guards were taken out by the local mortuary. Their bodies were put into the hearses with much respect, and a state funeral was held for each. The prisoners who killed the guards were loaded into a horse-drawn wagon and dumped into a mass grave on Woodpecker Hill without any fanfare or service.

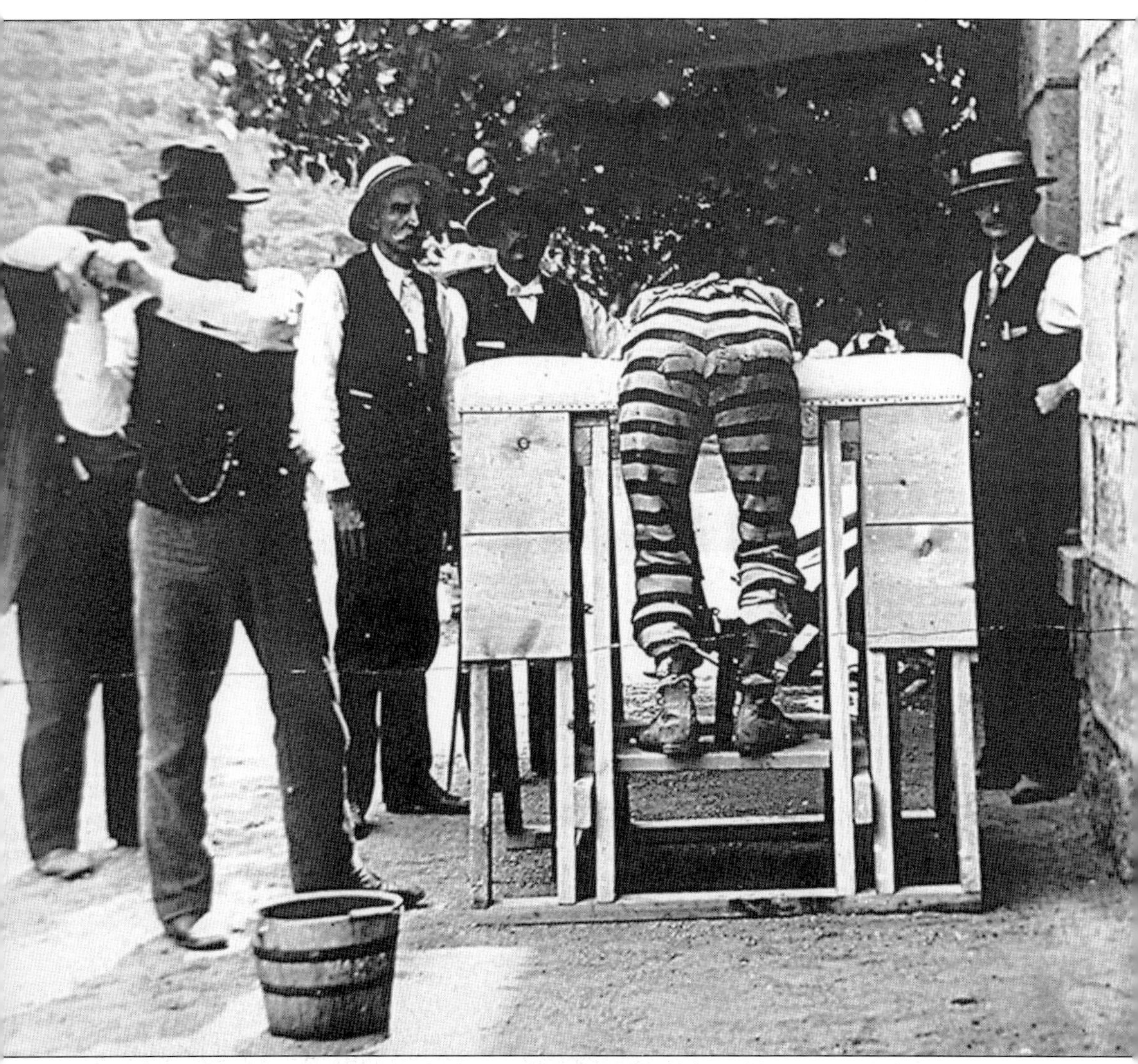

Most credit warden Roy Best with the implementation of the Old Gray Mare, but the whipping post actually began in the 1800s as a punishment tool for unruly prisoners. When Roy Best oversaw the Mare procedure, he stopped overzealous guards from using it on prisoners who talked back or committed minor infractions. He believed that the Mare should only be used in the most serious cases. A prisoner was strapped to the post by his feet on one side and laid over with his hands attached on the other side. He was beaten with a wooden paddle as many as 20 times, with the exact number depending on the seriousness of his crime. The paddle shred his pant seat, caused bruising, and sometimes drew blood. One guard witnessed one beating and said it was the worst thing he had ever seen. The Old Gray Mare was abolished in 1952.

In the early 1900s,
inmates tried to escape
through the Tower 6 gate
by ramming it with a
prison vehicle. The act
did not entirely work,
but the force opened the
gate enough for them to
run through. They were
captured shortly after.

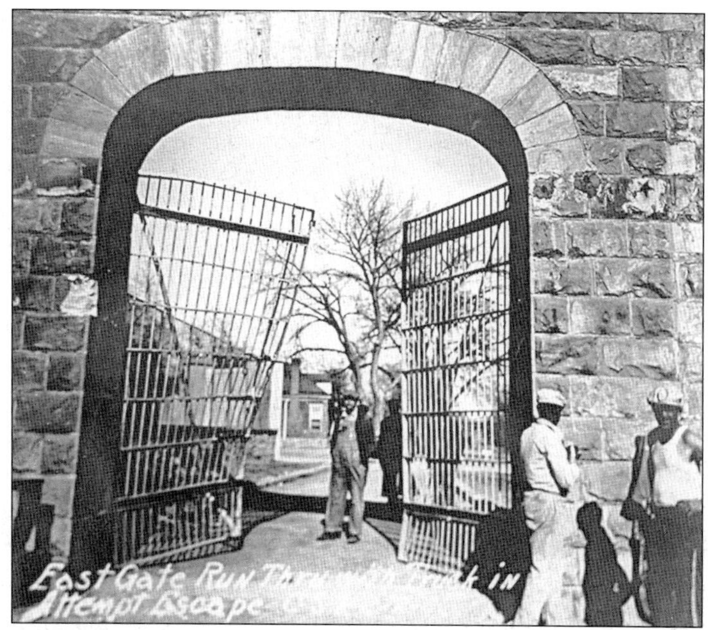

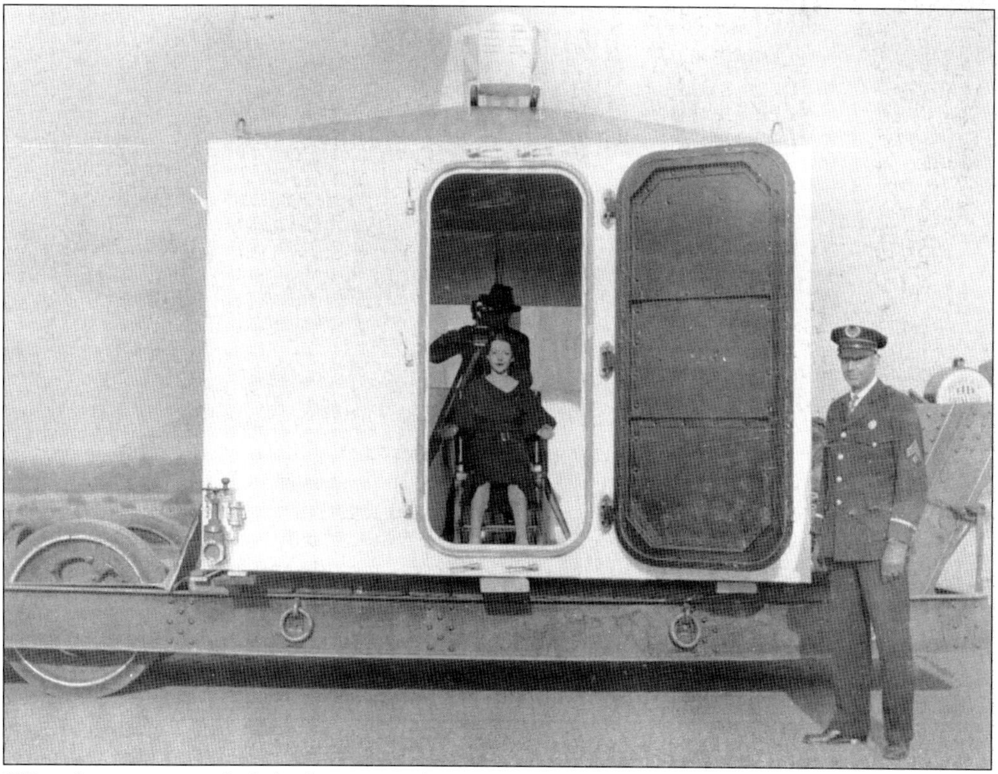

When hanging was abolished in 1932, the new method of execution became the gas chamber.
The new chamber was installed in its own properly ventilated building before being moved to
the maximum-security Cell House 3. This chamber, bearing two seats, was responsible for the
deaths of 24 male prisoners. When it was retired, a modern chamber was used for 8 more deaths,
bringing the total to 32.

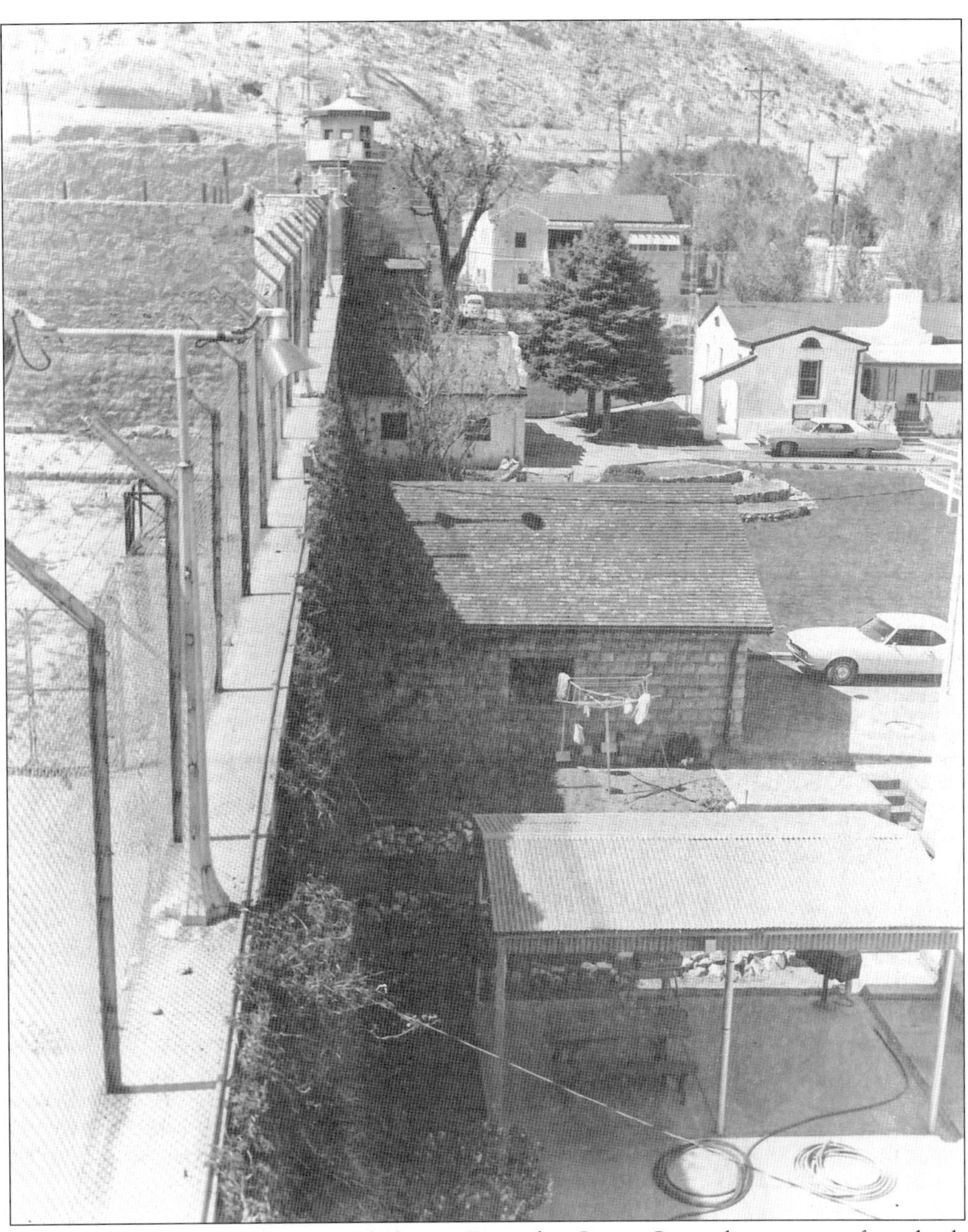

In 1971, during the annual Music and Blossom Festival in Cañon City, a daring escape from death row was almost successful. Prisoners Ernest Leroy Alsip, No. 40177, and Michael John Bell, No. 35299, attempted to escape from Cell House 3 at Old Max, Colorado State Penitentiary. The escape route was out the roof of the cell house, down a drainpipe, and across to the wall, where they climbed atop a shed and managed to make it along the big wall to Tower 6. Alsip and Bell dropped to the garage roof on the east side of the wall and planned to run into the large crowd gathered for the parade, the carnival, and the booths and vendors set up and down Main Street. They came very close.

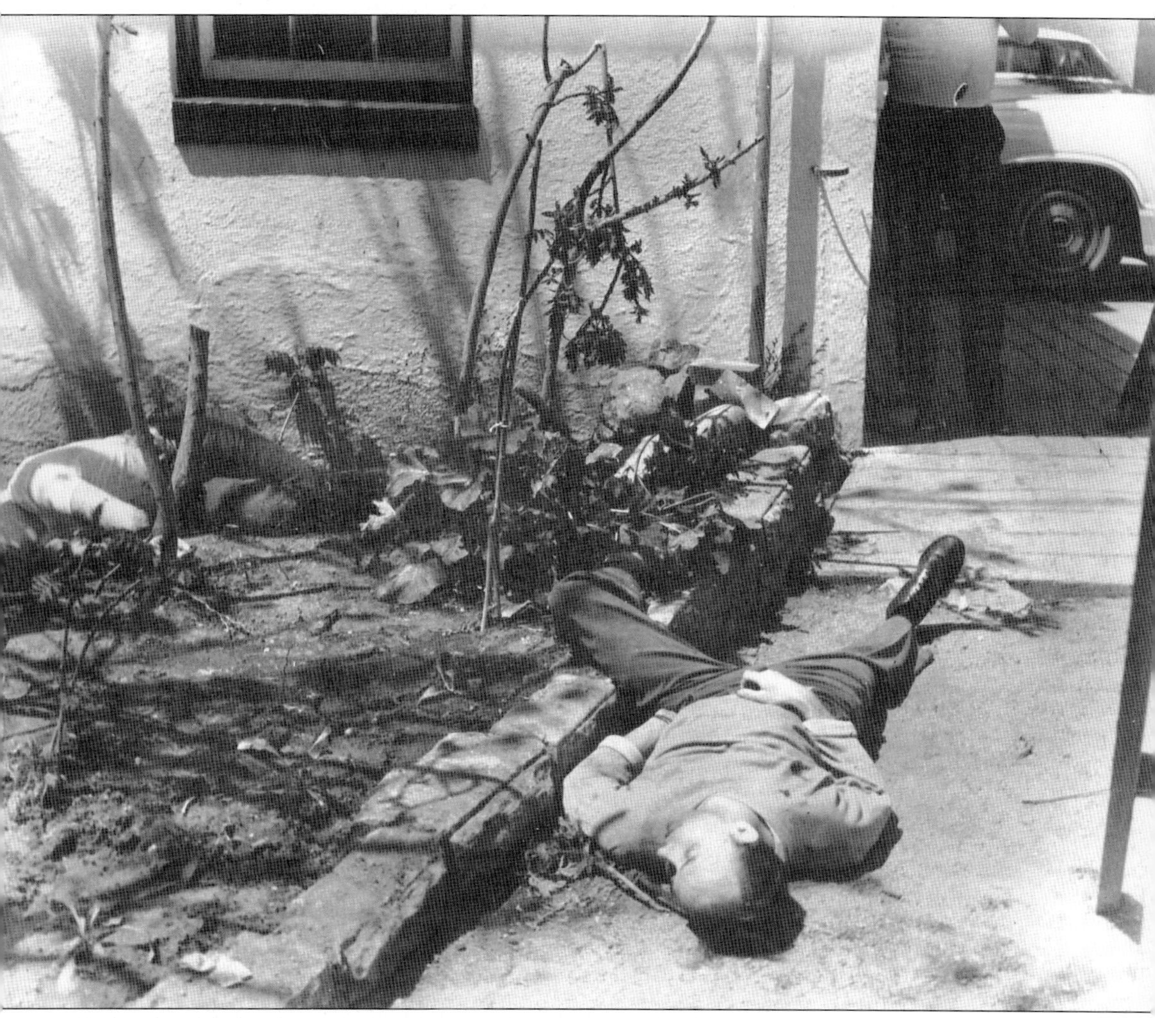

High school kids who were lined up in the street, waiting their turn to march in the parade, observed the prisoners as they dropped down on the garage roof. Alert tower guards noticed the prisoners as well and shot both Alsip and Bell, killing them instantly. Alsip fell into a garden and Bell onto a street leading into the prison. Guards rushed to the area and had to keep the onlookers back to secure the scene. The onlookers and the high school bands believed that a movie was being filmed and they had just witnessed one of the scenes. They clapped, screamed, and yelled when it was over, impressed by the great show put on for their entertainment.

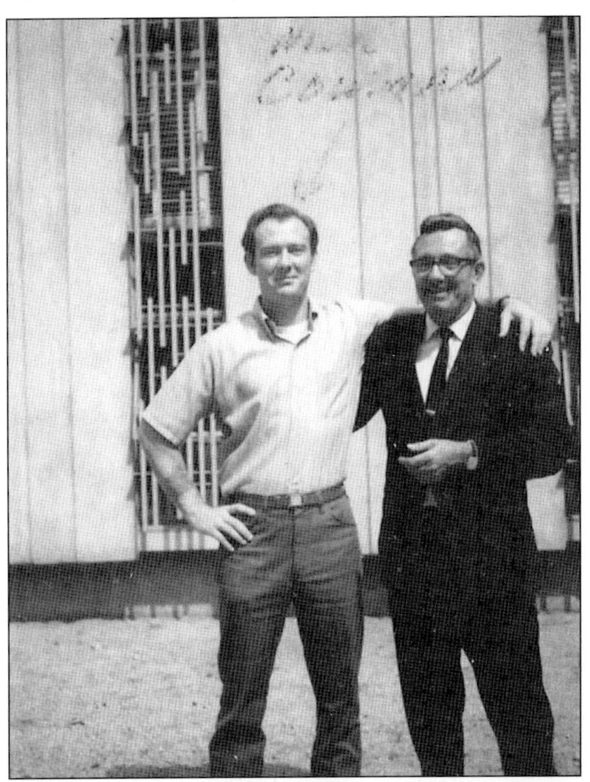

Prisoner Nicholas Cowman was serving a 35-to-45-year sentence for aggravated robbery in 1962. He played on the prison football team and was written up only once for sniffing glue. During his first two years in prison, he planned an escape down to the smallest details.

In the summer of 1974, Cowman escaped and disappeared for over a year. On July 30, 1975, he was finally located at a campsite in California, where he had been since the previous winter. Unfortunately for him, the reason he had remained there so long was that he had frozen to death in his sleeping bag.

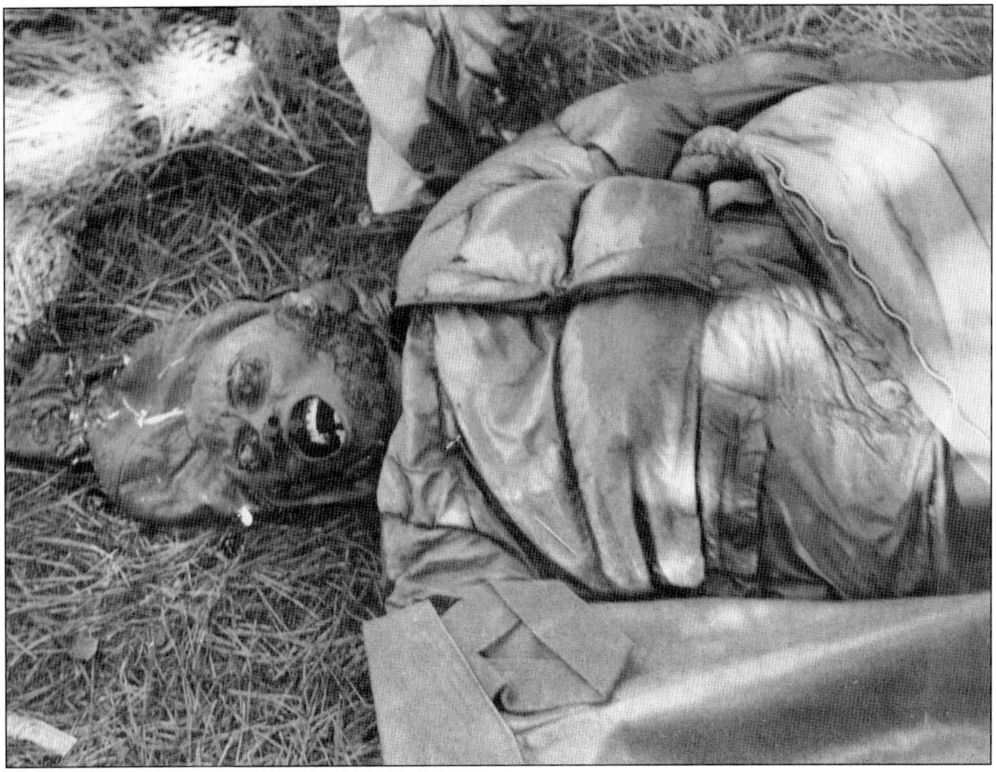

Seven

SOON THERE WILL BE NINE

Cañon City started off with one facility in 1871 and is now home to eight—soon to be nine—prisons. People ask why there are so many state prisons in this area, and there is really no set answer. Most people think it is because of the availability of space on the state-owned land that makes it economically feasible to build here. Others believe that the citizens of Cañon are comfortable with the prisons, so what will one more hurt? Whatever the reason, the local economy profits from them. The prisons are the number one employer in the county, and staff members have job security. Cañon City is a close-knit community where everyone knows someone who works at one of the facilities.

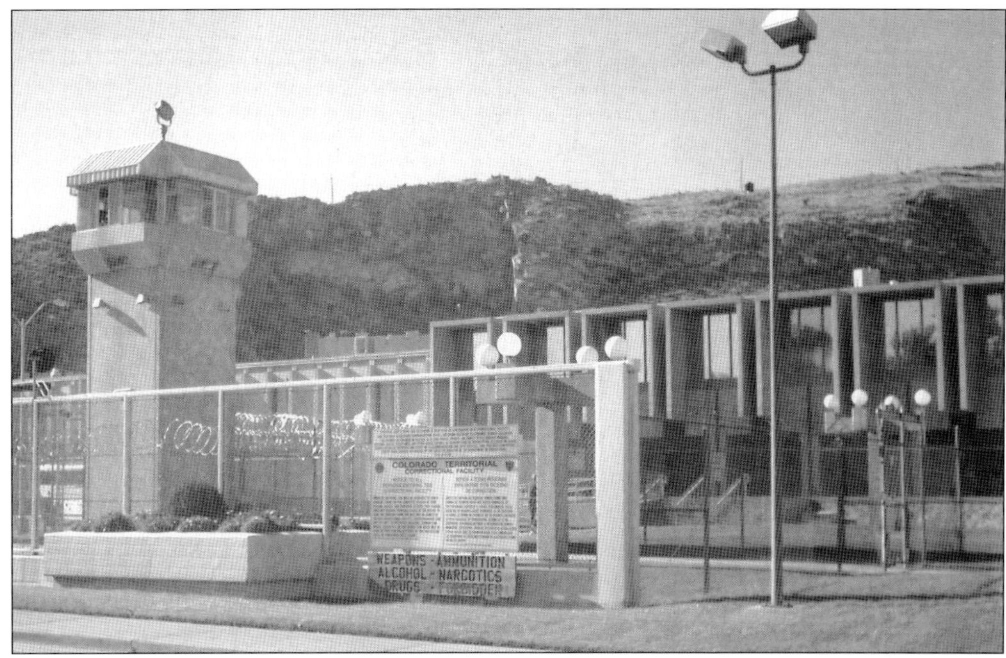

Colorado Territorial Correctional Facility (CTCF) was opened in 1871 and became a state prison in 1876, the year of statehood. The land was originally donated by Jonathan Draper. Constructed of native stone from the quarry on the hill behind it, the prison houses the Receiving/Diagnostic Unit and business offices. It is now a Level 3 facility with 786 beds.

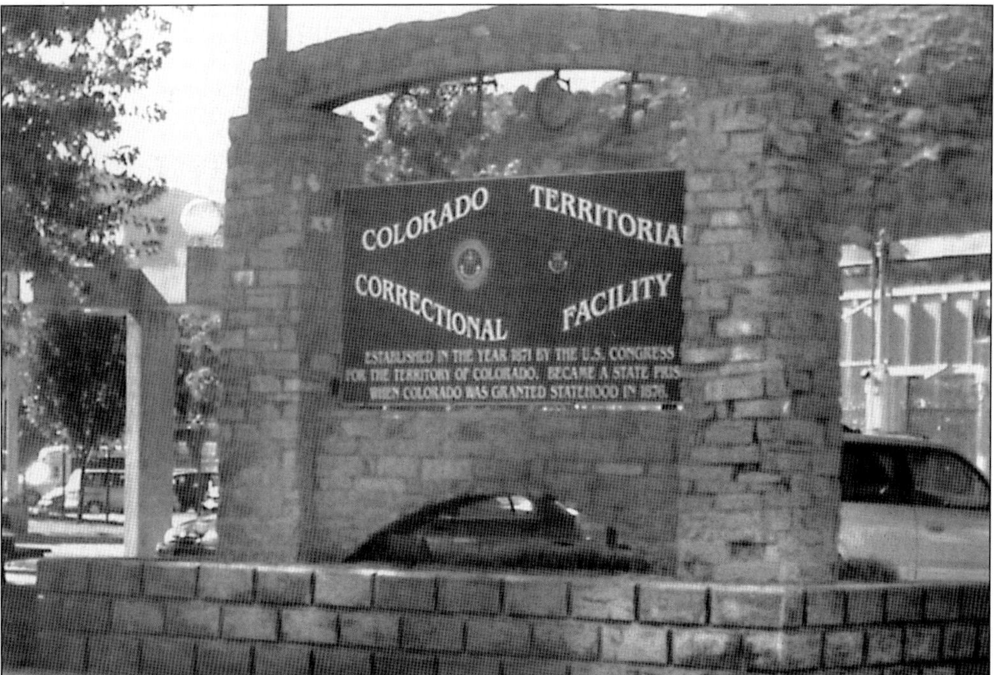

This sign sits in front of CTCF and is located on the highway entrance to the facility. The signs to each prison were made by inmate labor with use of the available area stone. Territorial and Women's signs can be seen from the roads leading to the facilities.

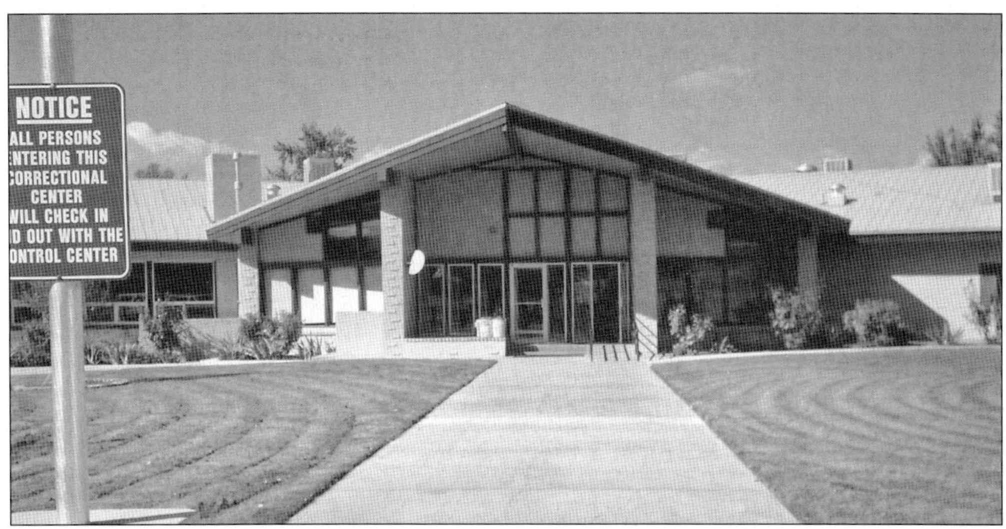

Skyline Correctional Center (SCC) was opened in 1956 with 60 beds. Through years of construction and double-bunking, it now has a capacity for 249 inmates. As a Level 1 facility, it is not surrounded by a wall or fence. No violent offenders are housed at this level.

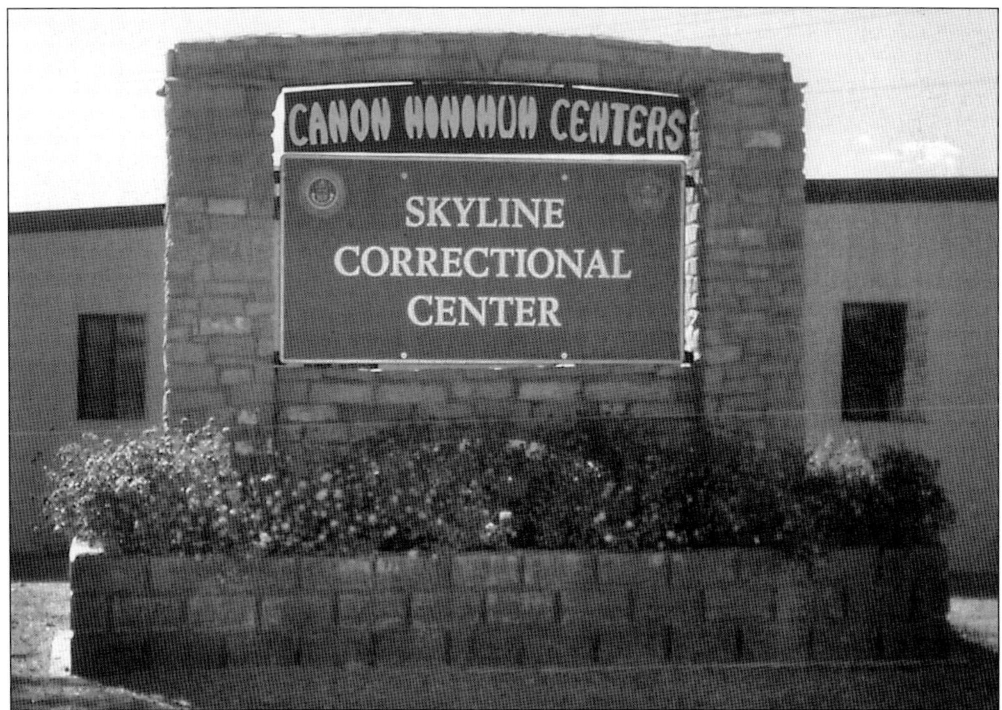

Each of the signs presenting the facility is new and all have been added in the last few years. For years plain wooden signs identified the prison. The signs representing the facilities in the East Cañon Complex are not visible to the public.

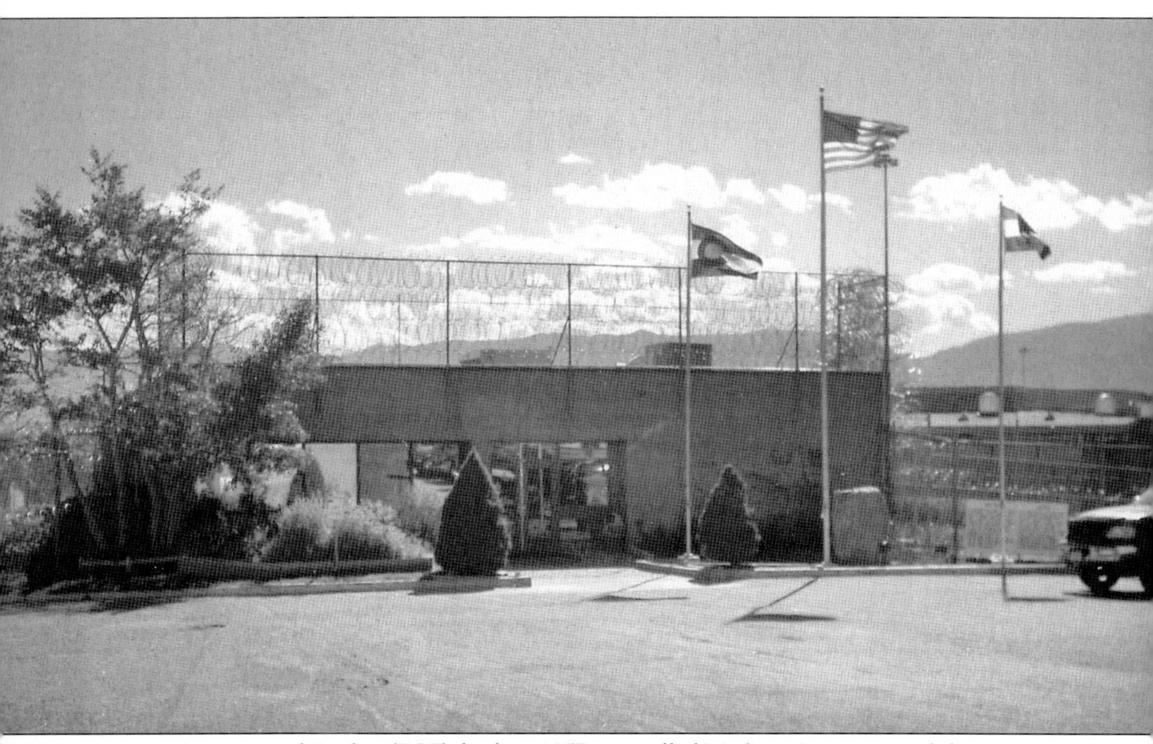

Fremont Correctional Facility (FCF), built in 1957, was called Medium Security until the name was changed in the 1970s. The FCF land was once owned by the Holy Cross Abbey of Cañon City. This facility operates the Correctional Industries Furniture Shop, a machine shop, a welding program, and the sheet metal works. It is a Level 3 facility and has a capacity for 1,471 offenders.

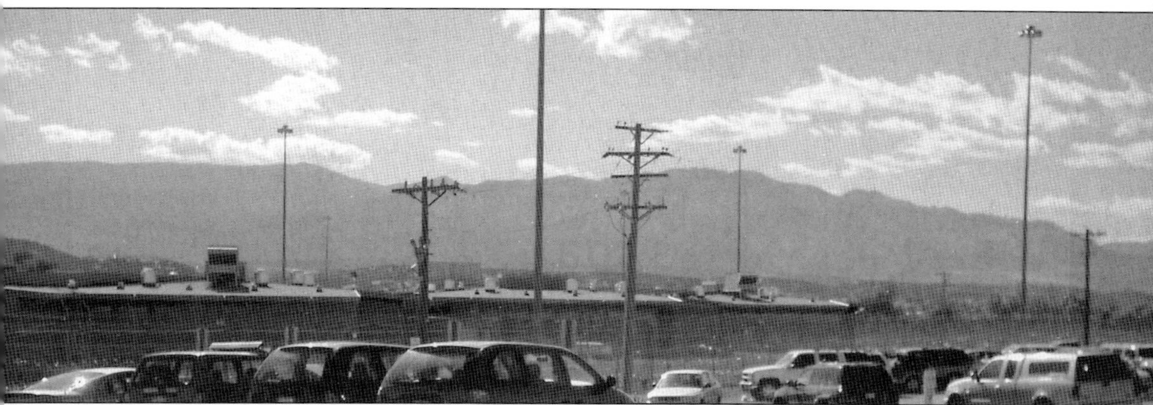

In 1980, Shadow Mountain Correctional Facility (SMCF), a Level 4 closed prison, was constructed directly west of Fremont. It ran on its own for the next 11 years until merging with Fremont in 1991. SMCF originally had four cell houses, its own big yard, and a wooden freestanding tower that stood just south of the yard and was only manned when inmates were outside. It ran independently from Fremont even though the two facilities shared a common fence line. Fremont's Tower 2, at the back gate of the facilities, admitted traffic to both Fremont and Shadow Mountain and helped Shadow Mountain keep watch on the big yard. When the merge occurred, the prison became the largest in the state. That honor now belongs to Sterling Correctional Facility in Sterling, which can hold more than 2,500 offenders.

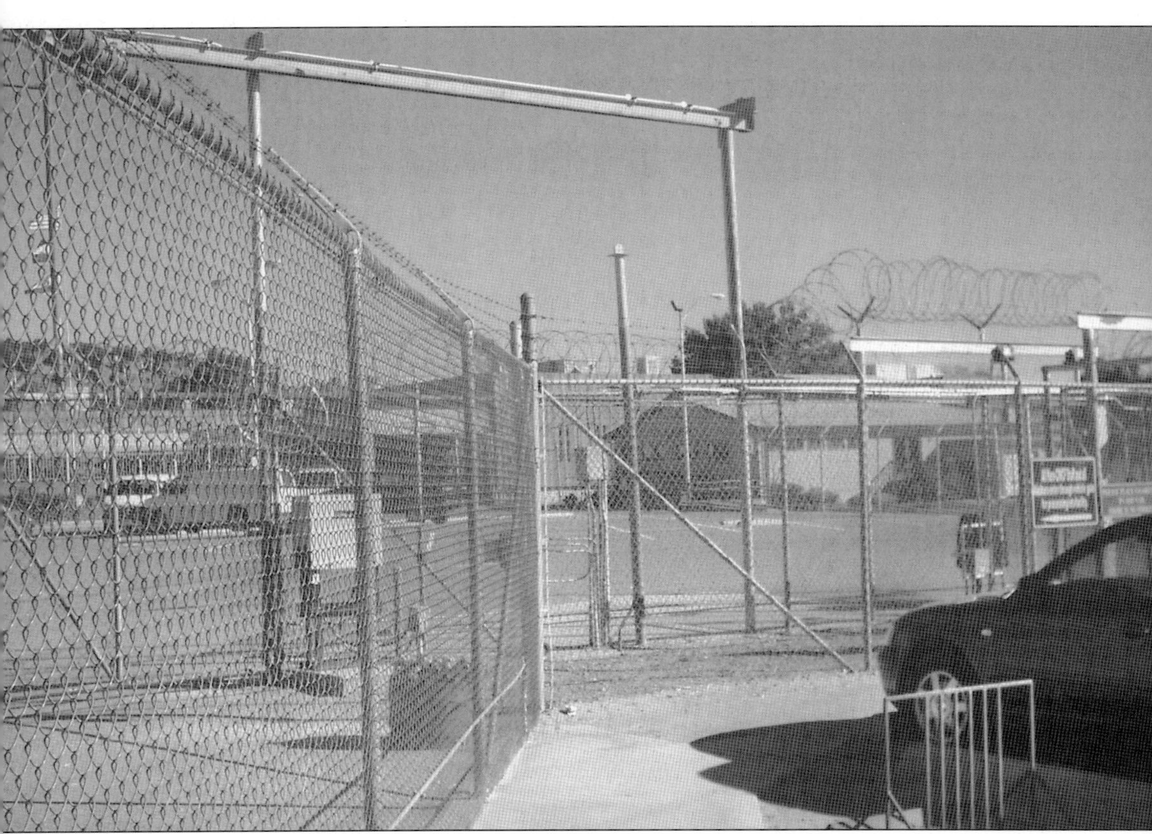

The original women's facility was a cell house inside the walls at Territorial that held female prisoners. In 1935, warden Roy Best had a new women's facility built outside the east wall of the prison called Colorado Women's Institute, later Cell House 4. It could hold 42 women and was contained by fences and razor wire. Watched over by Tower 6, the new facility had its own warden and staff, most of whom were women—a first for the prison system. It also included a clinic, a dining hall, and its own laundry services. The facility ran until 1968, when it became too small and was replaced by a larger women's space. For the next 10 years, the building housed protective-custody male prisoners and is now home to the Museum of Colorado Prisons, open since 1988.

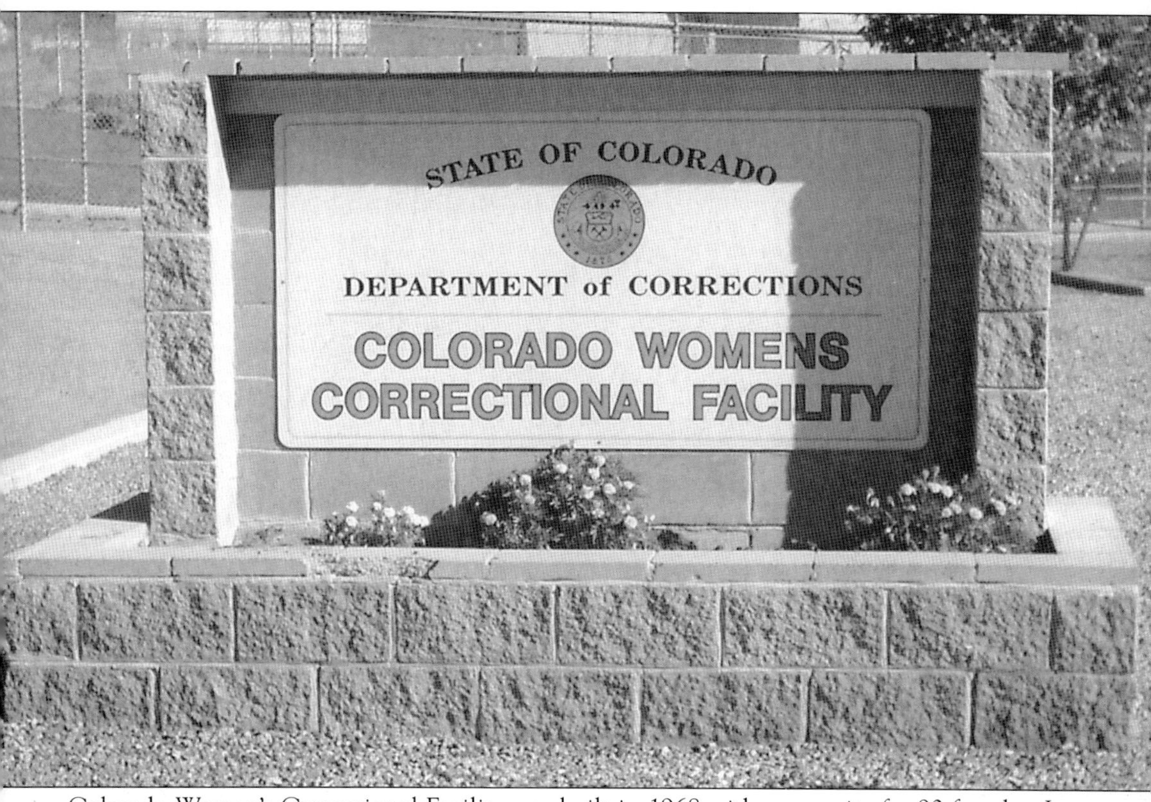

Colorado Women's Correctional Facility was built in 1968 with a capacity for 90 females. It staffed 37 female officers and had an average daily inmate population of 50 to 60. The population has fluctuated over the years when buildings were added and temporary trailers were used and then taken out. Double-bunking increased the population of the facility, which can currently house 210 general-population offenders, plus 14 segregation beds. The convictions at the Level 4 facility include violent crimes with sentences ranging from 12 months to life. At one time, women from the facility were used to run the prison gardens. Now both male and female officers watch over the population and are trained in dealing with the unique problems that can occur with female offenders.

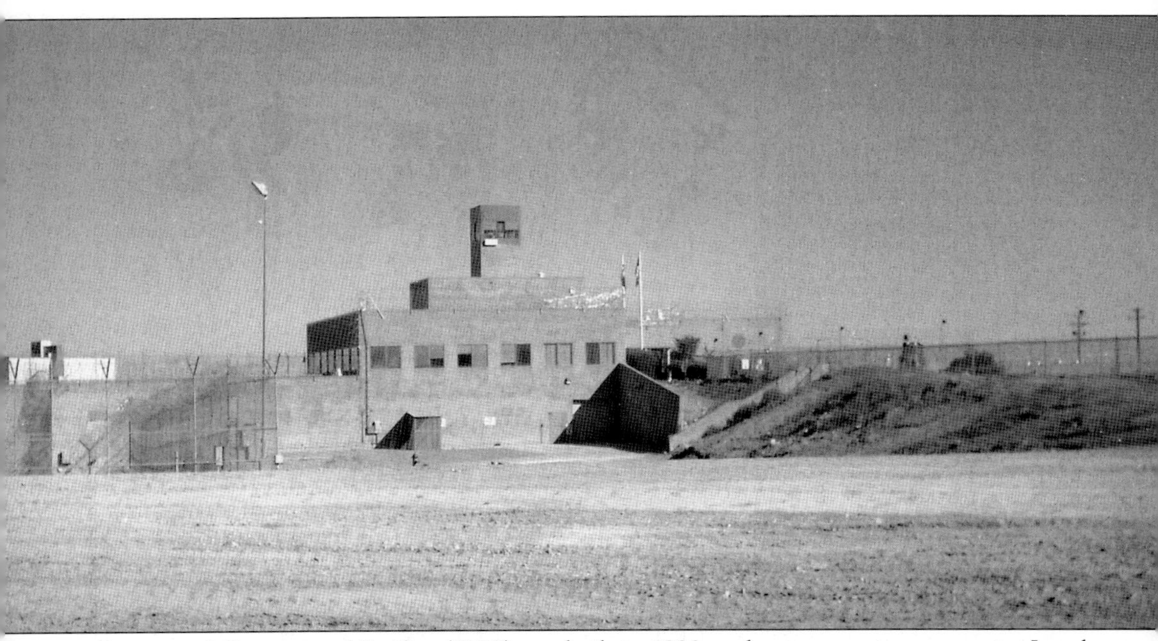

Centennial Correctional Facility (CCF) was built in 1980 as the new maximum-security Level 5 prison for the state. From 1980 until 1993, it was called Max until the new maximum-security facility, Colorado State Penitentiary, was built directly across the road. It is now a Level 4 security correctional institution for adult males, with a capacity of 336 close-custody offenders. A staff of 169 works directly with the offenders, along with 16 other employees such as library, administration, and maintenance personnel. Located on the East Complex, the 166,085-square-foot CCF sits on approximately 22 acres of land. Colorado State Penitentiary II will stand south of CCF and connect to the building by way of the old print shop. CCF has transitioned into a program-based facility providing the Progressive Reintegration Opportunity (PRO) Unit Program and the Diversion Program. This unit is used to ease offenders from administrative segregation into the general population.

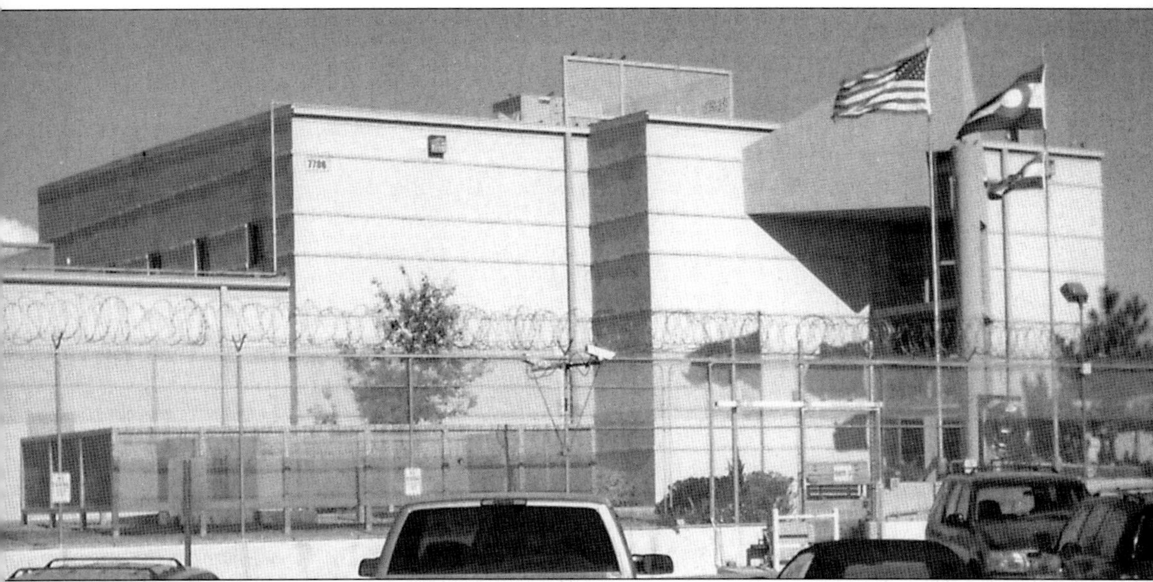

Four Mile Correctional Center (FMCC) came online in 1983 with a bed count of 52. A Level 2 facility in Cañon City, it was originally opened as a modular unit to support the Correctional Industry Dairy. FMCC is a work center that requires its offender population to maintain employment. Most programs are offered at night and include adult basic education, GED, English as a second language, courses through Adams State College, and vocational janitorial and vocational culinary arts. FMCC also provides drug and alcohol counseling and life skills and anger management classes through the mental health department. With the implementation of double-bunking, the facility has a capacity for 499 offenders. Menus for the day are developed by a registered dietitian, and specialized diets are available to meet medical and religious needs. Sack lunches are provided to those who work outside the perimeter of the facility.

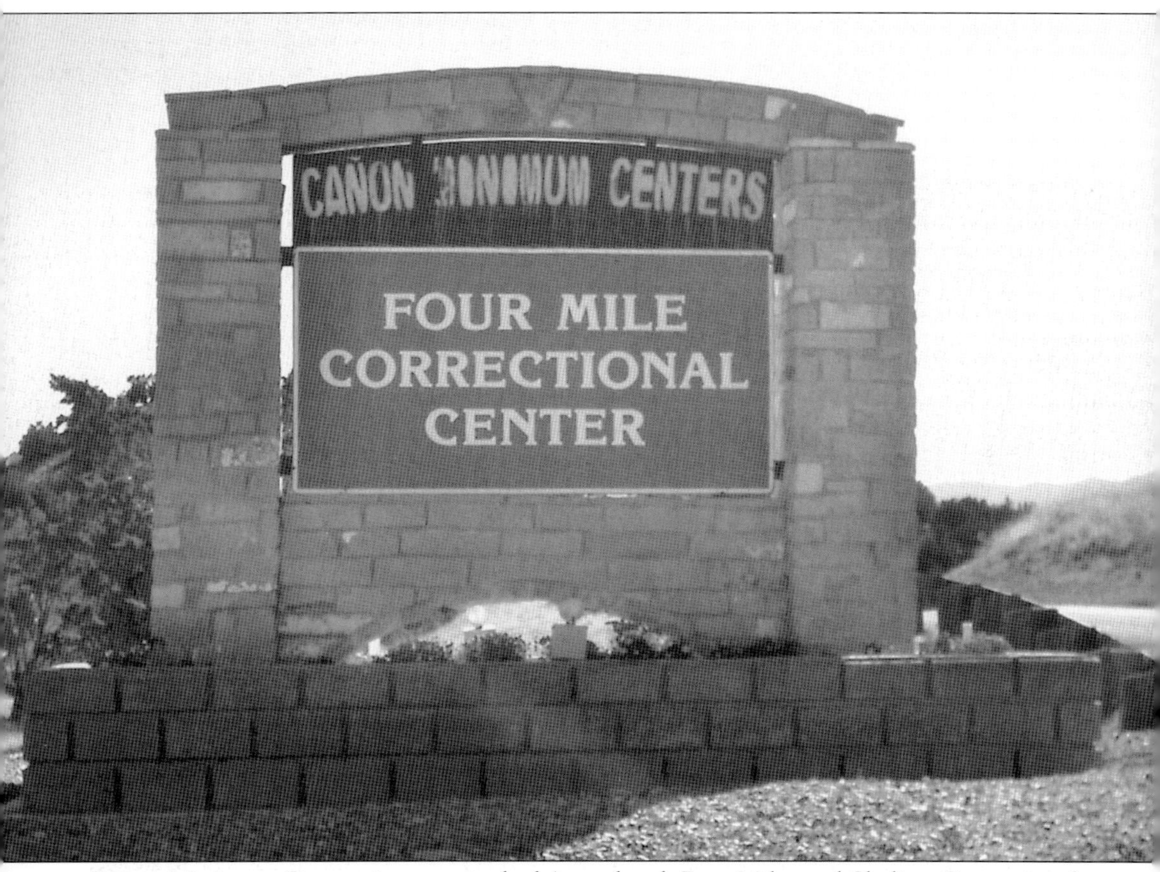

Cañon Minimum Centers is comprised of Arrowhead, Four Mile, and Skyline Correctional Centers. These are all minimum and minimum-restrictive centers, meaning that the offenders are required to hold jobs. Many inmates work off grounds at other facilities, on road crews, and at the weigh station that handles the trucks entering the East Cañon Complex. Minimum Center offenders are used in a variety of positions throughout the facilities in the Cañon area. Those from FMCC are employed at the Colorado State Penitentiary kitchen for cooking, cleaning up, and loading food carts for distribution to each pod or offender living unit. They are also used in the laundry at CSP and for cleaning the prison's administration section. The Visiting Center is cleaned by an offender brought over from one of the Minimum Centers during the week.

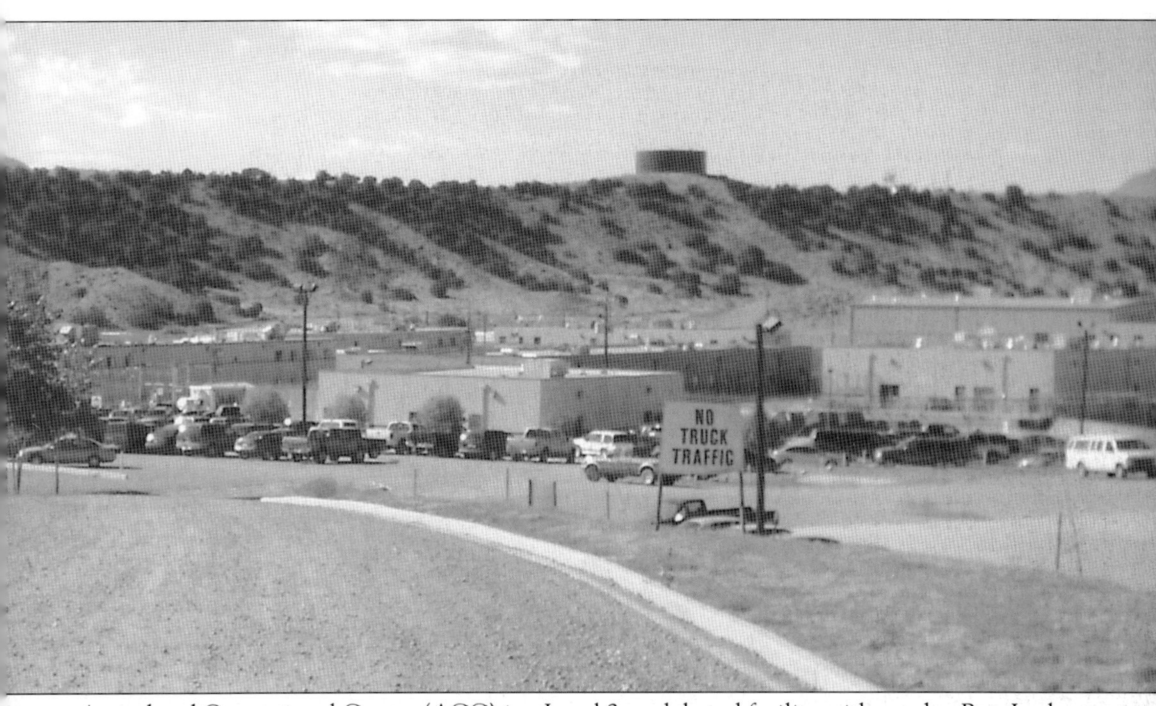

Arrowhead Correctional Center (ACC) is a Level 2 work-based facility with warden Ron Leyba overseeing the 494 offenders. This minimum-restrictive facility employs 119 line staff and 45 other staff. ACC applied for and received its initial American Correctional Association (ACA) accreditation in 1993 and has maintained national accreditation since then. Most programs are offered at night so that the offender population can be employed during the day. Programs at ACC include adult basic education, secondary education or GED, English as a second language, courses through Adams State College, and vocational janitorial. The facility opened n 1989 with a capacity of 288. Through construction and double-bunking, the capacity has risen to 484. Among the staff are associate warden Bobby Allen, custody control manager Ray Masse, physical plant manager Dennis Corbin, and support services manager Sue Buchanan.

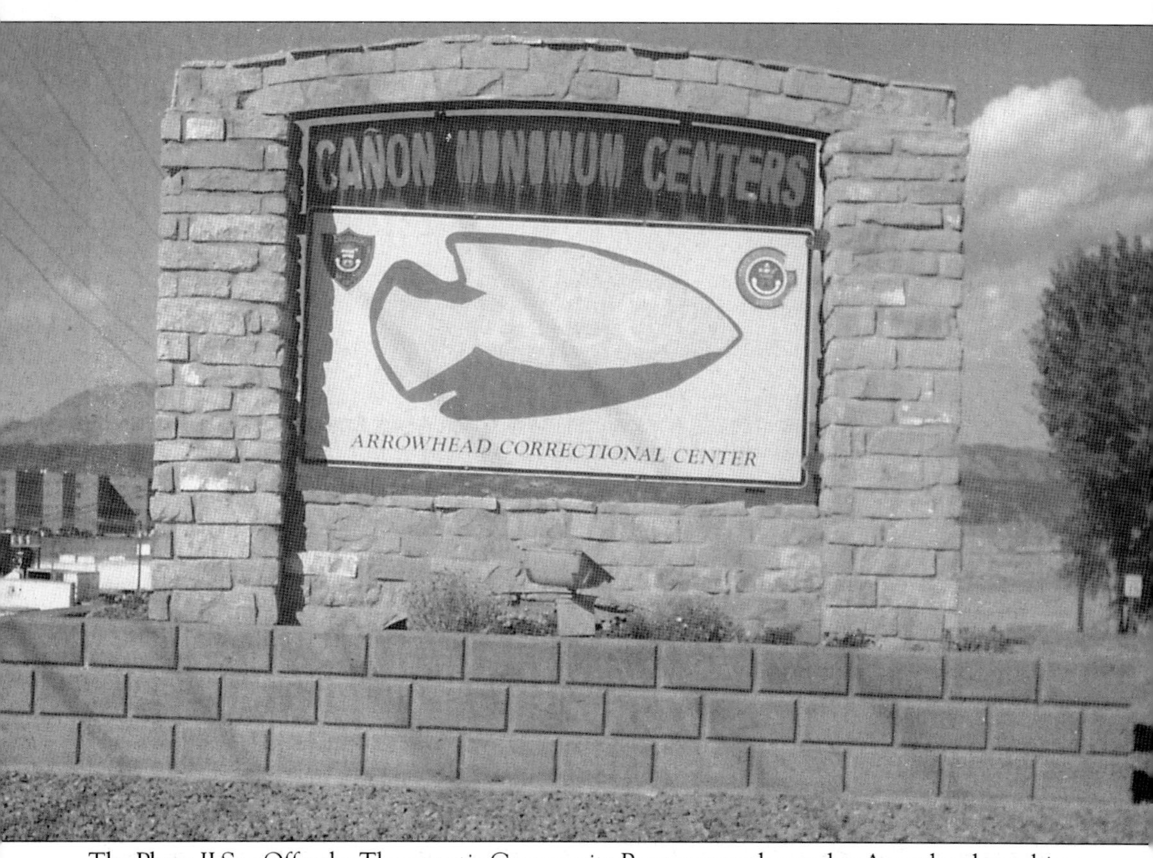

The Phase II Sex Offender Therapeutic Community Programs are located at Arrowhead, resulting in special housing and program arrangements. Those who are enrolled are housed separately and are required to follow strict guidelines to stay in the program. Oftentimes the completion of the program is mandatory for parole. Admission of guilt and taking responsibility for one's actions are required. If an offender is thrown out of the Phase II program, he must begin again at Phase I and is put on a waiting list, which can be lengthy. ACC also offers drug and alcohol counseling, anger management, and life skills treatment for general-population offenders.

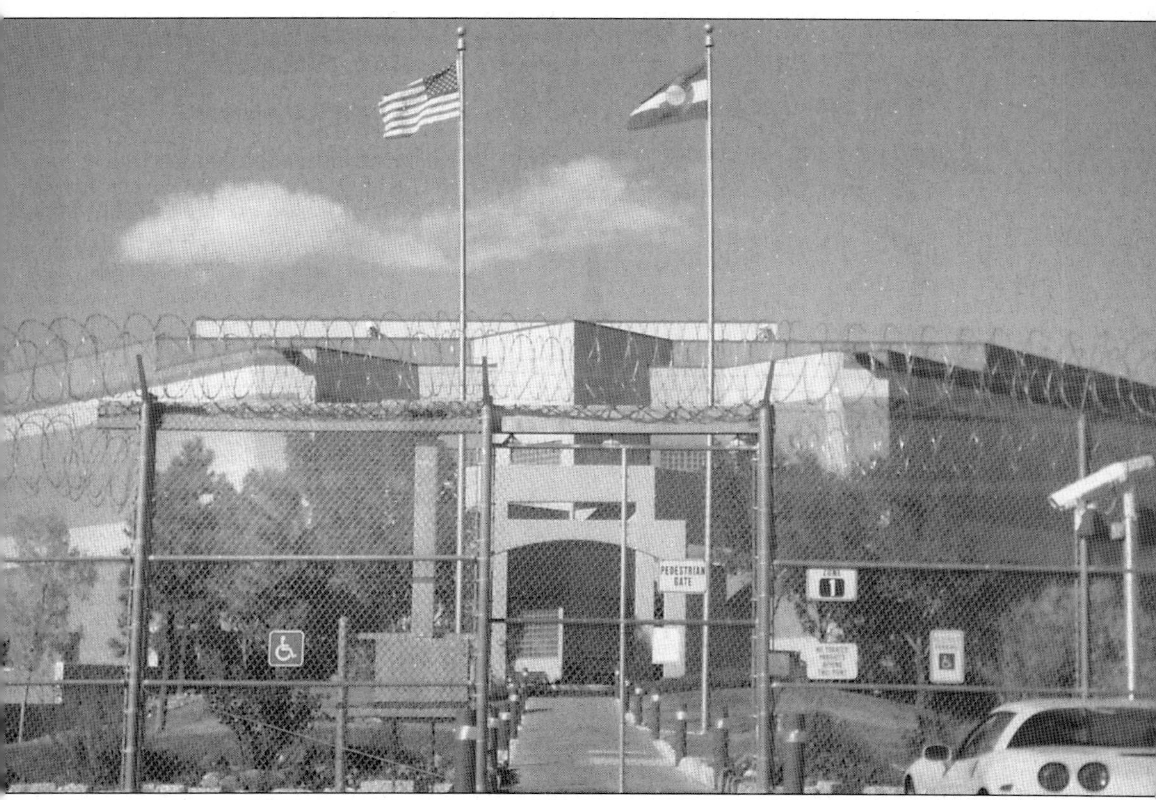

For many years, Cell House 3 at Territorial was the Max unit. In 1980, when Centennial Correctional Facility opened, Max was relocated there. For the next 13 years, CCF was the state Max unit until Colorado State Penitentiary was built and opened on August 16, 1993. When first opened, it had a capacity for 504. In January 1998, Phase II brought an additional 252 beds. In May 2002, CSP and CCF merged administration, programming, and operations into Colorado's High Security Management System. Warden Susan Jones oversees the operations of both CSP and CCF. A Level 5 security correctional institution for adult males, CSP sits on about 80 acres, with approximately 470,000 square feet of floor space. Capacity at the facility is now 756 with very few beds to spare.

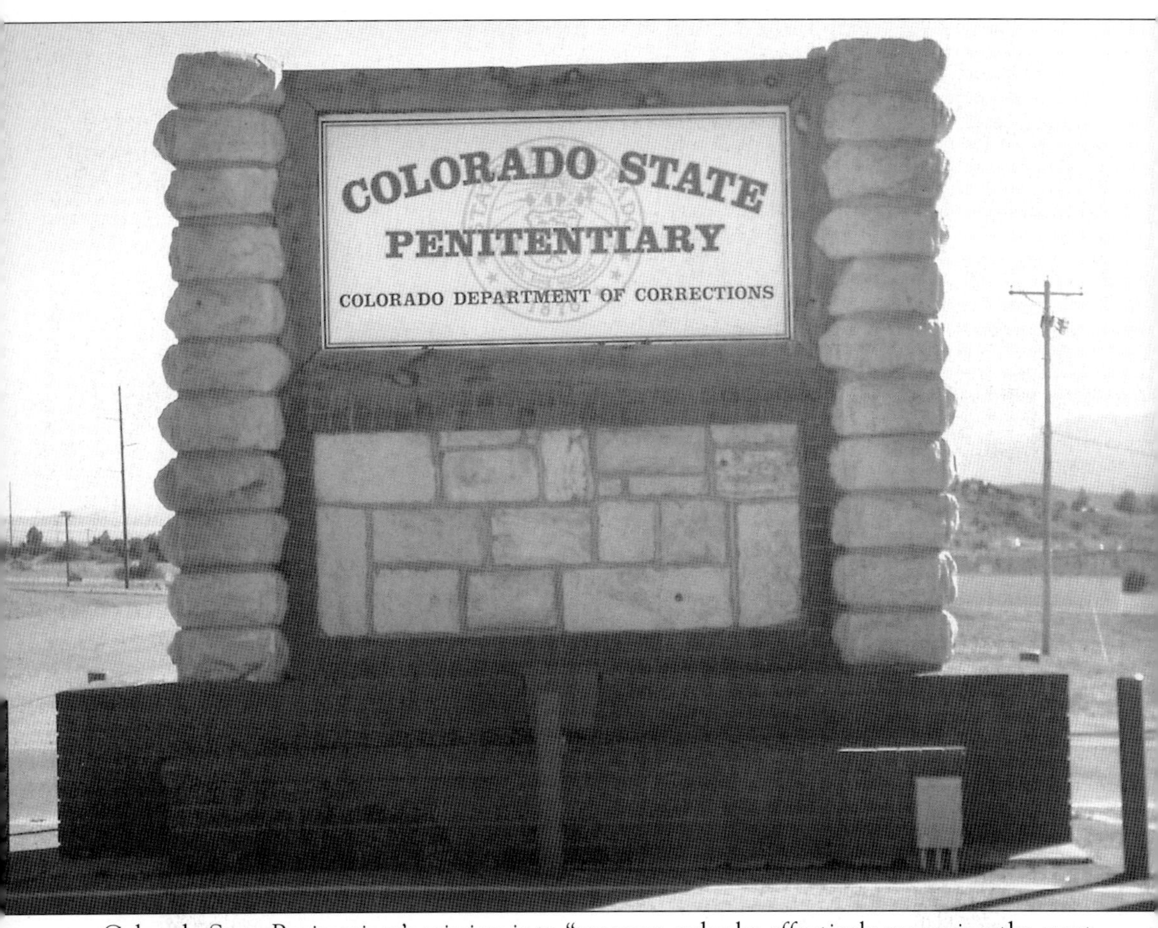

Colorado State Penitentiary's mission is to "preserve order by effectively managing the most disruptive offenders who have demonstrated the inability to function at a less secure facility by providing a safe, secure, and humane environment." CSP also "aims to change offender conduct through incentive-based behavior modification and cognitive programs which facilitate offender reintegration into less secure environments." Furthermore, CSP "strives to promote a safe work environment in a culture which mentors and encourages staff professionalism, career enhancements, positive morale, and pride." This is a very hard mission to accomplish when staff members are confronted with violent offenders who have spent years fighting the system every step of the way. The State of Colorado uses a point system to determine at what level facility an offender will be housed. All death row offenders are automatically sent to CSP, but points are determined by the crime, the history, and an offender's conduct while in prison. If an offender is a security problem, he will probably end up at Level 5 CSP.

In the last few years, the population has steadily risen along with the increasing rate of crime. The prisons are busting at the seams, and more and more facilities are being built to house the incoming offenders. Current laws are making it hard to keep up with the influx of drug dealers, habitual traffic offenders, drunk drivers, and immigration offenders, whom the state must hold throughout the hearing and deportation process. Overcrowding drives up the crimes happening within the facilities. The ground-breaking for CSPII occurred in August 2007. Another Level 5 facility, it will house the most violent and disruptive offenders in the prison system. It will be built from the same blueprints as CSP and will be located east of that facility. It will run just as CSP does, with the same type of offenders and the same programs offered.

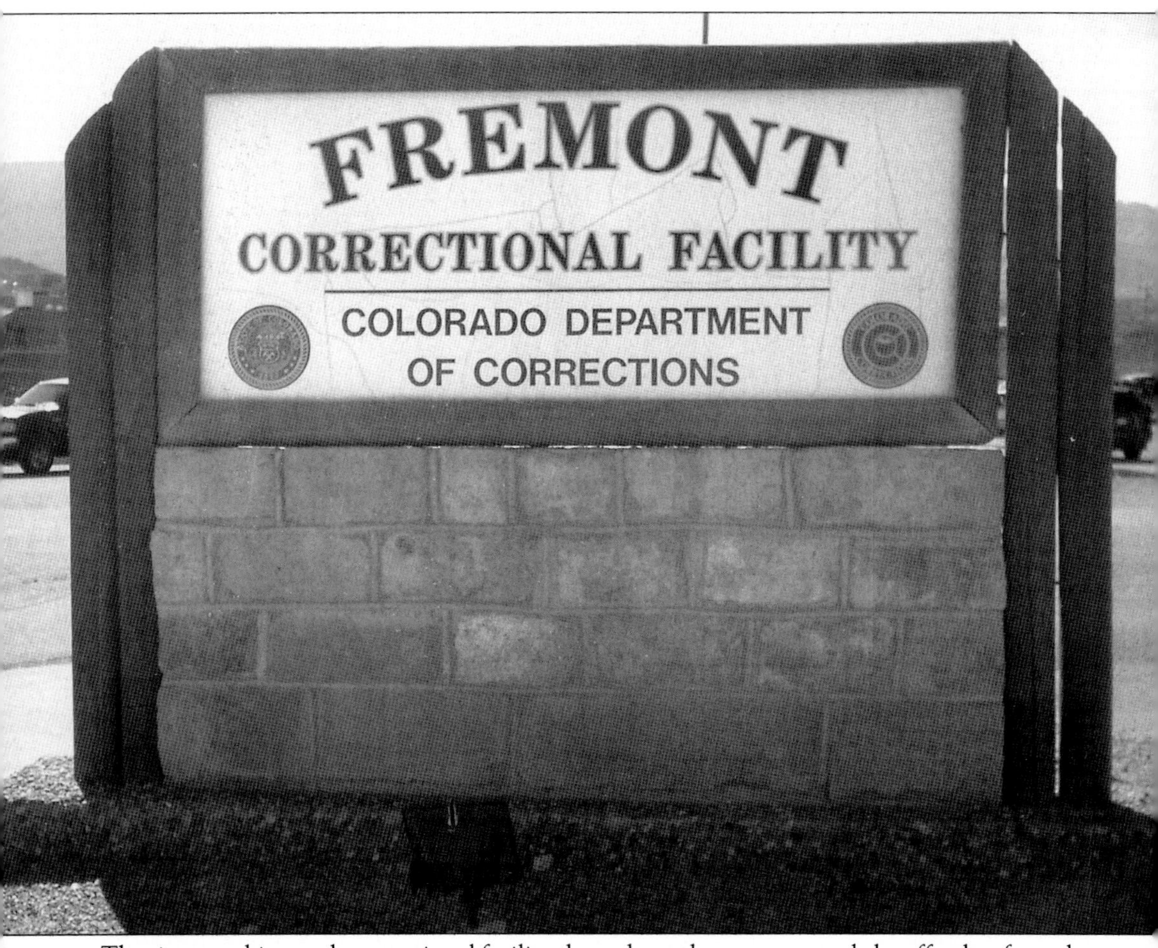

The signs marking each correctional facility throughout the state are made by offenders from the area's stone and rock. The CCF sign has been removed for the construction of CSPII, but a new one will be erected when the building is completed. Stone for most of the Cañon City signs was removed from the rock quarry behind CTCF. The markers for the facilities were erected in the last few years. Signs reading, "Do Not Pick Up Hitchhikers In The Area. They May Be Escaped Inmates," were visible at the east and west entrances to Cañon City on Highway 50 but have recently disappeared. Even with warning signs that clearly state the entrance to a correctional facility, civilians are still known to drive up to the facility thinking that they can tour the place. In the case of CTCF, which sits on the highway, they will walk in the front door asking to visit.

NOTICE TO ALL PERSONS ENTERING THIS CORRECTIONAL FACILITY

PRIOR TO ENTERING, YOU WILL BE REQUIRED TO SIGN A CONSENT FORM FOR THE COMPLETE SEARCH OF YOUR PERSON, VEHICLE AND PERSONAL EFFECTS. THIS SEARCH DOES NOT REQUIRE PROBABLE CAUSE. IF YOU REFUSE TO SIGN THE CONSENT FORM YOU WILL NOT BE ADMITTED TO THIS CORRECTIONAL FACILITY. UNDER COLORADO LAW, ANY ATTEMPT TO INTRODUCE WEAPONS, AMMUNITION, DRUGS, EXPLOSIVES OR ANY OTHER ITEM WHICH MAY BE USED TO THREATEN THE SECURITY OF THIS INSTITUTION SHALL BE PUNISHABLE AS A FELONY.

C.R.S. 18-8-203, 18-8-204, 18-8-204.1 AND 18-8-204.2

EFFECTIVE JULY 1, 2005, THE FOLLOWING IS IDENTIFIED AS CONTRABAND IN A CORRECTIONAL FACILITY: ANY PORTABLE ELECTRONIC COMMUNICATION DEVICE, INCLUDING CELLULAR TELEPHONES; CLONED CELLULAR TELEPHONES AS DEFINED IN SECTION 18-9-309; PUBLIC, PRIVATE, OR FAMILY-STYLE RADIOS; PAGERS; PERSONAL DIGITAL ASSISTANTS; ANY OTHER DEVICE CAPABLE OF TRANSMITTING OR INTERCEPTING CELLULAR OR RADIO SIGNALS BETWEEN PROVIDERS AND USERS OR TELECOMMUNICATION AND DATA SERVICES; AND PORTABLE COMPUTERS; EXCEPT THOSE DEVICES AUTHORIZED BY THE EXECUTIVE DIRECTOR OF THE DEPARTMENT OF CORRECTIONS.
C.R.S. 18-8-204

When a visitor or staff member enters a correctional facility, he is asked to sign a form that gives the facility the right to search him and his belongings. He is asked to walk through an electric monitor and to remove anything metal. Facilities today use the monitor at their front entrances, and the staff is required to enter and leave through the device.

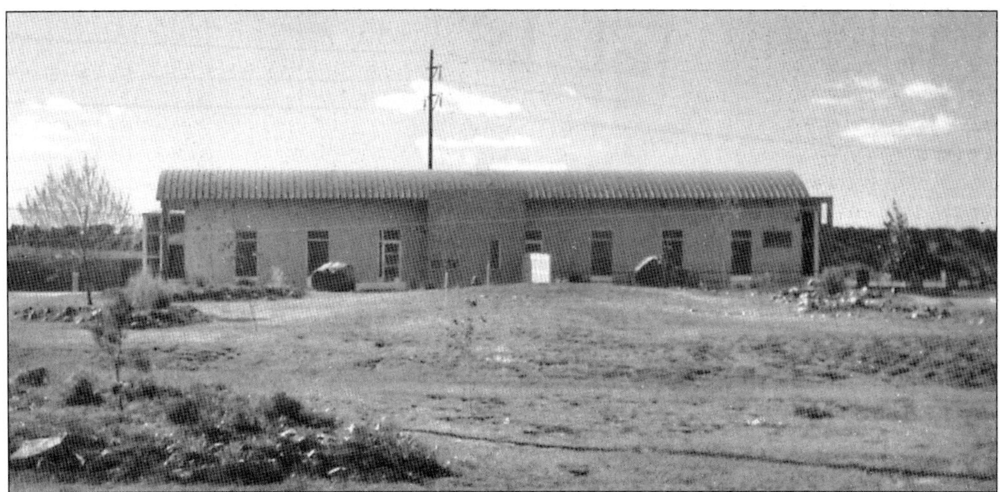

The Visitors Facility at the East Cañon Complex sits before a checkpoint. If a civilian wishes to visit with an offender, he must sign up in advance and then stop at the center and show photograph identification. Each visitor must go through the electric monitor, submit to a pat down, and then ride a bus to the specific facility.

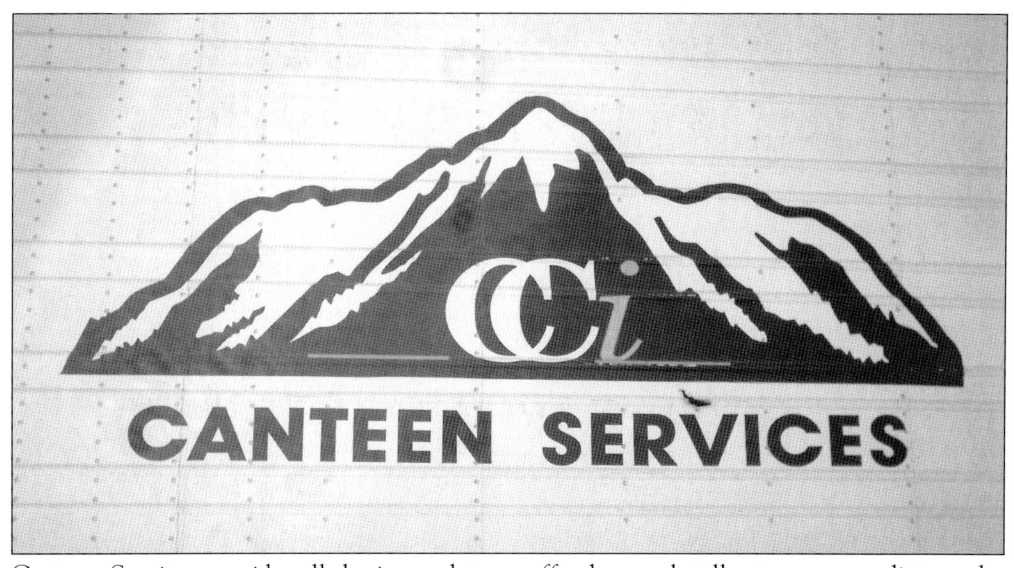

Canteen Services provides all the items that an offender can legally possess according to the Department of Corrections. The shop sells clothing that the state does not offer, such as sweats and tennis shoes, and has a wide variety of food items that offenders can buy to supplement their state-issue meals.

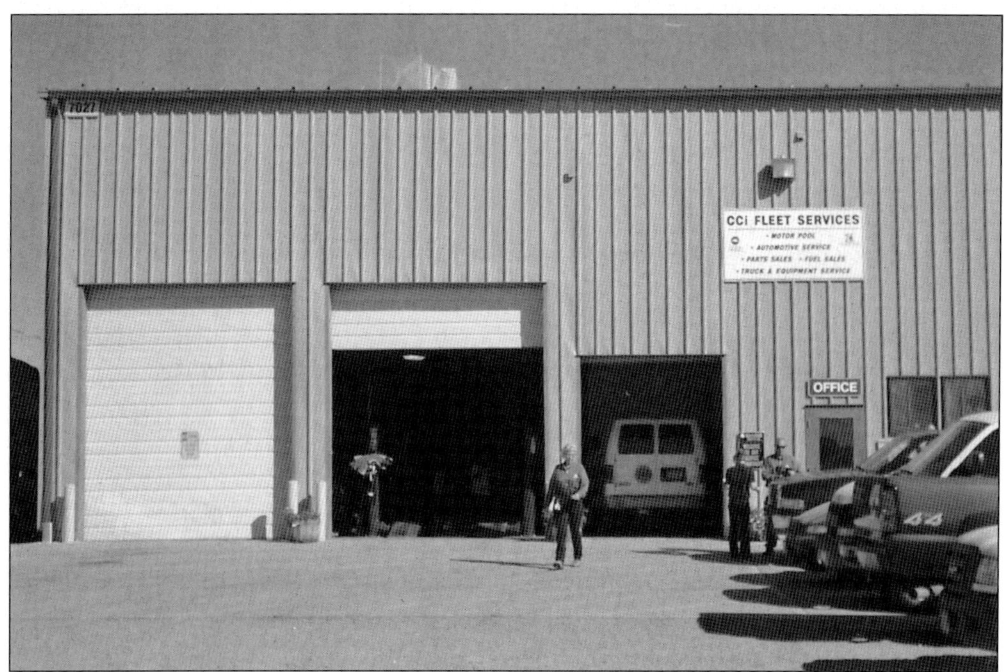

Located adjacent to Canteen Services, Fleet Services takes care of all the state vehicles in the Cañon City area. From performing mechanical work to fixing flats, the shop maintains all the vehicles that are used in the transportation of offenders and the completion of road maintenance, among others. Offenders are trained as mechanics in this area.

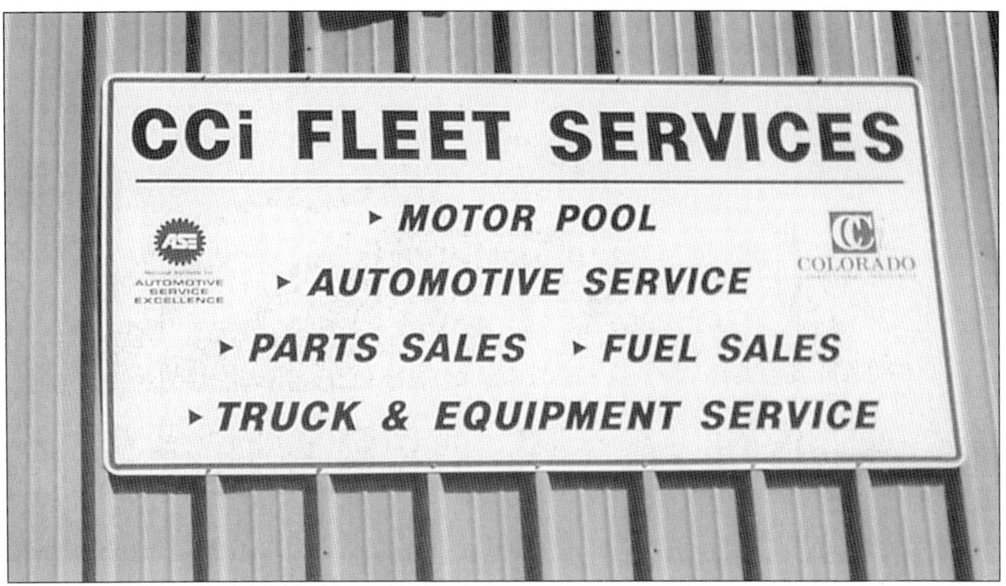

Fleet Services also provides a full-service filling station. When an employee needs transportation for business or training at another facility across the state, a vehicle can be checked out from this area.

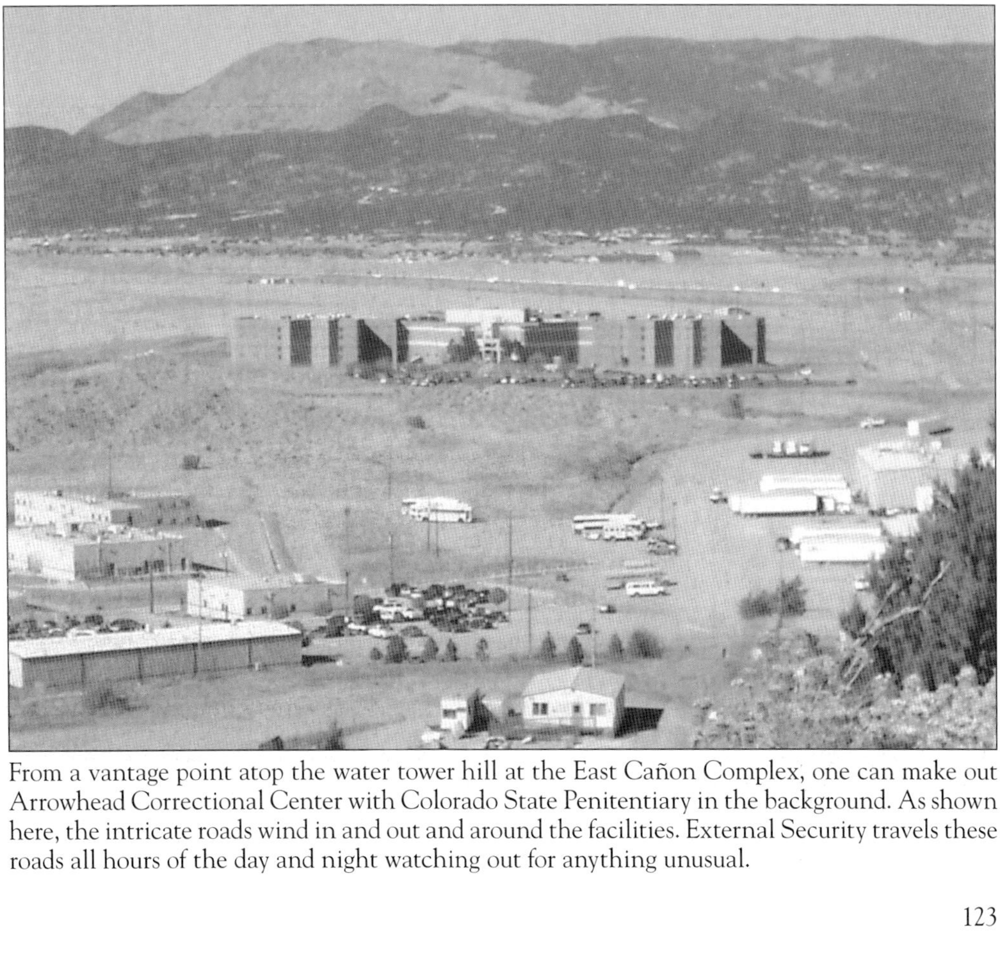

From a vantage point atop the water tower hill at the East Cañon Complex, one can make out Arrowhead Correctional Center with Colorado State Penitentiary in the background. As shown here, the intricate roads wind in and out and around the facilities. External Security travels these roads all hours of the day and night watching out for anything unusual.

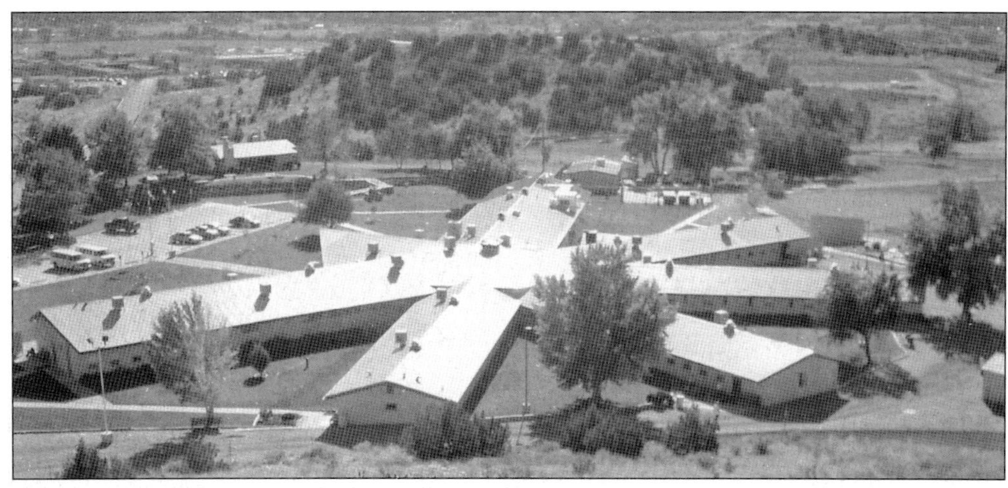

Skyline Correctional Facility looks small from this front shot, but from above it sections off into five different wings of offenders' cells. Skyline does not have a wall or high fence surrounding it, just a white wooden fence one can step over.

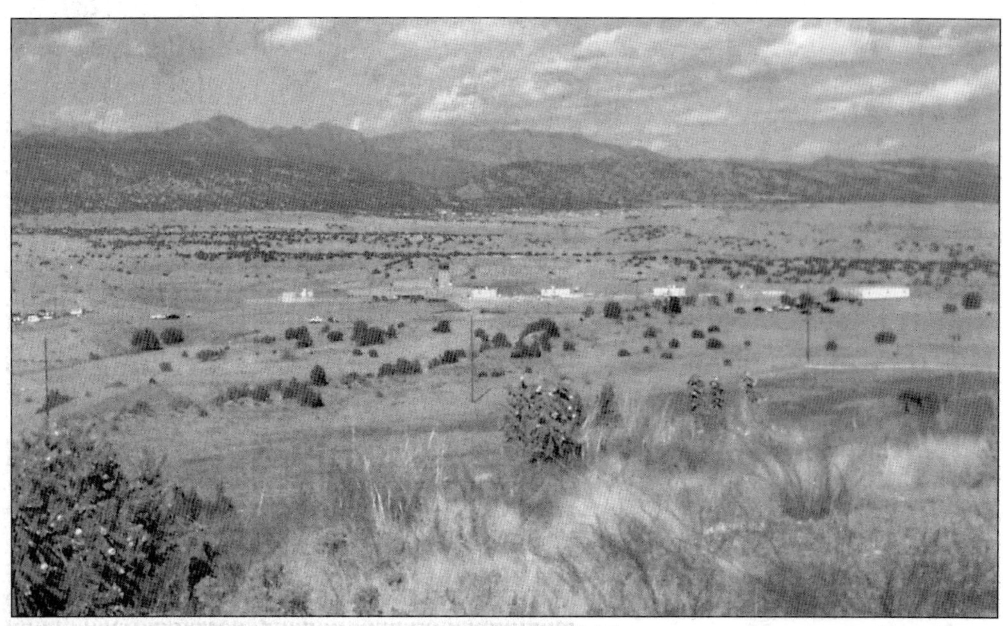

This aerial view shows the construction trailers for CSPII. The area encompassing the East Cañon Complex is state-owned restricted property. The new facility will be built next to Centennial.

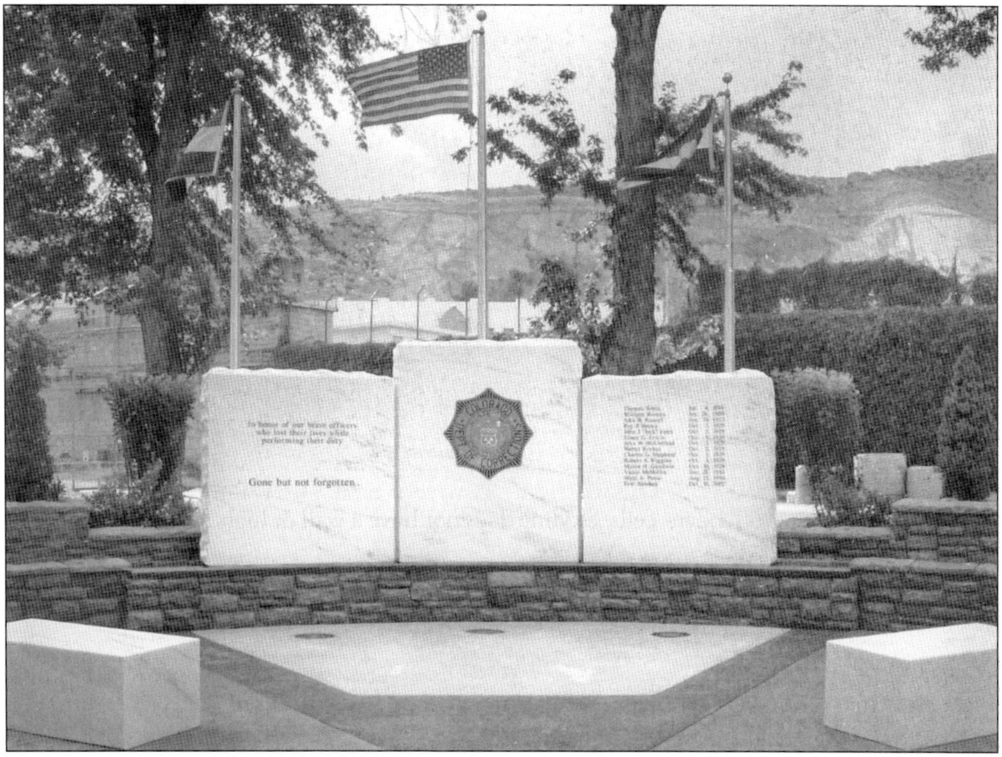

Dedicated in 2006 by then-director of prisons Joe Ortiz, the Correctional Peace Officers Memorial Wall stands on the front lawn of Territorial Correctional Facility. The names listed on the wall include the first officer killed in 1899, the eight officers murdered in the 1929 riot, and five others.

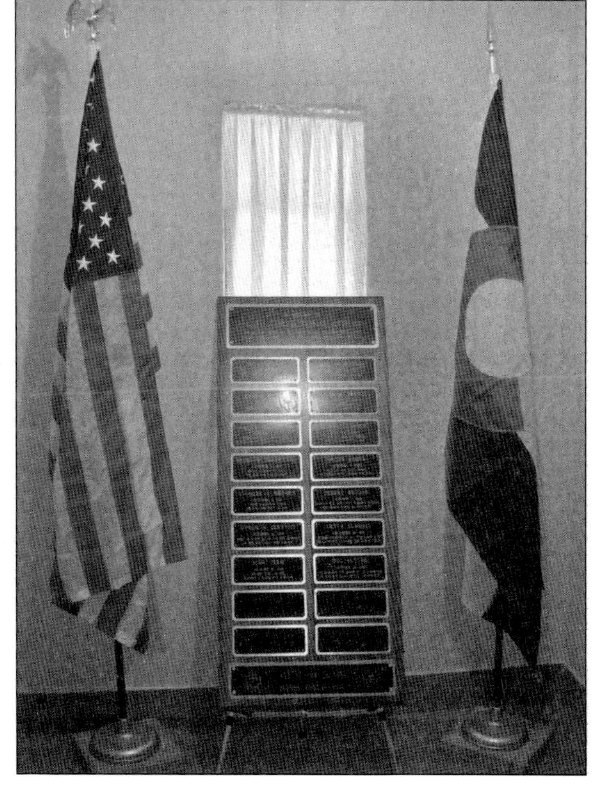

To those who made the ultimate sacrifice, may they rest in peace: Thomas Tobin, William Rooney, John Russell, Ray Brown, John Eeles, Elmer Erwin, John McClelland, Walter Rinker, Charles Shepherd, Robert Wiggins, Myron Goodwin, Victor McMillian, Marc Perse, and Eric Autobee.

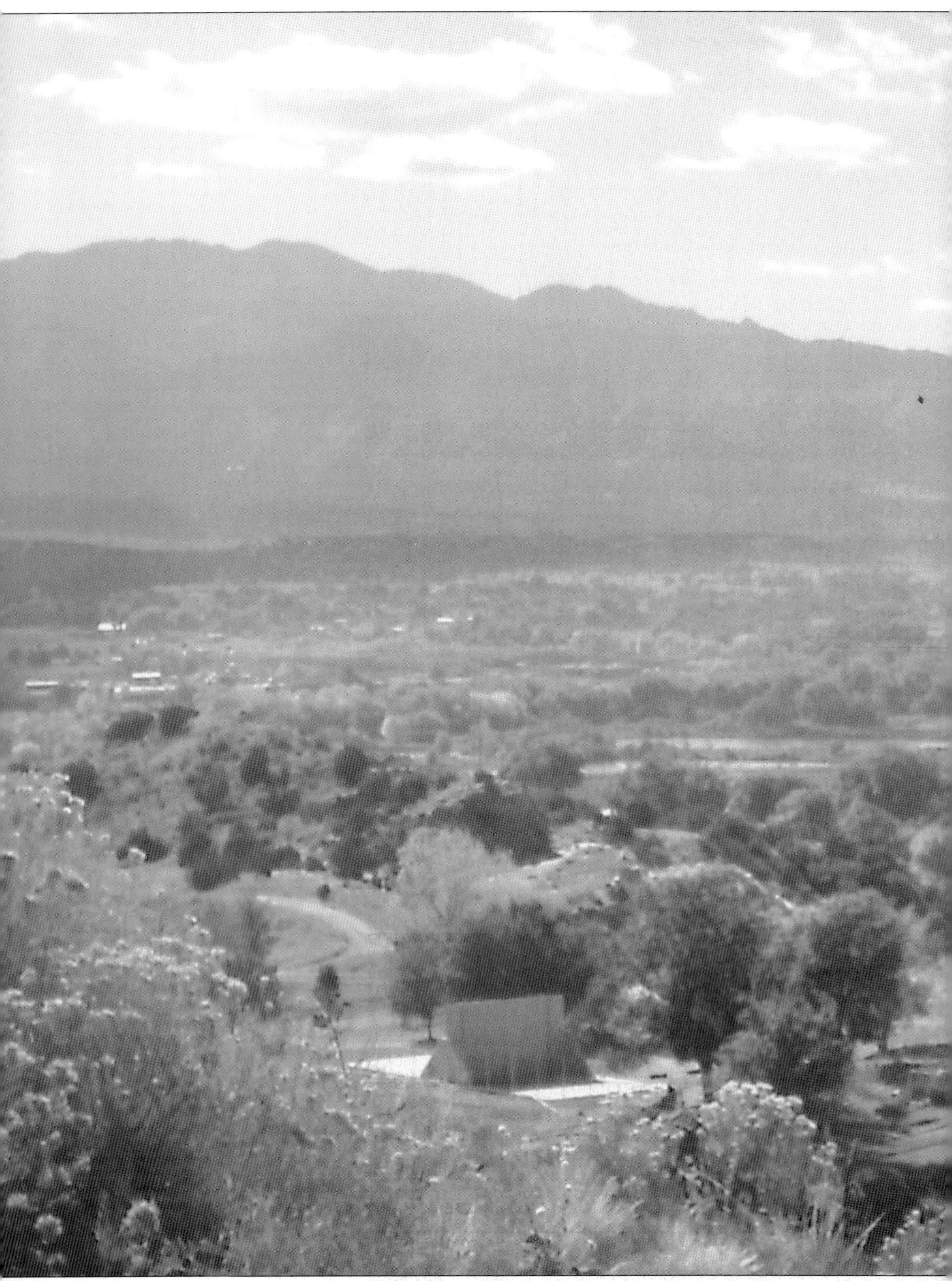

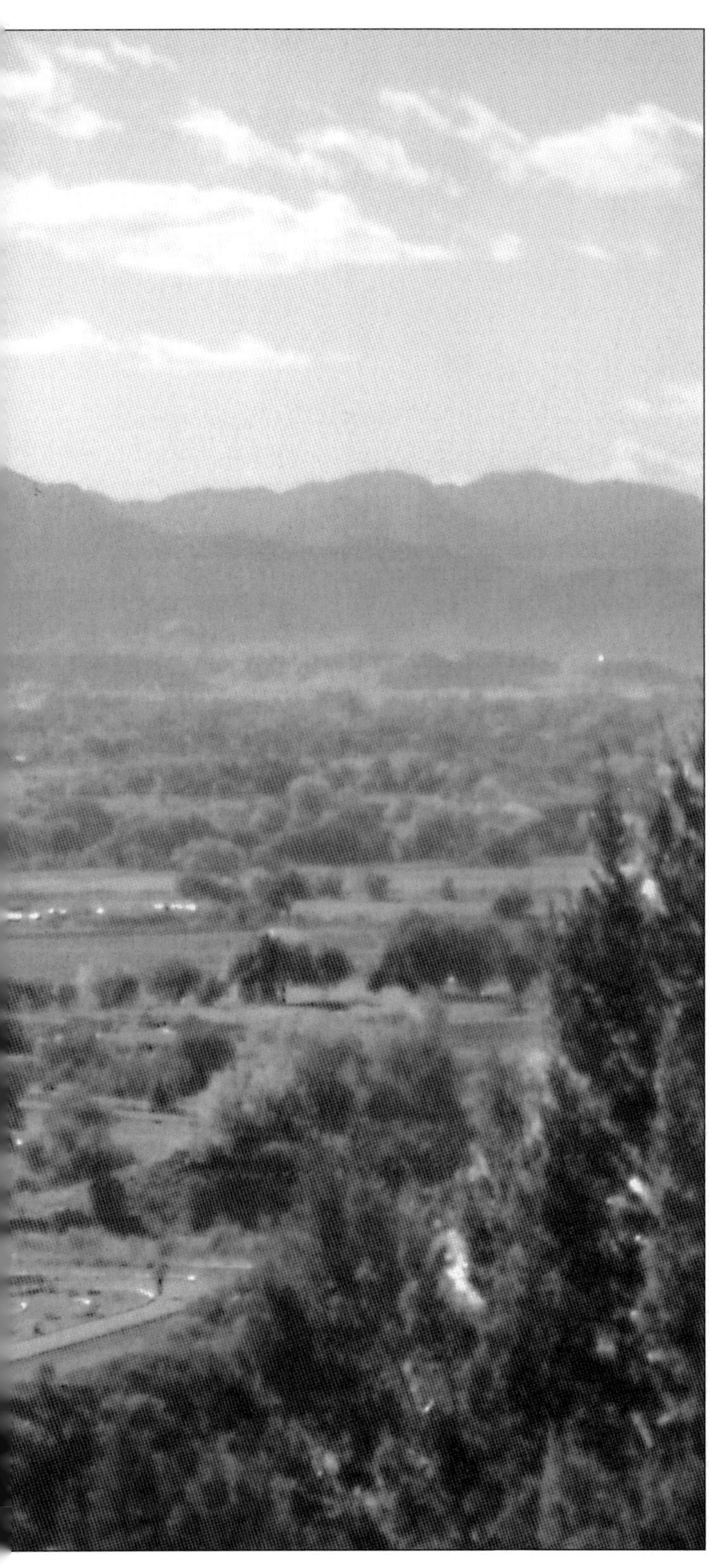

From atop the hill where
the East Cañon Complex
water tower stands, one
can see the spot where
the Colorado Department
of Corrections all began.
Sitting in a natural bowl
surrounded by picturesque
mountains, Cañon City has
grown from the small, one-
street town of the late 1800s
to the Prison Capital of the
World. One must not be
deceived by the friendliness
of the locals and the beauty
of the area. It is still a prison
town, and the locals are well
aware of those who dwell
behind the old stone walls
and razor-wire fences.

ACROSS AMERICA, PEOPLE ARE DISCOVERING SOMETHING WONDERFUL. THEIR HERITAGE.

Arcadia Publishing is the leading local history publisher in the United States. With more than 4,000 titles in print and hundreds of new titles released every year, Arcadia has extensive specialized experience chronicling the history of communities and celebrating America's hidden stories, bringing to life the people, places, and events from the past. To discover the history of other communities across the nation, please visit:

www.arcadiapublishing.com

Customized search tools allow you to find regional history books about the town where you grew up, the cities where your friends and family live, the town where your parents met, or even that retirement spot you've been dreaming about.

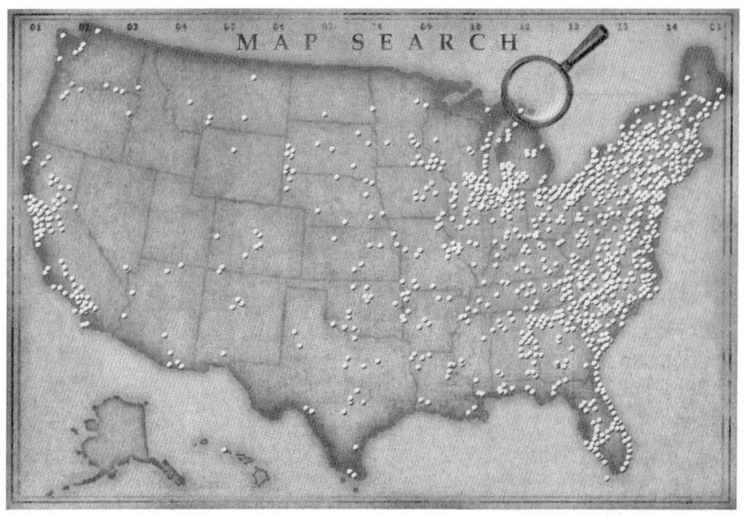